T

Recent Titles in
Bibliographies and Indexes in Law and Political Science

Scottish Nationalism and Cultural Identity in the Twentieth Century:
An Annotated Bibliography of Secondary Sources
Gordon Bryan, compiler

Edward S. Corwin and the American Constitution: A Bibliographical Analysis
Kenneth D. Crews

Political Risk Assessment: An Annotated Bibliography
David A. Jodice, compiler

Human Rights: An International and Comparative Law Bibliography
Julian R. Friedman and Marc I. Sherman, compilers and editors

Latin American Society and Legal Culture
Frederick E. Snyder, compiler

Congressional Committees, 1789-1982: A Checklist
Walter Stubbs, compiler

Criminal Justice Documents: A Selective, Annotated Bibliography of
U.S. Government Publications Since 1975
John F. Berens, compiler

TERRORISM,
1980–1987

A Selectively Annotated Bibliography

Compiled by
Edward F. Mickolus with Peter A. Flemming

Bibliographies and Indexes in Law and Political Science, Number 8

GREENWOOD PRESS
New York • Westport, Connecticut • London

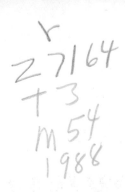

This book was produced from copy provided by the author and without editing or proofreading by the publisher.

Library of Congress Cataloging-in-Publication Data

Mickolus, Edward F.
   Terrorism, 1980-1987 : a selectively annotated bibliography / compiled by Edward F. Mickolus with Peter A. Flemming.
   p.   cm. — (Bibliographies and indexes in law and political science, ISSN 0742-6909 ; no. 8)
   Includes indexes.
   ISBN 0-313-26248-9 (lib. bdg. : alk. paper)
   1. Terrorism—Bibliography.   I. Flemming, Peter A.   II. Title.
III. Series.
Z7164.T3M54   1988
[HV6431]
016.3036'25—dc 19   87-32275

British Library Cataloguing in Publication Data is available.

Library of Congress Catalog Card Number: 87-32275
ISBN: 0-313-26248-9
ISSN: 0742-6909

First published in 1988

Greenwood Press, Inc.
88 Post Road West, Westport, Connecticut 06881

Printed in the United States of America

The paper used in this book complies with the Permanent Paper Standard issued by the National Information Standards Organization (Z39.48-1984).

10 9 8 7 6 5 4 3 2 1

Contents

vi Contents

Preface

This book updates a previous volume The Literature of
Terrorism: A Selectively Annotated Bibliography which
Greenwood Press published in 1980. Since then, international
terrorist attacks have, unfortunately, continued apace. So,
too, has the enormous outpouring of commentary and research
that such attacks inspire. This volume, like its predecessor,
attempts to impose some order on this literature and provide
researchers with a comprehensive survey of materials dealing
with various aspects of terrorism. As before, day-to-day
press reports have not been noted, although noteworthy news
analyses receive mention. Although the majority of the
entries are in English and written by Americans, numerous
citations from other languages are included to illustrate
contributions available around the world. When possible,
rough English translations of titles are provided. Although
this book attempts to provide a broad cross section of
research and opinion on terrorism, inclusion of any citation
or class of citation should in no way imply agreement of the
views presented by those authors.

Care has been taken to minimize duplicate listings,
although there may be some overlap between the previous volume
and this one. Most of this bibliography surveys literature
published between 1980-1986, but many items that were missed
in the earlier volume are included herein. We have also tried
to include items from publications that are not often cited in
terrorism studies, to give the reader an indication of the
breadth of material necessary, as well as an inkling of the
extent of the effects of terrorism in all aspects of life, not
just those upon which we most often comment.

Because some entries related to more than one category,
each item is placed under the heading deemed most appropriate
to the central theme of the book or article cited. Many of
the items have been annotated, although the compilers have not
been able to read and digest every piece cited. In some cases,
annotations given by authors or sponsoring organizations have
been quoted. Where appropriate, such instances are noted at
the beginning of a commentary.

The organization of this annotated bibliography closely parallels that of its predecessor, to permit the researcher to compare quickly developments in the literature on specific topics. The literature has changed since the 1970s, however, reflecting changes in the nature of the topic per se, our policy concerns, and the extent of our knowledge of the subject.

The General Treatments section includes books and articles discussing definitions, theories, the history of terrorism, notes on terrorist tactics, trends in various forms of terrorism, and how to go about studying the phenomenon. The Tactics of Terrorists section has five subcategories: Assassinations includes works on the killing of highly placed political leaders, as well as murders of lesser-known individuals for political reasons. Bombings notes articles on bombing campaigns, types of bombs, firebombs and arson attempts, letter bombs, and effects of bombing on civilian morale. Skyjackings includes general treatments on skyjacking and aerial sabotage, discussions of preventive security, international legal solutions, and structurally similar types of incidents which may involve non-aerial forms of transportation. Hostage-Taking includes works on kidnapping, barricade and hostage situations, extortionate threats made against individuals or installations, strategies of negotiation by terrorists and victims, and related issues. Nuclear and Other Forms of High-Technology Terrorism includes discussions of safeguards and measures against governmental and private diversion of nuclear materials, attack and theft of this material and types of demands that could be made. Reflecting the development of scholarly thought on this issue, the category has been expanded to include other threats against high-technology targets, as well as the use of non-nuclear advanced technology by terrorists. The Philosophical Approaches section includes books and articles by well-known terrorists, commentaries on their thoughts, and views on what terrorism as a social phenomenon means to democracy and civilization as a whole.

A comparatively new Terrorist Infrastructure section reflects our growing knowledge of how terrorist groups operate, and how they are assisted by like-minded individuals, groups, and governments. The Links of Terrorist Groups subsection includes articles on the funding, training, and exchanges of personnel between known organizations. State Support for Terrorism explores how governments aid and abet terrorist activity, the use of terrorism by government authorities, the effects of such state-sanctioned violence upon society and international relations, and examines suggestions for combatting such behavior. Narcotics Trafficking and Terrorism includes articles illustrating the growing narco-terrorist link.

The Terrorism by Geographic Area section is divided into six subcategories, with discussions of terrorism, revolutionary movements, and civil uprisings.

Having noted terrorist motivations and trends in their behavior, we move to a discussion of Responses, which is divided into four major sections. General treatments note governmental and societal reactions, and mutually reinforcing cycles of terrorism and counterterrorism. The effects on democracy of anti-terrorist responses are also included. Physical Security and Executive Protection notes guidelines on preventing attacks, how political risk studies should be conducted, and anti-terrorist hardware. The Military Responses section concentrates on the development of unilateral measures of self-help in dealing with terrorism, from kidnapping of fugitives to Entebbe-style paramilitary rescue teams. The International Legal Approaches section looks at international legal conventions, domestic law, trends in extradition, and suggestions for future measures.

Several miscellaneous sections complete the bibliography. The Media and Terrorism section includes arguments on the proper role of the media in the tactical and strategic response to terrorism. Psychological and Medical Approaches include studies of terrorist motivations, psychiatric notions about the causes of murderous behavior, selection of political targets, the effects of society upon unstable individuals, and the medical and psychiatric care of victims after the incident. Related Studies refer to behavioral science approaches to causes of political violence in general and criminal activity, defining relationships between forces, governments, and society. Fiction concentrates on contemporary novels on transnational terrorism, although a few earlier works and other forms of expression are represented. Bibliographies concentrate on compilations of works on terrorism in general. Listings on specialized topics are included in the appropriate regional or functional section of this bibliography. Author and title indexes are also included at the end of this volume. In the author index only the first author of co-authored works are listed.

The list of people who have aided the compilers by providing copies of their drafts and published works, as well as others who have provided leads in tracking down fugitive or obscure citations, is too extensive to list here. Rather let us offer a plenary thanks and invite the readers of this guide to send copies or citations of their recent works for inclusion in future editions of this bibliography.

Terrorism,
1980–1987

General Treatments

Adam, Frances Cruchley <u>Saints or Sinners: A Selective and Political Study of Certain Nonstate Terrorists</u> (University of Alberta, Ph.D. dissertation, 1979).

Adams, James <u>The Financing of Terror</u> (London: New English Library, 1986), 276 pp.
 Adams focuses on the funding of the IRA and the PLO, and gives detailed studies of how kidnap-ransoms and drug trafficking supplement terrorist incomes. Reviewed in 33, 12 <u>Playboy</u> (December 1986), p. 33.

Alexander, Arthur J. "Getting the Most from Scarce Resources" 5, 2 <u>TVI Journal</u> (Fall 1984), pp. 26-31.

Alexander, Yonah, Paul Baum and Raphael Danziger "Conference Report: Terrorism: Future Threats and Responses" 7, 4 <u>Terrorism</u> (1985), pp. 367-410.

Alexander, Yonah and John M. Gleason, eds. <u>Behavioral and Quantitative Perspectives on Terrorism</u> (New York: Pergamon, 1981), 396 pp.

Anand, Vijay Kumar <u>Terrorism and Security</u> (New Delhi: Deep and Deep, 1984), 283 pp.

Arostegui, Martin C. "Special Reports of Risks International" 7, 4 <u>Terrorism</u> (1985), pp. 417-430.

"An Atlas of Terrorism" 6, 2 <u>Assets Protection</u> (1981), pp. 26-36.
 A collection of the major charts and graphics from CIA papers on terrorism.

Avery, W. P. "Terrorism and the International Transfer of Conventional Armaments" in Yonah Alexander and John M. Gleason, eds. <u>Behavioral and Quantitative Perspectives on Terrorism</u> (New York: Pergamon, 1981), pp. 329-339.

Barker, Ralph <u>Not Here, But in Another Place</u> (New York: St. Martin's, 1980), 356 pp.

Barnard, Neil "Be Vigilant and Faithful" 22, 3 <u>Roeping en Riglyne</u> (September 1974), pp. 2-3.

Barnard, Neil "International and Urban Terrorism" 13 <u>Tydskrif vir Christelike Wetenskap</u> (First Quarter, 1977), pp. 13-30.

Barnard, Neil "Terrorism as Threat to Our Christian Civilization" 3, 2 <u>Riglyne</u> (August 1972), pp. 34-36.

Barrett, Michael J. "Patterns in Terror" 4, 3 <u>Defense and Diplomacy</u> (March 1986), pp. 40-43.
    Barrett, a CIA assistant general counsel, provides the CIA's statistics for international terrorist attacks committed between 1970-1985.

Bartsch, Gunter <u>Terrorismus</u> (Zurich: Schweizerischer Aufklarungs-Dienst, 1978), 56 pp.

BDM Corporation <u>The BDM Corporation's Terrorism Data Base</u> (McLean, Va.: The BDM Corporation, 1980).

Becker, Jillian "The Most Important Question: Review Article" 4 <u>Terrorism</u> (1980), pp. 311-322.

Becker, Jillian, et al. <u>British Perspectives on Terrorism</u> (London: Allen and Unwin, 1981).

Becker, Jillian, et al. <u>Contemporary Terror: Studies in Sub-State Violence</u> (New York: Macmillan, 1981).

Beer, D. "Terrorism" 45, 6 <u>Social Education</u> (1981), pp. 480-482.

Beichman, Arnold "An Angry Fancy: The 'Politics' of Terror" 2 <u>Lugano Review</u> (1975), pp. 18-24.
 Revolution is passe, but terrorism is not.

Blackmore, John "The Dowager and the Hitman" <u>Police Magazine</u> (November 1978), pp. 2-3.

Bonanate, Luigi <u>Dimensioni del Terrorismo Politico: Aspetti Interni e Internazionali, Politici e Giuridici; introduzione di Filippo Barbano</u> (Turin, Italy: University Institute of Political Science, 1979), 346 pp.

Bonanate, Luigi "Some Unanticipated Consequences of Terrorism" 16, 3 <u>Journal of Peace Research</u> (1979), pp. 197-212.

Bonanate, Luigi "Terrorism and Governability" 13, 1 <u>Rivista Italiana di Scienza Politica</u> (April 1983), pp. 37-64.

Bonanate, Luigi "Terrorism and International Political Analysis" 3, 1-2 <u>Terrorism</u> (1979), pp. 47-67.
 Bonanate attempts to explain the success of forms of international terrorism and the failures of domestic terrorism.

Bonanate, Luigi and P. Gastaldo, eds. Il Terrorismo Nell-eta Contemporanea (Firenze: Le Monnier, 1981).

Bookbinder, Paul "Terrorism: Left and Right" 13 Present Tense (Spring 1986), pp. 54-56.

Brainerd, Gideon R., Jr. "Terrorism: The Theory of Differential Effects" 5, 3 Conflict (1984), pp. 233-244.

Braungart, Richard G. and Margaret M. Braungart "International Terrorism: Background and Response" 9, 2 Journal of Political and Military Sociology (Fall 1981), pp. 263-288.
A review of 14 major books on terrorism.

Brown, Gene, ed. The Great Contemporary Issues: Terrorism (New York Times/Arno Press, 1979), 378 pp.
A collection of major articles which appeared in the New York Times.

Buckley, Alan D., Daniel D. Olson and Stephen Sloan, eds. International Terrorism: Current Research and Future Directions (Wayne, New Jersey: Avery Publishing Group, 1980), 113 pp.

Burton, John Deviance, Terrorism and War: The Process of Solving Unsolved Social and Political Problems (New York: St. Martin's, 1979), 240 pp.
Reviewed by Glenn D. Paige 75, 1 American Political Science Review (March 1981), pp. 262-263.

Byford, Lawrence "Terrorism and Democracy" in Donald E. J. MacNamara and Philip John Stead, eds. New Dimensions in Transnational Crime (New York: John Jay, 1982).

Carlton, David and Carlo Schaerf, eds. Contemporary Terror: Studies in Substate Violence (New York: St. Martin's and London: Macmillan, 1981), 231 pp.
Proceedings of the Seventh Conference of the International School on Disarmament and Research on Conflicts, Ariccia, Italy, 1978.

Cavanagh, F.J. "Political Terrorism" in John T. O'Brien and Marvin Marcus, eds. Crime and Justice in America: Critical Issues for the Future (Elmsford, New York: Pergamon, 1979).

Center for Contemporary Studies "The International Arms Trade and the Terrorist" 7 Contemporary Affairs Briefing (London: CCS, 1981).
The paper shows that terrorists frequently steal from the arsenals of the American armed forces in West Germany.

Lord Chalfont "Terrorism and International Security" 5, 4 Terrorism (1982), pp. 309-324.

Chandler, Jerome Greer "Terrorism: A Case of False Security" 113 American Legion (July 1982), pp. 18-22.

Cheason, J. M. "A Bayesian Framework for the Determination of Terrorist Risk Exposure in Third World Countries" paper presented to the third annual Third World Conference, Omaha, Nebraska, October 1979.

Cheason, J. M. "Terrorist Risk Exposure: A Bayesian Approach", paper presented at the national meeting of the Academy of Criminal Justice Sciences, Oklahoma City, March 1980.

Cherne, Leo "U.S. Intelligence Requirements for the Late 1980's; Terrorism and the Soviet Union" 52 Vital Speeches (April 1, 1986), pp. 370-374.

Christopher, Maura "Terrorism's Brutal Impact - In Dollars and Cents; At Next to No Costs, Terrorists Can Provoke a Hugely Expensive Reaction" 118 Scholastic Update (May 16, 1986), pp. 23-24.

Clarke, Thurston By Blood and Fire (New York: Putnam, 1981), 304 pp.

Clifford, W. "Terrorism and Overkill" 5, 3 Terrorism (1981), pp. 281-286.

Cline, Ray S. "Endemic Nature of Political Terrorism in the 1980s" paper presented at the Conference on Political Terrorism and Energy: The Threat and Response, Washington, D.C., Georgetown University Center for Strategic and International Studies, May 1, 1980

Clutterbuck, Richard "Terrorism and Urban Violence" 34, 4 Proceedings of the Academy of Political Science (1982), pp. 165-175.

"Colby College Conference Report" 8, 1 Terrorism (1985), pp. 79ff.

Collins, John M. "Definitional Aspects", in Yonah Alexander and Charles K. Ebinger, eds. Political Terrorism and Energy: The Threat and Response (New York: Praeger, 1982).

"Combatting Terrorism: Publishing Customer Data" 5 Kriminalistik (1980), p. 203.

Cooper, H. H. A. Evaluating the Terrorist Threat: Principles of Applied Risk Assessment (Bureau of Operations and Research, International Association of Chiefs of Police, 1979).

Cooper, H.H.A. "Terrorism: New Dimensions of Violent Criminality" 9 Cum. Law Review (1978), pp. 369ff.

Cooper, H.H.A. "Woman as Terrorist" in Freda Adler and Rita James Simon, eds. The Criminology of Deviant Women (Boston: Houghton Mifflin, 1979), pp. 150-157.

Cordes, Bonnie, Bruce Hoffman, Brian Michael Jenkins, Konrad Kellen, Sue Moran and William Sater Trends in International Terrorism, 1982 and 1983 (Santa Monica, California: The Rand Corporation, R-3183-SL, 1984).

Cordes, Bonnie, Brian Michael Jenkins and Konrad Kellen "A Conceptual Framework for Analyzing Terrorist Groups" (Santa Monica: The Rand Corporation, R-3151, June 1985).

Corrado, Raymond R. "Female Terrorists: Competing Perspectives" in Curt T. Griffiths and Margit Nance, eds. Female Offender (Simon Fraser University Criminology Research Center, Canada, 1980), pp. 37-50.

Corsi, Jerome R. "Terrorism as a Desperate Game: An Analytic Step Toward Comprehension of Fear, Bargaining, and Communication in the Terrorist Event" paper presented at the Third Biennial Meeting of the International Society for Research on Aggression, Washington, D.C., September 23, 1978, 47 pp., published as "Terrorism as a Desperate Game" 25 Journal of Conflict Resolution (1981), pp. 47-85.
The author distinguishes between types of terrorist events, and explores how decision trees can be used to organize a discussion of bargaining in hostage situations. Problems in applying formal game theory are also given attention.

Crater, Col. John F., USA "Terrorism: A Beneficiary of Arms Proliferation" (National Defense University, National War College research project, March 15, 1979), 37 pp.

Crenshaw, Martha "The Causes of Terrorism" 13, 4 Comparative Politics (July 1981), pp. 379-399.

Crenshaw, Martha "Incentives for Terrorism" in Outthinking The Terrorist: An International Challenge: Proceedings of the 10th Annual Symposium on the Role of Behavioral Science in Physical Security (Washington, D.C., April 23-24, 1985), pp. 15-24.

Crenshaw, Martha "The Meaning of Terrorism for World Order", paper presented to the 24th annual convention of the International Studies Association, Mexico City, April 5-9, 1983.

Crenshaw, Martha "An Organizational Approach to the Analysis of Political Terrorism" 29, 3 Orbis (Fall 1985), pp. 465-488.

Crenshaw, Martha "The State of Terrorism as an International Problem" paper presented to the annual meeting of the International Studies Association, Los Angeles, March 18-22, 1980.

Crozier, Brian "Transnational Terrorism" 1 Clandestine Tactics and Technology (Gaithersburg, Maryland: International Association of Chiefs of Police, n.d.).

Darby, Phillip "Violence: The Contagion of Terrorism" 24 Optima (1974), pp. 48-55.
A history of terrorism since World War II.

Des Pres, Terrence "Terror and the Sublime" 5, 2 Human Rights Quarterly (May 1983), pp. 135-146.

Deutsch, Antal "On the Economics of Terrorism" 5, 4 Terrorism (1982), pp. 363-366.

Devine, Philip E. and Robert J. Rafalko "On Terror" 463 <u>Annals of the American Academy of Political and Social Science</u> (September 1982), pp. 39-53.

Dimitrijevic, Vojin "Is There Nowadays Terrorism Which Is Not International?" 34, 3-4 <u>Medunarodni Problemi</u> (July-December 1982), pp. 337-346.

Dimitrijevic, Vojin "Medjunarodni Terorizam" <u>Arhiv za Pravne i Drustvene Nauke</u> (1980), pp. 23-44.

Dimitrijevic, Vojin <u>Terorizam u Unutrasnoj i Medjunarodnoj Politici</u> (Belgrade: Radnicka Stampa, 1982), 220 pp.

Dissing, Karen <u>Terrorismen</u> (Copenhagen: Gyldendal, 1982), 215 pp.

Dobson, Christopher and Ronald Payne <u>The Terrorists: Their Weapons, Leaders and Tactics</u> (New York: Facts on File, 1982), 262 pp.
The book also covers who supports them, how they are trained and financed, and who's who.

Dobson, Christopher and Ronald Payne <u>War Without End--The Terrorists: An Intelligence Dossier</u> (London: Harrap, 1986), 279 pp.

Dziak, John J. "Military Doctrine and Structure" in Uri Ra'anan, Robert L. Pfaltzgraff, Jr., Richard H. Shultz, Ernst Halperin, and Igor Lukes <u>Hydra of Carnage: International Linkages of Terrorism: The Witnesses Speak</u> (Lexington, Mass.: Lexington Books, 1986), pp. 77-92.

Eddy, Art "Let's Hear it for Failures at Terrorism" 27 <u>Handling and Shipping Management</u> (October 1986), p. 7.

Emerson, Ryan Quade <u>Who's Who in Terrorism: US and International</u> (Purcellville, Va.: International Intelligence Center, 1984).
1985 and 1986 volumes are also available.

Erling R. <u>Terror: Soklen Mobbing ei Empirisk Undersuknung</u> (1980), 139 pp.

Evron, Yair, ed. <u>International Violence: Terrorism, Surprise and Control</u> (Jerusalem: The Jerusalem Academic Press, 1979).

"Faces of Terrorism" 118 <u>Scholastic Update</u> (May 16, 1986).

Farrell, William R. "High Risk Violence and Terrorism: A Distinction with a Difference?" paper presented to the panel on the Role of High Risk Violence in Ethnic Nationalism at the annual meeting of the International Studies Association/South, University of Florida at Gainesville, October 29-31, 1981, also presented at the spring conference of the National Capital Area Political Science Association and the International Studies Association-D.C. Chapter, Mount Vernon College, Washington, D.C., February 27, 1982.

Farrell, William R. "Terrorism is...?" 32 <u>Naval War College Review</u> (May-June 1980), pp. 64-72.

Fattah, Ezzat A. "Terrorist Activities and Terrorist Targets: A Tentative Typology" in Yonah Alexander and John M. Gleason, eds. <u>Behavioral and Quantitative Perspectives on Terrorism</u> (New York: Pergamon, 1981), pp. 11-32.

"Female Terrorists: A Growing Phenomenon" 1, 3 <u>Executive Risk Assessment</u> (January 1979), 6 pp.

Field Marshall D.C. "On Organizing Urban Guerrilla Units" 2 <u>Clandestine Tactics and Technology</u> (Gaithersburg, Maryland: International Association of Chiefs of Police, n.d.).

Flemming, Peter A. "Terrorist Typologies: A Quantitative Perspective" paper presented at the annual convention of the International Studies Association/Midwest, Chicago, 1985.

Flemming, Peter A., Alex P. Schmid and Michael Stohl. "The Theoretical Utility of Typologies of Terrorism: Lessons and Opportunities" in Michael Stohl, ed. <u>The Politics of Terrorism</u>; Third Edition: Revised and Expanded. (New York: Marcel Dekker, 1987).

Fornari, Franco "Stampa e terrorismo in relazione alle centrali estere" 12, 3/4 <u>Giustizia e Costituzione</u> (1981), pp. 23-27.

Foster, Charles R. "The Future of High Risk Conflict in World and National Politics" paper presented to the panel on the Role of Terrorism in Ethnic Nationalism at the annual convention of the International Studies Association/South, University of Florida, October 29-31, 1981.

Fowler, William W. "An Agenda for Quantitative Research on Terrorism" (Santa Monica: The Rand Corporation, P-6591, July 1980), 11 pp.

Fowler, William W. "Terrorism Data Bases: A Comparison of Missions, Methods and Systems" paper presented to the convention of the International Studies Association, Los Angeles, March 18-22, 1980, also available as (Santa Monica: The Rand Corporation, N-1503-RC, March 1981), 42 pp.
A discussion of the major datasets which are publicly and commercially available, including the RAND files and ITERATE.

Fowler, William W. and Helen E. Purkitt "Temporal Trends in International Terrorism 1968 to 1979: An Analysis Using Poisson and Contagion Models" paper delivered to the annual Convention of the International Studies Association, March 1980.

Freed, Donald and Fred Simon Landis <u>Death in Washington</u> (Westport, Conn.: Lawrence Hill, 1980).

Freedman, Lawrence Zelic and Yonah Alexander, eds. <u>Perspectives on Terrorism</u> (Wilmington, Delaware: Scholarly Resources, Inc., 1983), 254 pp.

Freeman, Charles Terrorism (London: Batsford Academic and Educational, Ltd., 1981), 72 pp.

Friedlander, Robert A. Terror-Violence, Aspects of Social Control (London: Oceana, 1983), 299 pp.

Frostmann, Herbert M. International Political Terrorism and the Approaching Emergence of the Authoritarian State (American Classical College Press, 1981), 146 pp.

Galleni, Mauro Rapporto Sul Terrorismo (Milano: Rizzoli, 1981), 552 pp.

Galtung, Johan "On Violence in General and Terrorism in Particular" (Oslo: Universitetet i Oslo, Professoratet i Konflikt-og fredsforskning, 1978), 27 pp.

Garrigan, Timothy B. and George A. Lopez Terrorism: A Problem of Political Violence (New York: Council on International and Public Affairs, Consortium for International Studies Education, 1984).
A learning package consisting of materials to be used in a course on political violence.

Gazit, Shlomo and Michael Handel "Insurgency, Terrorism, and Intelligence" in Intelligence Requirements for the 1980s: Counterintelligence (New York: National Strategy Information Center, 1980).

Geismar, Alain L'Engrenage Terroriste (Paris: Fayard, 1981), 179 pp.

Georges-Abeyie, D. E. "Political Crime and Terrorism: Toward an Understanding" in Graeme R. Newman, ed. Crime and Deviance (Beverly Hills: Sage Annual Reviews of Studies in Deviance, Vol. 4, 1980), pp. 313-332.

Gilboa, Eytan "The Use of Simulation in Combatting Terrorism" 5, 3 Terrorism (1981), pp. 265-279.

Gleason, John M. "Third World Terrorism: Perspectives for Quantitative Research" paper presented at the joint national meeting of the Operations Research Society of America and the Institute for Management Sciences, Los Angeles, November 13-15, 1978, reprinted in Yonah Alexander and John M. Gleason, eds. Behavioral and Quantitative Perspectives on Terrorism (New York: Pergamon, 1981), pp. 242-255.

Godfrey, David "Terrorism and Banking" 5, 4 Terrorism (1982), pp. 353-362.

Govea, Rodger M. "Distinction Without Purpose: The Study of Political Terrorism", paper presented to the 24th annual convention of the International Studies Association, Mexico City, April 5-9, 1983.

Govea, Rodger M. "Is Terrorism Contagious?" (Cleveland State University, Department of Political Science, unpublished mimeo, 1983).

Govea, Rodger M. "Terrorism as a Political Science Offering" 8, 1 <u>Teaching Political Science</u> (October 1980), pp. 3-20.

Graham, David M. "Terrorism: What Political Status?" 284 <u>Round Table</u> (October 1981), pp. 401-403.

Graham-Yooll, Andrew <u>A Matter of Fear</u> (Westport, Conn.: L. Hill, 1982), 128 pp.

Green, Leslie C. "Aspects of Terrorism" 5, 4 <u>Terrorism</u> (1982), pp. 373-400.
A look at League of Nations and UN attempts and failures to define and combat terrorism.

Groebel, Jo and Hubert Feger "Analyse von Strukturen terroristischer Gruppierungen" in Wanda Baeyer-Katte et al., <u>Gruppenprozesse: Analysen zum Terrorismus 3</u> (Opladen, West Germany: Westdeutscher Verlag, 1982).

Grosscup, Beau "Terrorism, Neoconservatism and the Crisis of Liberal Democracy" paper presented to the American Political Science Association convention, Washington, D.C., August 1980, 29 pp.

Gurr, Ted Robert "Empirical Research on Political Terrorism: The State of the Art and How It Might be Improved" May 1986 manuscript, 55 pp., to be published in Robert O. Slater and Michael Stohl, eds. <u>Current Perspectives on International Terrorism</u> (New York: St. Martin's and London: Macmillan, 1986).

Gutteridge, William, ed. <u>Contemporary Terrorism</u> (New York: Facts on File, 1986), 225 pp.
Reviewed in <u>Foreign Affairs</u> (Fall, 1986), p. 180.

Haggman, Bertil <u>Terrorism: Var Tids Krigforing (Terrorism: Warfare of Our Times)</u> (1978).

Hamilton, Lawrence D. "Dynamics of Insurgent Violence: Preliminary Findings" in Yonah Alexander and John Gleason, eds. <u>Behavioral and Quantitative Perspectives on Terrorism</u> (New York: Pergamon, 1981), pp. 229-241.

Hamilton, Lawrence D. and James D. Hamilton "Dynamics of Terrorism" (University of New Hampshire Department of Sociology and University of California at Berkeley Department of Economics, August 1980), 22 pp., later published in 27, 1 <u>International Studies Quarterly</u> (March 1983), pp. 39-54.
After discussing theories of terrorism by practitioners, government officials, and academics, the authors build new models of contagion, finding differences across countries not previously explored. Using stochastic analysis of ITERATE data, the authors found that the contagion of terrorism is more easily reversed in less democratic, poorer, and less well-educated societies.

Hamilton, Peter Espionage, Terrorism and Subversion in an Industrial Society (Surrey: Bookmag, 1979).

Han, Henry Hynwook, ed. Terrorism, Political Violence, and World Order (Lanham, Md.: University Press of America, 1984), 767 pp.
Reviewed by George A. Lopez 9 Maryland Journal of International Law and Trade (Fall 1985), pp. 237-239.

Harris, Jonathan The New Terrorism: Politics of Violence (New York: Julian Messner, 1983), 197 pp.

Hayes, David Terrorists and Freedom Fighters (Hove: Wayland, 1980), 96 pp.

Hazelip, A. Charles Twelve Tenets of Terrorism: An Assessment of Theory and Practice (Florida State University, Ph.D. dissertation, 1980), 344 pp.

Hazlewood, Leo A. "Research Gaps in Crisis Management of Terrorist Incidents" (Arlington, Va: CACI-Federal, contract with the US Department of Defense, Office of Naval Research, 1978).
According to an executive summary, "the objective of the proposed effort is to analyze the potential for research related to terrorism-induced crises, to document existing research on terrorism, to identify research gaps and opportunities relevant to new and existing crisis management goals, and to evaluate the potential for significant accomplishments as a result of crisis management/terrorism research."

Hayes, Richard E. and R. Mahoney "Design of a Prototype Interactive Terrorism Data System" (Arlington, Va.: CACI-Federal, proposal to the US Department of Defense, Office of Naval Research, 1980).
This proposed "to systematize prior work on terrorism and put it in a form that can be accessed and used efficiently and quickly by a decision-maker faced with a terrorist attack."

Hellebusch, Charles M., ed. The International Terrorism Newsletter
Published in the 1980s, the ITN frequently needs better editing, has too broad a view of the scope of inquiry, but often has nuggets which are not easily found elsewhere.

Helms, Andrea R. C. "Democracy Under Fire: Liberalism and the Terrorist Challenge" (Fairbanks: University of Alaska, 1981).

Herold, H. "Trends in International Search for Terrorists" 4 Kriminalistik (1980), pp. 165-171.

Herz, Martin F., ed. Diplomats and Terrorists: What Works, What Doesn't: A Symposium (Washington, D.C.: Institute for the Study of Diplomacy, Edmund A. Walsh School of Foreign Service, Georgetown University, 1982), 69 pp.

Hess, H. "Terrorismus und Terrorismus-Diskurs." Tijdschrift voor Criminologie (1981), 4 pp.

Heyman, Edward S. "The Diffusion of Transnational Terrorism" in Richard H. Shultz, Jr. and Stephen Sloan, eds. Responding to the Terrorist Threat: Security and Crisis Management (New York: Pergamon, 1980), pp. 190-244.

Heyman, Edward S. "Monitoring the Diffusion of International Terrorism" (Gaithersburg, Maryland: International Association of Chiefs of Police, 1980), 36 pp.

Heyman, Edward S. and Edward Mickolus "Comment: Observations on 'Why Violence Spreads'" 24, 2 International Studies Quarterly (June 1980), pp. 299-305.
A critique of the data and analysis used in the Midlarsky et al. piece which appears elsewhere in this issue.

Heyman, Edward S. and Edward F. Mickolus "Imitation by Terrorists: Quantitative Approaches to the Study of Diffusion Patterns in Transnational Terrorism" paper presented to the joint national meeting of the Operations Research Society of America and the Institute for Management Sciences, New York City, May 1-3, 1978, reprinted in Yonah Alexander and John Gleason, eds. Behavioral and Quantitative Perspectives on Terrorism (New York: Pergamon, 1981), pp. 175-228.
The article shows how to use Markov chains and adjacency maps to study contagion.

Hippchen, Leonard Joseph and Yong S. Yim Terrorism, International Crime, and Arms Control (Springfield, Illinois: Thomas, 1982), 293 pp.

Hitchens, Christopher "Wanton Acts of Usage: Terrorism: A Cliche in Search of a Meaning" 273 Harpers (September 1986), pp. 66-70.

Hopple, Gerald W. "Transnational Terrorism: Prospectus for a Causal Modeling Approach" 6, 1 Terrorism (1982), pp. 73-100.

Hurt, Henry "Search for a Terrorist Gang" 127 Reader's Digest (December 1985), pp. 166-174.

Ignatius, David "Terrorism by the Numbers: The Threat Has Changed Less Than Our Perceptions of It" Washington Post (April 13, 1986), p. C5.
    An associate editor of the Post offers statistics from the Department of State and Federal Aviation Administration showing that statistically, international terrorism has been fairly stable in the last few years.

Im, Eric Iksoon, Jon Cauley and Todd Sandler "Cycles and Substitutions in Terrorist Activities: A Spectral Approach" (mimeo, in preparation, 1987), 24 pp.

"International Terrorism" Gist (Washington, D.C.: US Department of State, Bureau of Public Affairs, September 1984), 2 pp.
A quick summary of statistics on international terrorism and US policy initiatives through 1983.

"International Terrorism" (Washington, D.C.: US Department of State, Bureau of Public Affairs Selected Documents No. 24, 1986, 16 pp.
Texts of an address by President Reagan, statements and an address by Ambassador Robert B. Oakley, Acting Ambassador at Large for Counter-Terrorism, and a statement by Ambassador Parker W. Borg, Deputy, Office of the Ambassador at Large for Counter-Terrorism. Includes statistical tables and chronologies of terrorist incidents.

International Terrorism in 1979 (Washington, D.C.: National Foreign Assessment Center, Central Intelligence Agency, April 1980, PA 80-10072U), 25 pp.
The study found a carryover of the trends in terrorism in 1978--attacks on diplomats and business interests, simple operations, targeting in industrialized democracies. Although there were few attacks, both worldwide and against Americans, most casualties resulted.

Ivianski, Zeev "Provocation at the Center: A Study in the History of Counter-Terror" 4, 1-4 Terrorism (1980), pp. 53-88.

Jaeger, Herbert, et al. Lebenslaufanalysen: Analysen zum Terrorismus 2 (Opladen, West Germany: Westdeutscher Verlag,1981).

Jenkins, Brian Michael "Diplomats on the Front Line" paper presented at the Conference on International Terrorism: The Protection of Diplomatic Premises and Personnel, Bellagio, Italy, 1982 (published by Santa Monica, California: The Rand Corporation, P-6749, March 1982), 11 pp.
Paper provides an overview of terrorist attacks on diplomats and diplomatic facilities, which increased 60 percent in 1980 and 1981 over the previous two-year period.

Jenkins, Brian Michael "Introduction and Overview" in Brian Michael Jenkins, conference director Terrorism and Beyond: An International Conference on Terrorism and Low-Level Conflict (Santa Monica: The Rand Corporation, R-2714-DOE/DOJ/DOS/RC, December 1982), pp. 3-29.

Jenkins, Brian Michael "New Modes of Conflict" 28, 1 Orbis (Spring 1984), pp. 5-15.
Jenkins sees the last 20 years of armed conflict as involving conventional war, guerrilla war, and international terrorism, the latter of which will increase.

Jenkins, Brian Michael "Statements About Terrorism" 463 Annals of the American Academy of Political and Social Science (September 1982), pp. 11-23.

Jenkins, Brian Michael "The Study of Terrorism: Definitional Problems" paper presented to the joint national meeting of the Operations Research Society of America and the Institute for Management Sciences, New York City, May 1-3, 1978, reprinted in Yonah Alexander and John M. Gleason, eds. Behavioral and Quantitative Perspectives on Terrorism (New York: Pergamon, 1981), pp. 3-10, also available as (Santa Monica: The Rand Corporation, P-6563, December 1980), 10 pp.

Jenkins, Brian Michael "Talking to Terrorists" (Santa Monica, California: The Rand Corporation, P-6750, March 1982), 15 pp.

Jenkins, Brian Michael, Conference Director Terrorism and Beyond: An International Conference on Terrorism and Low-Level Conflict: prepared for the US Department of Energy, the US Department of Justice, the US Department of State (Santa Monica: The Rand Corporation, R-2714, 1982), 287 pp.

Jenkins, Brian Michael "Terrorism in the 1980s" (Santa Monica: The Rand Corporation, P-6564, December 1980), 13 pp.

Jenkins, Brian Michael "Terrorism Outlook for the 80's" 25, 1 Security Management (January 1981), pp. 14-21.
Address given at the 26th annual American Society for Industrial Security seminar and exhibits in Miami Beach, Florida, September 25, 1980.

Johnson, Chalmers "Terror" 15 Society (November-December 1977), pp. 48-52.
Johnson notes that terrorism has risen due to new targets, new technologies, and a new toleration of the terrorists.

Johnson, Paul "The Cancer of Terrorism" in Benjamin Netanyahu, ed. Terrorism: How the West Can Win (New York: Farrar, Straus, Giroux, 1986), pp. 31-38.

Johnson, Paul "The Seven Deadly Sins of Terrorism" 28, 5 NATO Review (October 1980), pp. 28ff.

Jubelius, W. "Frauen und Terror: Erklaerungen, Difamierungen" Kriminalistik (June 1981), pp. 247-255.

Kahn, E. J., Jr. "How do We Explain Them?" 54 New Yorker (June 12, 1978), pp. 37-62.
A biography of Richard L. Clutterbuck, terrorism expert.

Karber, Phillip A. and Russell William Mengel "Political and Economic Forces Affecting Terrorism" in Patrick J. Montana and George S. Roukis, eds. Managing Terrorism: Strategies for the Corporate Executive (Westport, Conn.: Quorum Books, 1983), pp. 23-40.

Karstedt-Henke, S. "Soziale Bewegung und Terrorismus: Alltagstheorien und Sozialwissenschaft-Liche Ansaetze zur Erklaerung des Terrorismus" in E. Blankenburg, ed. Politik der Inneren Sicherheit (Frankfurt, 1980).

Kellen, Konrad "On Terrorists and Terrorism" (Santa Monica: The Rand Corporation, N-1942-RC, 1982).

Kellett, Anthony International Terrorism: A Retrospective and Prospective Examination, ORAE Report No. R-78 (Ottawa: Department of National Defence, 1981).

Kempe, Frederick "Violent Tactics" Wall Street Journal (April 19, 1983).
The author interviewed leading academic and professional researchers on terrorism.

Kern, J. W. "Terrorism and Gunrunning" (Gaithersburg, Maryland: International Association of Chiefs of Police, n.d.), 15 pp.

Kirk, Richard M. "Political Terrorism and the Size of Government: A Positive Institutional Analysis of Violent Political Activity" 40, 1 Public Choice (1983), pp. 41-52.

Koch, Noel C. "Terrorism! The Undeclared War" Defense 85 (March 1985).

Koffler, Judith S. "Terror and Mutilation in the Golden Age" 5, 2 Human Rights Quarterly (May 1983), pp. 116-134.

Kupperman, Robert H. "Terrorism in the Decade Ahead: Adaptation, Technology and Response" in The 1980s: Decade of Confrontation? Proceedings of the Eighth Annual National Security Affairs Conference 13-15 July 1981, cosponsored by the National Defense University and the Under Secretary of Defense for Policy (Washington, D.C.: National Defense University Press, Fort Lesley J. McNair, 1981), pp. 265-284.

Laingui "Histoire de la Lutte Internationale Contre le Terrorisme (History of the International Battle Against Terrorism)" 2 Quaderni (1978).

Lallemand, Roger Terrorisme et Democratie (Brussels: Institut Emile Vandervelde, 1979), 74 pp.

Laqueur, Walter "The Futility of Terrorism; Second Thoughts on Terrorism" in The Political Psychology of Appeasement: Finlandization and Other Unpopular Essays (New Brunswick and London: Transaction/Holt Saunders, 1980), pp. 101-125.

Laqueur, Walter "Reflections on Terrorism" 65 Foreign Affairs (Fall 1986), pp. 86-100.

Laurent, Roland L'internationale Terroriste Demasquee (Nice: A. Lefeuvre, 1981), 300 pp.

Leaney, B. K. "Terrorism: A Summary" 34, 2 Australian Police Journal (April 1980), pp. 100-104.

Lefever, Ernest W. "Terrorism: A National Issues Seminar" 146 World Affairs (Summer 1983).

Leites, Nathan "Understanding the Next Act" 3, 1-2 Terrorism (1979), pp. 1-46.
 Leites attempts to explore terrorist actions and motivations by looking at the statements of several small contemporary groups.

Leonard, Leonard A., ed. Global Terrorism Confronts the Nations (New York University, 1979).

Letman, Sloan T. and Francis G. Spranza "Political Alienation and Terrorism" (Loyola University of Chicago, 1978).

Levine, Herbert M. "Is Terrorism an Effective Political
Instrument?", Chapter 15 in World Politics Debated: A Reader
in Contemporary Issues (New York: McGraw-Hill, 1983).

Liakhov, E. G. Problemy Sotrudnichestva Gosudarstv v Borbe s
Mezhdunarodnym Terrorizmom (Moscow: Mezhdunar. otnosheniia,
1979), 168 pp.

Livingstone, Neil C. "Is Terrorism Effective?" International
Security Review (Fall 1981), pp. 389-409.

Livingstone, Neil C. "The Wolves Among Us: Reflections on the
Past Eighteen Months and Thoughts on the Future" 146, 1 World
Affairs (Summer 1983), pp. 7-22.
A look at changes in tactics of the IRA, ASALA, PLO, and
other terrorists.

Livingstone, Neil C. and Terrell E. Arnold "Democracy Under
Attack" in Neil C. Livingstone and Terrell E. Arnold, eds.
Fighting Back: Winning the War Against Terrorism (Lexington:
Lexington Books, 1986), pp. 1-10.

Lodge, Juliet, ed. Terrorism: A Challenge to the State
(Oxford: M. Robertson, and New York: St. Martin's, 1981), 247
pp.

Lopez, George A. "Dealing with Terrorism in the '80s: A World
Order Approach", paper presented to the 24th annual convention
of the International Studies Association, Mexico City, April
5-9, 1983.

Lopez, George A. "Teaching About Terrorism: Notes on Methods
and Materials" 3, 1-2 Terrorism (1979), pp. 131-145.
Lopez offers a set of educational objectives, as well as a
discussion of the uses of library research exercises, films,
simulations, and values clarification approaches.

Lopez, George A. "Terrorism, Worldviews and Problems of
Policy" paper presented to the International Studies
Association Annual Meeting, Cincinnati, Ohio, March 1982.

Lyakhov, Yevgeniy Grigoryevich Problemy Sotrudnichestva
Gosudarstv V Bor'be Mezhdunarodnym Terrorizmom (Moscow:
Mexhdunar. otnosheniya, 1979), 166 pp.

Mack, Andrew "The Utility of Terrorism" Australia and New
Zealand Journal of Criminology 14, 4 (December 1981), pp. 197-
224, updated paper presented to the 24th annual convention of
the International Studies Association, Mexico City, April 5-9,
1983.

MacKellar, William Terror Run (New York: Dodd, Mead, 1982),
189 pp.

Manor, F. S. "The New World Disorder: If Terrorism is War by
Other Means, We Aren't Even Holding Our Position" 13 American
Spectator (June 1980), pp. 19-21.

Marchese, Stelio "Alle origini del terrorismo strategico" 21, 2 Storia e Politica (June 1982), pp. 257-275.

Markides, Kyriacos "Terrorism: The Functional Equivalent of War", paper presented to the 24th annual convention of the International Studies Association, Mexico City, April 5-9, 1983.

Martin, L. John "Violence, Terrorism, Non-Violence: Vehicles of Social Control" in Joseph S. Roucek, ed. Social Control for the 1980s: A Handbook for Order in a Democratic Society (Westport, Conn.: Greenwood, 1978).

Matz, Ulrich and Gerhard Schmidtchen, eds. Gewalt und Legitimitaet: Analysen zum Terrorismus 4/1 (Opladen, West Germany: Westdeutscher Verlag, 1983).

McBride, James D. "Terrorism: Book Reviews" 40 Humanist (May-June 1980), pp. 39-40.
A review of a book edited by Yonah Alexander, David Carlton and Paul Wilkinson.

McClure, Brooks "The Dynamics of Terrorism" 3 Clandestine Tactics and Technology (Gaithersburg, Maryland: International Association of Chiefs of Police, n.d.).

McGeorge, Harvey J., II "Kinetics of Terrorism" 146, 1 World Affairs (Summer 1983), pp. 23-41

Meltzer, Milton The Terrorists (New York: Harper and Row, 1983), 216 pp.

Merari, Ariel "L'internationalisation du terrorisme politique" 49, 1 Rivista di Studi Politici Internazionali (January-March 1982), pp. 129-134.

Merari, Ariel, ed. On Terrorism and Combatting Terrorism (Tel Aviv University Jaffee Center for Strategic Studies, and University Publications of America, 1986).

Meyer, Edward C. "Low-Level Conflict: An Overview" in Brian Michael Jenkins, conference director Terrorism and Beyond: An International Conference on Terrorism and Low-Level Conflict (Santa Monica: The Rand Corporation, R-2714-DOE/DOJ/DOS/RC, December 1982), pp. 38-44.

Mickolus, Edward F. "International Terrorism in 1979" paper presented to the annual convention of the Academy of Criminal Justice Sciences, Oklahoma City, March 19890.

Mickolus, Edward F. "Studying Terrorism in the 1980s: Looking Backward and Forward" presentation to the Symposium on International Terrorism, Defense Intelligence College, Washington, D.C., December 2-3, 1985.

Mickolus, Edward F. "Studying Terrorist Incidents: Issues in Conceptualization and Data Acquisition" paper presented at the annual meeting of the International Studies Association, Los Angeles, March 18-22, 1980, 31 pp.

Mickolus discusses the development of an early version of the CIA's computerized dataset on international terrorist events, and how this experience led to the creation of an improved system for monitoring terrorist activities.

Mickolus, Edward F. "Tracking the Growth and Prevalence of International Terrorism" in George S. Roukis and Patrick J. Montana, eds. Managing Terrorism: Strategies for the Corporate Executive (Westport, Conn.: Quorum, 1983), pp. 3-22.
Statistics through 1980 on international terrorist attacks.

Mickolus, Edward F. Transnational Terrorism: A Chronology of Events, 1968-1979 (Westport: Greenwood Press, and London: Aldwych, 1980), 967 pp.
An exhaustive chronology of incidents from Biblical times through 1979, with lists of organizations and acronyms, indexes by location and date, by type of attack and date, and groups involved in the attack.

Mickolus, Edward F. and Edward S. Heyman "ITERATE: Monitoring Transnational Terrorism" paper presented to the joint national meeting of the Operations Research Society of America and the Institute for Management Sciences, New York City, May 1-3, 1978, later published in Yonah Alexander and John M. Gleason, eds. Behavioral and Quantitative Perspectives on Terrorism (New York: Pergamon, 1981), pp. 153-174.
Discusses how the variables of the dataset were created, lists the sources and summarizes the data codebook.

Mickolus, Edward F., Edward S. Heyman, and James Schlotter "Responding to Terrorism: Basic and Applied Research" in Stephen Sloan and Richard Shultz, eds. Responding to the Terrorist Threat: Prevention and Control (New York: Pergamon, 1980), pp 174-189.
The authors provide an overview of the types of research which has been conducted on terrorism.

Mickolus, Edward F., Todd Sandler, and Jeanne Murdock International Terrorism in the 1980s: A Chronology (in preparation).
A detailed chronology of international and major foreign internal terrorist attacks, with an econometric analysis of trends.

Mickolus, Edward F., Todd Sandler, Jeanne Murdock and Peter A. Flemming ITERATE III: Attributes of Terrorist Events, 1978-1987 (Falls Church, Va.: Vinyard Software, 1988).
A set of microcomputer disks and codebooks which offer numerical information on the material which appears in the authors' International Terrorism in the 1980s: A Chronology.

Midlarsky, Manus I., Martha Crenshaw and Fumihiko Yoshida "Why Violence Spreads: The Contagion of International Terrorism" 24 International Studies Quarterly (June 1980), pp. 262-298.
The authors look at terrorism as a general phenomenon and a set of subtypes, and use the ITERATE dataset to examine copycat violence. A companion piece by Heyman and Mickolus discusses why ITERATE may be an inappropriate dataset for this research, to which Midlarsky et al offer a rejoinder.

Miller, Abraham H. "On Terrorism" Public Administration Review (July/August 1977), pp. 429-434.

Monday, Mark "TVI Update" 5, 1 TVI Journal (Summer 1984), pp. 39ff., same title in 5, 2 (Fall 1984).

Monti, Daniel J. "The Relation Between Terrorism and Domestic Civil Disorders" 4, 1-4 Terrorism (1980), pp. 123-142.

Motley, James Berry "International Terrorism: A New Mode of Warfare" International Security Review 6, 1 (Spring 1981), pp. 93-123.

Motley, James Berry "Terrorism" National Defense (January 1985).

Motley, James Berry "Terrorist Warfare: Formidable Challenges" 9 Fletcher Forum (Summer 1985), pp. 295-306.
 Motley offers an incremental phases model of potential conflict.

Moynihan, Daniel Patrick "Terrorists, Totalitarians, and the Rule of Law" in Benjamin Netanyahu, ed. Terrorism: How the West Can Win (New York: Farrar, Straus, Giroux, 1986), pp. 41-43.

Muenkler, H. "Guerillakrieg und Terrorismus" 25, 3 Neue Politische Literatur (1980), pp. 299-326.

Naimark, Norman M. Terrorists and Social Democrats (Cambridge: Harvard, 1983).

Nanes, Allan "International Terrorism" Issue Brief (Washington, D.C.: Library of Congress, CRS, August 18, 1981), 16 pp.

Nathan, James A. "The New Feudalism" Foreign Policy (Spring 1981), pp. 156-166.

Neier, Aryeh "Ten Years of Terrorism: Book Review" 38 Bulletin of the Atomic Scientists (March 1982), pp. 31-33.

Neue Zuercher Zeitung (Redaktion der-) Blutspur der Gewalt. Bilanz Eines Jahrzehnt des Terrorismus (Zurich: Buchverlag Dernzz, 1980), 185 pp.

"New Rand Publications Study Options on Terrorism" 12, 26 Security Systems Digest (December 23, 1981), pp. 6-8.

"New Wrinkle for Terrorism May Well be Hypnotized Commandos" Security Systems Digest (April 25, 1979), p. 3.

Newhouse, John "A Freemasonry of Terrorism" The New Yorker (July 8, 1985).

Newhouse, John "International Terrorism in the Social Studies" Social Studies (1980), pp. 14-17.

Netanyahu, Benjamin "Defining Terrorism" in Benjamin Netanyahu, ed. Terrorism: How the West Can Win (New York: Farrar, Straus, Giroux, 1986), pp. 7-15.

Netanyahu, Benzion "Terrorists and Freedom Fighters" in Benjamin Netanyahu, ed. Terrorism: How the West Can Win (New York: Farrar, Straus, Giroux, 1986), pp. 25-30.

The 1980s: Decade of Confrontation? Proceedings of the Eighth Annual National Security Affairs Conference 13-15 July 1981, cosponsored by the National Defense University and the Under Secretary of Defense for Policy (Washington, D.C.: National Defense University Press, Fort Lesley J. McNair, 1981), 312 pp.

Nogueres, Henri "Le Terrorisme" Apres-Demain (Fall 1979), pp. 3-48.
 A collection of articles.

Norton, Augustus R. "Review Essay on Terrorism and the Liberal State" 7, 4 Armed Forces and Society (Summer 1981), pp. 598-625.

O'Brien, Conor Cruise "Thinking About Terrorism" Atlantic Monthly (June 1986), pp. 62-66.

Patterns of International Terrorism (Washington: US Department of State, Office for Combatting Terrorism, 1983), 21 pp.
 These annual studies give statistics on international terrorism: targets, victims, locations, types of attacks.

"Patterns of International Terrorism: 1980: A Research Paper" (Washington, D.C.: US Central Intelligence Agency, National Foreign Assessment Center, PA 81-10163U, April 1981), 17 pp.
 Summarized in "Patterns of International Terrorism: 1980" Defense and Economy World Survey (July 20, 1981), pp. 46-57.

"Patterns of International Terrorism: 1981" 82 Department of State Bulletin (August 1982), pp. 8-21, also available as separate publication (July 1982), 23 pp.

Perez, Frank H. "The Impact of International Terrorism" 340 Current Policy (US Department of State, October 29, 1981).
 Text of address by the Acting Director of the Office for Combatting Terrorism before the Conference on Violence and Extremism: A Leadership Response in Baltimore, Maryland.

Perez, Frank H. "Terrorist Target: The Diplomat" 82, 2065 Department of State Bulletin (August 1982), pp. 22-30, also available in 402 Current Policy (June 10, 1982), 4 pp.
 Presentation to the Instituto de Cuestiones Internacionales Terrorism Conference, June 1982.

Perrault, Giles Un Homme a Part (Paris: B. Barrault, 1984), 586 pp.

Petrakis, G. "Terrorism as a Transnational Phenomenon" 28, 5 Law and Order (May 1980), pp. 26-36.
 Part 1 of a 7-part series.

Pilat, J. F. "Terrorism" 8, 77 <u>Washington Papers</u> (1980), pp. 53-64.

Pontara, G. "Violenza e Terrorismo. Il Problema della Definizione e della Giustificazione" in Luigi Bonanate, ed. <u>Dimensioni del Terrorismo Politico</u> (Milano, 1979), pp. 25-98.

Possony, Stefan T. "Kaleidoscopic Views on Terrorism" 4, 1-4 <u>Terrorism</u> (1980), pp. 89-122.

"Prospective sul Terrorismo" 2 <u>Quaderni</u> (1978).
The entire issue is devoted to the proceedings of a conference on terrorism.

Purkitt, Helen "International Terrorism: A Systematic Study of Past, Present, and Future Trends in Transnational Violence" paper presented to the annual convention of the International Studies Association, Los Angeles, March 18-22, 1980.

Purnell, Susanna W. and Eleanor S. Wainstein <u>The Problems of U.S. Businesses Operating Abroad in Terrorist Environments</u> (Santa Monica: Rand R-2842-DOC, 1981), 103 pp.

Pyle, Christopher H. "Defining Terrorism" <u>Foreign Policy</u> (Fall 1986), pp. 63-78.
A discussion of legal and political aspects of terrorism, the legal status of revolutionaries, extradition, and the right of asylum.

Quainton, Anthony C. E. "Opening Address" in Brian Michael Jenkins, conference director <u>Terrorism and Beyond: An International Conference on Terrorism and Low-Level Conflict</u> (Santa Monica: The Rand Corporation, R-2714-DOE/DOJ/DOS/RC, December 1982), pp. 30-37.

Quainton, Anthony C. E. "Terrorism and Political Violence: A Permanent Challenge to Governments" paper presented to the Sesquicentennial Symposium on Terrorism: The Challenge to the State, Wesleyan University, January 28-30, 1982, 26 pp.

Rana, Swadesh "International Terrorism: A Mode of Combat?" 34, 3 <u>India Quarterly</u> (October-December, 1978), pp. 491-502.

Raufer, Xavier <u>Terrorisme</u> (Paris: Garnier, 1982), 336 pp.

Raynor, Thomas P. <u>Terrorism: Past, Present, Future</u> (New York: F. Watts, 1982), 152 pp.

Reinares-Nestares, Fernando, comp. <u>Terrorismo y Sociedad Democratica</u> (Madrid: Akal, 1982), 185 pp.

Risks International "Special Report: Significant Regional Developments, October-December 1984" 8, 2 <u>Terrorism</u> (1985), pp. 165-184.

Risks International "Terrorism, January-September 1981" 5, 4 <u>Terrorism</u> (1982), pp. 371-372.

Romerstein, Herbert "Political Doctrine and Apparatus" in Uri Ra'anan, Robert L. Pfaltzgraff, Jr., Richard H. Shultz, Ernst Halperin, and Igor Lukes <u>Hydra of Carnage: International Linkages of Terrorism: The Witnesses Speak</u> (Lexington, Mass.: Lexington Books, 1986), pp. 59-76.

"Rooting out a Root of Terror" 4, 10-12 <u>TVI Journal</u> (Winter 1983), pp. 7-10.

Rootes, C. "Living With Terrorism" 6-7 <u>Social Alternatives</u> (1980), pp. 46-49.

Rosenau, James N. "Le Touriste et le Terroriste ou les Deux Extremes du Continuum Transnational (The Tourist and the Terrorist: Two Extremes on a Transnational Continuum)" 10, 2 <u>Etudes Internationales</u> (June 1979), pp. 219-232.

Rubenstein, Richard E. <u>Alchemists of Revolution: Terrorism in the Modern World</u> (New York: Basic Books, 1987), 266 pp. Reviewed by John Prados "Making Sense of Modern Terrorism" <u>Washington Post</u> (April 24, 1987), p. B4. The author looks at theories of the causes of terrorism, but ultimately does not offer empirical data to back his observations.

Rupprecht, Reinhard "Reflections on Elucidating the Causes of Terrorism from a Police Perspective" in Hans-Dieter Schwind, et al, eds. <u>Causes of Terrorism in the FRG</u> (Berlin: Walter de Gruyter, 1978), pp. 154-168.

Russell, Charles A. and Bowman H. Miller "Transnational Terrorism: Terrorist Tactics and Techniques" 4 <u>Clandestine Tactics and Technology</u> (Gaithersburg, Maryland: International Association of Chiefs of Police, n.d.).

Russett, Bruce M. "Who Are Terrorists" 17, 5 <u>Society</u> (1980), pp. 16-17.

Rymph, Raymond C., David L. Taylor, Marsha A. Yaggie, and Michele L. Marzoni "Terrorism and Social Reaction: A Model Derived from Five Case Studies" paper presented to the North Central Sociological Association, 1978, available from the authors at Purdue University, West Lafayette, Indiana 47907. The authors look at terrorism in Argentina, Turkey, West Germany, and the US (by the Hanafis and Weathermen).

Sablier, Edouard <u>Le Fil Rouge: Histoire Secrete du Terrorisme International</u> (Paris: Plon, 1983), 308 pp.

Saddy, Fehmy "International Terrorism, Human Rights, and World Order" 5, 4 <u>Terrorism</u> (1982), pp. 325-352.

Salcedo, Jose Maria "El papel del terrorismo y el terrorismo de papel" <u>QueHacer</u> (January-February 1981), pp. 38-45.

Sandler, Todd, et. al "Economic Methods and the Study of Terrorism" in Paul Wilkinson, ed. <u>Research on Terrorism</u> (Aberdeen, Scotland: University of Aberdeen Press, 1987).

Sandler, Todd, John T. Tschirhart and Jon Cauley "A Theoretical Analysis of Transnational Terrorism" 77, 1 American Political Science Review (March 1983), pp. 36-54.
Abstract reads: "This article presents some 'rational-actor' models that depict the negotiation process between terrorists and government policy makers for those incidents where hostages or property are seized and demands are issued. The models account for the objectives and constraints faced by both the terrorists and the policy makers. Uncertainty is introduced through probability constraints (i.e., chance constraints) requiring a specific likelihood of some event occurring. Implications are subsequently extracted from the comparative static analysis as the models' parameters are changed. The last part of the article presents a club theory analysis concerning the sharing of transnational commando forces."

Santoro, Victor Disruptive Terrorism (Port Townsend, Washington: Loompanics Unlimited, 1984), 135 pp.

Sayre, Robert M. "International Terrorism: A Long Twilight Struggle" 84 Department of State Bulletin (October 1984), pp. 48-50, also available as 608 Current Policy (August 15, 1984), 3 pp.
The State Department's chief counter-terrorist outlines US policy.

Schamis, Gerardo Jorge War and Terrorism in International Affairs (New Brunswick, New Jersey: Transaction Books, 1980), 89 pp.

Scherer, John L. Terrorism, An Annual Survey, Volume I (Minneapolis, Scherer, 1982).
Volume II, 216 pp., published in 1983.

Schmid, Alex Peter Political Terrorism: A Research Guide to Concepts, Theories, Data Bases and Literature (Amsterdam: North-Holland Publishing, and New Brunswick, New Jersey: Transaction Books, 1984), 585 pp.
An invaluable reference work, which includes a directory of the world's terrorist groups, a 4091-item annotated bibliography by A. J. Jongman which is perhaps the best available on European writings on terrorism, a survey of 200 of the world's leading experts on terrorism regarding "invisible colleges" of students of political violence, and an exposition on data bases and theories.

Schmidtchen, Gerhard "Jugend und Staat" in Ulrich Matz and Gerhard Schmidtchen, eds. Gewalt und Legitimitaet: Analysen zum Terrorismus 4/1 (Opladenn, West Germany: Westdeutscher Verlag, 1983).

Schmidtchen, Gerhard "Terroristische Karrieren" in Herbert Jaeger, et al., Lebenslaufanalysen: Analysen zum Terrorismus 2 (Opladen, West Germany: Westdeutscher Verlag, 1981).

"Secretary-General Notes 'Steady Increase' in Politically Motivated Violence" 21 UN Monthly Chronicle (October 1984), pp. 86-87.

Sederberg, P. C. "Defining Terrorism" (Columbia: University of South Carolina, 1981 mimeo), 5 pp.

Selzer, Michael <u>Terrorist Chic: An Exploration of Violence in the Seventies</u> (New York: Hawthorn, 1979).

Shuja, Sharif M. "Terrorism--A Special Problem: National or Transnational?" 31, 1 <u>Pakistan Horizon</u> (1978), pp. 102ff.

Shultz, George P. "The Challenge to the Democracies" in Benjamin Netanyahu, ed. <u>Terrorism: How the West Can Win</u> (New York: Farrar, Straus, Giroux, 1986), pp. 16-24.

Shultz, George P. "Terrorism and the Modern World" 7, 4 <u>Terrorism</u> (1985), pp. 431ff.

Shultz, George P. "Terrorism: The Problem and the Challenge" 84 <u>Department of State Bulletin</u> (August 1984), pp. 29-30, reprinted in 586 <u>Current Policy</u> (June 13, 1984), 3 pp.
  A transcript of the Secretary of State's presentation to the House Foreign Affairs Committee.

Shultz, Richard H. "Conceptualizing Political Terrorism: A Typology" in A. D. Buckley and D. D. Olson, eds. <u>International Terrorism: Current Research and Future Directions</u> (Wayne, New Jersey: Avery Publishing Group, 1980), pp. 9-18.

Shultz, Richard H., Jr. "Recent Regional Patterns" in Uri Ra'anan, Robert L. Pfaltzgraff, Jr., Richard H. Shultz, Ernst Halperin, and Igor Lukes <u>Hydra of Carnage: International Linkages of Terrorism: The Witnesses Speak</u> (Lexington, Mass.: Lexington Books, 1986), pp. 95-124.

Shultz, Richard H., Jr. and Stephen Sloan "International Terrorism: The Nature of the Threat" in Richard H. Shultz, Jr. and Stephen Sloan, eds. <u>Responding to the Terrorist Threat: Security and Crisis Management</u> (New York: Pergamon, 1980), pp. 1-17.

Shultz, Richard H., Jr. and Stephen Sloan "Terrorism: An Objective Act, A Subjective Reality" in Richard H. Shultz, Jr. and Stephen Sloan, eds. <u>Responding to the Terrorist Threat: Security and Crisis Management</u> (New York: Pergamon, 1980), pp. 245-254.

Simon, Jeffrey D. "The Future of Political Risk Analysis" 5, 2 <u>TVI Journal</u> (Fall 1984), pp. 23-25.

Simon, Jeffrey D. "TVI Update" 5, 4 <u>TVI: Terrorism Violence Insurgency Journal</u> (Spring 1985), pp. 54ff.

Simon, Jeffrey D. "TVI Update (As of September 1, 1985)" 6, 1 <u>TVI: Terrorism Violence Insurgency Journal</u> (Summer 1985), pp. 52-56.

Singh, Baljit "Some Values and Social Issues in Political Terrorism" 6, 1 <u>Ohio Northern University Law Review</u> (1979), pp. 82-88.
  Singh argues that terrorism studies have attempted to

describe, diagnose, and prescribe, without attempting to explain behavior. He argues that actions must be assessed in their social context, which varies across cultures. He notes that there are great asymmetries between governments and peoples, many of whom do not have their own states. Several tables illustrating this phenomenon are presented.

Slater, Robert O. and Michael Stohl, eds. Current Perspectives on International Terrorism (London: Macmillan and New York: St. Martin's, 1986), 240pp.
This book provides an indepth analysis of seven salient perspectives on international terrorism: psychological factors in terrorism; goals and objectives of terrorism; empirical research on terrorism; support mechanisms for terrorists; state response to terrorism; and future trends in terrorism. It provides systematic analysis of terrorism making it useful for government policy makers and scholars alike.

Sloan, Stephen "The Anatomy of Non-Territorial Terrorism: An Analytical Essay" 4 Clandestine Tactics and Technology (Gaithersburg, Maryland: International Association of Chiefs of Police, n.d.).

Sloan, Stephen "International Terrorism: Conceptual Problems and Implications" 17, 2 Journal of Thought (1982), pp. 19-29.

Sloan, Stephen Simulating Terrorism (Norman: University of Oklahoma, 1981), 158 pp.
Reviewed by Edward Mickolus in 75, 4 American Political Science Review (December 1981), p. 1027; R. L. Kavanaugh 49, 4 Police Chief (1982), pp. 64-65.

Smith, W. H. "International Terrorism: A Political Analysis" 31 Year Book of World Affairs (London: Stevens, 1977), pp. 140-141.

Snitch, Thomas "Political Separatism and Terrorism: A Global Overview" paper presented to the panel on the Role of Terrorism in Ethnic Nationalism at the annual convention of the International Studies Association/South, University of Florida, October 29-31, 1981.

Soustelle, Jacque "Liberty or License?" in Benjamin Netanyahu, ed. International Terrorism: Challenge and Response (Jerusalem: Jonathan Institute, 1980).

Sozialprotest, Gewalt, Terror (Stuttgart: Klett-Cotta, 1982), 476 pp.

St. John, P. "Analysis and Response of a Decade of Terrorism" International Perspectives (September 1981), pp. 2-5.
Cites 7 types of terrorists: Latin American, nationalist-separatist, urban leftists, the Carlos network, the KGB's allies, criminals, and psychotics.

"Statistics: Terrorism, October 1981--March 1982", 6, 1 Terrorism (1982), p. 105.

Sterling, Claire <u>Terror Decade: A Biopsy on International Terrorism, 1970-80</u> (New York: Holt, Rinehart, 1981).

Stinson, James L. and Edward S. Heyman "Analytic Approaches for Investigating Terrorist Crimes" (Gaithersburg, Maryland: International Association of Chiefs of Police, n.d.), 43 pp.

Stohl, Michael "Demystifying Terrorism: Myths and Realities of Contemporary Political Terrorism" in Michael Stohl, ed. <u>The Politics of Terrorism</u>; Third Edition Revised and Expanded. (New York: Marcel Dekker, 1987).

Stohl, Michael "Fashions and Phantasies in the Study of Political Terrorism" (Dubrovnik: Inter-University Center, 1981), 18 pp.

Stohl, Michael, ed. <u>The Politics of Terrorism</u> Third Edition. (New York: Marcel Dekker, 1987), 672 pp.
 This updated and expanded edition focuses on major theories, concepts, strategies, ideologies and implications of terrorism. Placing terrorists and terrorist action within their socio-political settings, this text and reference includes essays dealing with various geographical and topical aspects of terrorism. It also examines recent and longstanding controversies regarding the political consequences and causes of terror.

Stohl, Michael "Three Worlds of Terrorism" (Dubrovnik: Inter-University Center, 1981), 20 pp.

Stohl, Michael "The Three Worlds of Terrorism" 3, 6 <u>TVI, Terrorism, Violence, Insurgency</u> (July 1982), pp. 4-11.
 Updated version of "Three Worlds of Terrorism".

Sulevo, Kari "Terrori ja poliittinen jarjestelma (Terrorism and the Political System)" 4 <u>Politiikka</u> (1979), pp. 305-318.

Sundberg, Jacob W. F. "Operation Leo" 5, 3 <u>Terrorism</u> (1981), pp. 197-232.

Sussman, Deborah "Five Who Support Terrorism and Five Who Fight It" 118 <u>Scholastic Update</u> (May 16, 1986), pp. 17-18.

Szmidt, Longin Tadeusz <u>Terroryzm a Panstwo</u> (Lublin, Wydaw Lubelskie, 1979), 358 pp.

Tabakova, Vesela <u>Kogo Ubivat Teoristite</u> (Sofiia, Nar. mladezh, 1979), 138 pp.

Taylor, D. L. "Terrorism and Criminology: The Application of a Perspective" (West Lafayette, Indiana: Purdue University Institute for the Study of Social Change, 1978).

"Terrorism Begins at Home" 49 <u>Progressive</u> (August 1985), pp. 9-10.

<u>Terrorisme et Culture</u> (Paris: Fondation pour les Etudes de Defense Nationale, 1981), 213 pp.

"Terrorism: Origins, Directions and Support" (Washington, D.C.: 97th Congress, Hearings of the Subcommittee on Security and Terrorism, Committee on the Judiciary, April 24, 1981).

"Terrorism: Pure and Complex" 111 Commonweal (December 14, 1984), pp. 675-676.

"Terrorism: Special Issue" 10, 2 Conservative Digest (1984), 48 pp.

"Terrorism: A National Issues Seminar: The Brookings Institution Advanced Study Program" 146, 1 World Affairs (Summer 1983), pp. 79-113.

Terrorismo y Sociedad Democratica (Madrid: Akal, 1982), 185 pp.

Terroryzm Polityczny (Warsaw: Panstowowe Wydawn, Nauk, 1981), 353 pp.

"Terrorist Attacks Against Diplomats: A Statistical Overview of International Terrorist Attacks on Diplomatic Personnel and Facilities from January 1968 to June 1981" (Washington, D.C.: US Department of State, December 1981), 16 pp.

"Terrorist Incident Charts (1980)" 5, 3 Terrorism (1981), pp. 287-292.

"Terrorist Operational Patterns" 3, 1 Executive Risk Assessment (January 1981).

Thackrah, J. Richard "Contemporary Terrorism" 17, 1 Government and Opposition (Winter 1982), pp. 127ff.

Thackrah, John Richard Dictionary of Terrorism (London: Routledge and Kegan Paul, 1986).
Thackrah is connected with the Police Staff College, Bramshill House, Hampshire, England.

"Theme Issue: Worldwide Chronology of Terrorism 1981" 6, 2 Terrorism (1982).

"Through the Barrel of a Gun" 69 The Middle East (July 1980), pp. 8-15.
After discussing the recent history of guerrilla and terrorist campaigns, the author concludes that terrorist operations and cooperation will decline.

Todd, William Hoskins: The Artist as Terrorist (Ehling Clifton Books, 1982), 180 pp.

Touster, Saul "Comments (on Precursors on Terrorism)" 5, 2 Human Rights Quarterly (May 1985), pp. 147-150.

Trent, Darrell M. "The New Religion: Terrorism" Saturday Night (1980), pp. 41-49, also available in 8 Human Rights (Winter 1980), pp. 10-13, 47-48.

Trent, Darrell M. "United States and Transnational Terrorism" address at the Town Hall of California, Los Angeles, 1979 (Stanford: Hoover Institution, 1980), 15 pp.

Tromp, Hylke "A Survey of the Contemporary Spread of Terrorism", paper presented to the 24th annual convention of the International Studies Association, Mexico City, April 5-9, 1983.

Truby, J. David How Terrorists Kill: The Complete Terrorist Arsenal (Boulder: Paladin, 1978), 87 pp.

Truby, J. David "Improvised/Modified Small Arms Used by Terrorists" (Gaithersburg, Maryland: International Association of Chiefs of Police, n.d.), 16 pp.

Truby, J. David "Women as Terrorists" 3 Clandestine Tactics and Technology (Gaithersburg, Maryland: International Association of Chiefs of Police, n.d.).

Turk, Austin T. "Social Dynamics of Terrorism" 463 Annals of the American Academy of Political and Social Science (September 1982), pp. 119-128.

US Department of State Patterns of Global Terrorism 1983 (Washington, D.C.: US Department of State, 1984).

US Department of State, Office for Combatting Terrorism "Terrorist Attacks Against U.S. Business" 8, 2 Terrorism (1985), pp. 185ff.

US House of Representatives, Committee on the Judiciary, Subcommittee on Civil and Constitutional Rights Report on Domestic and International Terrorism (Washington, D.C., April 1981), 36 pp.

US Senate, Committee on the Judiciary, Subcommittee on Security and Terrorism "Terrorism: Origins, Direction and Support: Hearing" (Washington, D.C.: April 24, 1981), 92 pp.

Vaurio, Elaine L. The Efficacy of Terrorism (American University, College of Public and International Affairs, Master's Thesis, December 1979), 136 pp.
Vaurio uses quantitative content analysis of newspaper editorials and letters to the editor with events data analysis to study the efficacy of terrorist bargaining strategies.

Virtanen, Michael "Analyst Calls Terror Risk a Long Shot for Travelers" 45 Travel Weekly (February 20, 1986), pp. 1-2.
The analyst is Eugene Mastrangelo.

Virtanen, Michael "Government Officials See Tourism as Weapon Against Terrorism" 45 Travel Weekly (February 27, 1986), p. 59.
A summary of presentations by Ambassador Robert Oakley and Donna Tuttle.

Vitiuk, V. V. "Mezhdunarodnyi Terrorizm (Understanding International Terrorism)" 2 Sotsiologicheskie Issledovaniia (USSR) (1982), pp. 59-68.

Vitiuk, V.V. "Toward an Analysis and Evaluation of the Evolution of Terrorism" 18, 3 Soviet Sociology (Winter 1979-1980), pp. 22-43.

Wardlaw, Grant Political Terrorism: Theory, Tactics, and Counter-Measures (Cambridge University Press, 1982), 218 pp.

Watkins, James D., Admiral "Countering Terrorism: A New Challenge to our National Conscience" Sea Power (November 1984).

Watson, Francis M., Sr. "Terrorist Propaganda" 2 Clandestine Tactics and Technology (Gaithersburg, Maryland: International Association of Chiefs of Police, 1976).

Waugh, William L., Jr. "The Value of Violence: Organizational and Political Objectives of Terrorist Groups" Conflict Quarterly (Summer 1983).

Wedziagolski, Karol and Tadeusz Swietochowski, eds. Boris Savinkov: Portrait of a Terrorist (Kingston Press, 1985), 250 pp.

Weil, Sherri L. "Terrorist Expert Yonah Alexander: Scholar in an Uncharted Field" Georgetown Magazine (March-April, 1983), pp. 10-12.

Whitaker, Reg "Who are the Real Terrorists?" 20 Canadian Dimension (July-August 1986), p. 40.

Wilkinson, Paul The New Fascists (Marston Book Service, 1981), 192 pp.

Wilkinson, Paul, ed. Research on Terrorism (Aberdeen, Scotland: University of Aberdeen Press, 1987).

Wilkinson, Paul "Terrorism: International Dimensions--Answering the Challenge" 113 Conflict Studies (November 1979), pp. 1-14.

Wilkinson, Paul "Terrorism: Weapon of the Weak" Encyclopaedia Britannica Book of the Year (1979), pp. 128-137.

Wilson, James Q. "Thinking About Terrorism" 72 Commentary (July 1981), pp. 34-39.

Wolf, John B. "Economic Aspects of Terroristic Threats" (Gaithersburg, Maryland: International Association of Chiefs of Police, 1979).

Wolf, John B. "Organizational and Operational Aspects of Contemporary Terrorist Groups" 6, 3 Update Report (Gaithersburg, Maryland: International Association of Chiefs of Police, 1980).

Wolf, John B. "Terrorism: The Scourge of the 1980s" (Gaithersburg, Maryland: International Association of Chiefs of Police, 1980).

Wolfgang, Marvin E., special editor International Terrorism (Beverly Hills: Sage, 1982), 206 pp.

Woods, B. F. "Terrorism: The Continuing Crisis: Observations on the Potential Consequences of International Terrorism" 48, 5 Police Chief 48, 5 (1981), pp. 48-49.

Wooton, Barbara "When is a War not a War?" New Society (August 27, 1981), pp. 339-341.

"World Directory on Dissent and Insurgency 2 TVI Journal (1981), pp. 4-50.

"World Terrorism Intelligence Report" 12, 26 Security Systems Digest (December 23, 1981), pp. 10-12.

Wright, C.D. Terrorism (Fayetteville, Arkansas: Lost Roads Publishers, 1979).

Zamoyskiy, Lelliy Petrovich Taynyye pruzhiny mezhdunarodnogo terrorizma (Moscow: Mezhdunaroydnyye otnosheniya, 1982), 102 pp.

Zawodny, J. K. "Infrastructures of Terrorist Organizations" paper presented to the conference on Psychopathology and Political Violence: Terrorism and Assassination, sponsored by the University of Chicago, Department of Psychiatry and the Institute of Social and Behavioral Pathology, November 16-17, 1979, 22 pp., published in Lawrence Zelic Freedman and Yonah Alexander, eds. Perspectives on Terrorism (Wilmington: Scholarly Resources, Inc., 1983), pp. 61-70.
 Compared to the World War II resistance organizations, whose membership numbered in the hundreds of thousands, contemporary terrorist organizations are tiny. The WWII groups used a hierarchical structure, whereas modern groups are centrifugal. Zawodny points out 11 behavioral patterns inherent in this structure.

Zimmermann, Ekkart Political Violence, Crises, and Revolutions: Theories and Research (Cambridge, Mass.: Schenkman, 1983), 792 pp.

Tactics of Terrorists

ASSASSINATIONS

Alder, Douglas D. "Assassination as Political Efficacy: Two Case Studies from World War I" 12, 2 East European Quarterly (1978), pp. 209-231.
A look at the assassinations of Archduke Francis Ferdinand and Austrian Minister President Karkl Sturgkh.

"Ambush: Tool of Terror" 25 minute film (Motorola Teleprograms, Inc., 1974).

Bell, J. Bowyer Assassin (New York: St. Martins, 1979), 310 pp.

Branch, Taylor and Eugene M. Propper Labyrinth (New York: Viking, 1982), 623 pp.
Reviewed by Ross Thomas "The Anatomy of an Assassination" Washington Post Book World (March 28, 1982), p. 4. Another look at the Letelier assassination.

Cassidy, William L. "Planned Political Assassinations: An Introductory Overview" 2 Clandestine Tactics and Technology (Gaithersburg, Maryland: International Association of Chiefs of Police, 1977), 31 pp.

Clarke, James W. "American Assassins: An Alternative Typology" British Journal of Political Science (1981).

Clarke, James W. American Assassins: The Darker Side of Politics (Princeton University Press, 1982), 321 pp.
Reviewed by Edwin M. Yoder, Jr. "Taking Aim at Men of Power" Washington Post Book World (October 24, 1982), pp. 9, 13.

Clarke, James W. "Emotional Deprivation and Political Deviance: Some Observations on Governor Wallace's Would-Be Assassin, Arthur H. Bremer" paper presented at the annual meeting of the International Society of Political Psychology, Boston, June 4-7, 1980.

Clarke, James W. "Huey Long's Apolitical Assassin: The Subtle and Sometimes Tragic Boundary Between Political and Personal Life" paper presented to the annual meeting of the Southwestern Social Science Association, Houston, Texas, April 2-5, 1980.

Clarke, James W. "The Risks of Presidential Candidacy: The Perspective and Motive of Sirhan Sirhan" paper presented to the annual meeting of the American Political Science Association, Washington, D.C., August 27-31, 1980, 38 pp.
   Clarke argues that Sirhan does not fit models of the psychotic assassin, and believes that he was a politically motivated individual.

Cohen, Michael J. "The Moyne Assassination, November 1944: A Political Analysis" 15, 3 Middle Eastern Studies (October 1979), pp. 358-373.

Cooper, H. H. Anthony "Terroristic Fads and Fashions: The Year of the Assassin" 27, 3 Chitty's Law Journal (1979), pp. 92-97.

Dinges, John and Saul Landau Assassination on Embassy Row (New York: Pantheon, 1980), 411 pp.
   A look at the Letelier assassination of 1976. Reviewed by Patrick Breslin "Getting Away with Murder" 10, 27 Washington Post Book World (July 6, 1980), pp. 1-2.

Gordon, David "Political Murder: From Tyrannicide to Terrorism" 111 Library Journal (January 1986), p. 82.

Gurr, Ted Robert "Political Murder: From Tyrannicide to Terrorism (book reviews)" 23 Society (September-October 1986).

Heikal, Mohamed Autumn of Fury: The Assassination of Sadat (New York: Random House, 1983), 290 pp.
   Reviewed by Hermann Frederick Eilts "Anwar Sadat, Parade's End" 13, 31 Washington Post Book World (July 31, 1983), pp. 1-2, and Edward Mortimer "Accusations of an Ex-Adviser" New York Times Book Review (August 14, 1983), pp. 9, 26.

Hill, Gerald N. and Kathleen Thompson Hill Aquino Assassination: The True Story and Analysis of the Assassination of Philippine Senator Benigno S. Aquino, Jr. (Sonoma, California: Hilltop, 1983), 224 pp.

Hsu, Der-Ann and Richard E. Quandt "Statistical Analyses of Aircraft Hijacking and Political Assassination" (Princeton University, Econometric Research Program, 1976).

Krebs, Edward S. "Assassination in the Chinese Republican Revolutionary Movement" Ch'ing-shs wen-ti'i (China Studies) (December 1981), also available in Proceedings and Papers of the Georgia Association of History (1981), pp. 111-134.
   A look at assassinations during 1903-1907 and 1910-1912.

Lebow, R. Ned "Origins of Sectarian Assassination: The Case of Belfast, Northern Ireland" in Alan D. Buckley and Daniel D. Olson, eds. International Terrorism: Current Research and Future Directions (Wayne, New Jersey: Avery, 1980), pp. 41-53.

Lee, Martin A. and Kevin Coogan "Papal Shooting Probe Moves Into U.S.: 'Right-Wing Killers Coached Ali Agca to Finger Soviets,' Then Entered U.S." 22 National Catholic Reporter (January 24, 1986), pp. 7-10.

Perlstein, Gary R. "The Changing Face of Terrorism: From Regicide to Homicide" 30 International Journal of Offender Therapy and Comparative Criminology (December 1986), pp. 187-193.

Pope, Mark "Taking the Word to a Terror-Prone World: Missionaries at Risk" 30 Christianity Today (March 7, 1986), pp. 50-51.
Implications of the killing of missionary Chester Bitterman, and attacks on the Summer Institute of Linguistics.

Premo, Daniel L. "Political Assassination in Guatemala: A Case of Institutionalized Terror" 23, 4 Journal of Interamerican Studies and World Affairs (1981), pp. 429-456.

Reid, Donald M. "Political Assassination in Egypt, 1910-1954" 15, 4 International Journal of African Historical Studies (1982), pp. 625-651.

Rosenzweig, S. "On Assassination: A Democratic Outlook" 7 Aggressive Behavior (1981), pp. 265-274.

Schmookler, Andrew "Assassinations: The Problem is Not That the World is Sick" 5, 4 Terrorism (1982), pp. 367-370.

Snitch, Thomas H. "Assassinations and Political Violence, 1968-1978: An Events Data Approach" paper presented at the annual meeting of the National Capital Area Political Science Association and the International Studies Association, Washington, D.C., March 1980, also given at the annual meeting of the International Studies Association, Los Angeles, March 19, 1980, 37 pp.
Snitch discusses how to measure assassination events, problems in source coverage, and some preliminary findings.

Snitch, Thomas H. "Terrorism and Political Assassinations: A Transnational Assessment, 1968-1980" 463 Annals of the American Academy of Political and Social Science (September 1982), pp. 54-68.
Snitch looks at 721 political assassinations in 123 countries over a 13 year period, and finds shifts toward attacks against businessmen and diplomats, both of which were relatively unprotected targets.

Takeuchi, Jane, Fredric Solomon, and W. Walter Menninger, eds. Behavioral Science and the Secret Service: Toward the Prevention of Assassination (Washington: National Academy Press, 1981), 193 pp.

Turk, Austin T. "Assassination" in Sanford H. Kadish, ed. Encyclopedia of Crime and Justice (New York: Free Press/Macmillan, 1983).

BOMBINGS

The Arson Report (Washington, D.C.: National Crime Prevention Association).
An 8-page newsletter published 15 times per year to "help you meet the incendiary challenge in your community or business organization."

"Belgian Bombings: Terrorist at Defense-Related Organizations" 122 Aviation Week (May 6, 1985), p. 79.
Discusses actions by the Revolutionary Front for Proletarian Action, and bombings against the AEG-Telefunken AG in 1984 and the North Atlantic Assembly in 1985.

Biddle, Wayne "It Must be Simple and Reliable" 7 Discover (June 1986), pp. 22-31.
A discussion of the weapons and bombs used by terrorists, including a graphic on a pop-up obstacle for truck bombers.

Cockburn, Andrew "Can We Stop a Bomb Smuggler?" Parade (November 3, 1985), pp. 12-14.

Diamond, Stuart "Bomb Detectors" 3 Omni (November 1980), p. 40.

"Federal Law Enforcement Role at Issue in Abortion Bombings" 16 Criminal Justice Newsletter (February 1, 1985), pp. 7-8.

"Firebombs" 15 minute 16 mm. color film (Sacramento, California: MSM Studios, 1971).

"Keep It Simple and Reliable" 7, 6 Discover (June 1986), pp. 22-31.
A profusely illustrated cover story on the technology of terrorist bombs.

Maxwell, Evan "Bomb on the Loose! A Terrorists - and a Bomb-Were Reported on a Passenger Plane" 129 Reader's Digest (Canada) (July 1986), pp. 86-90.

McBee, Carol "Report on Explosives Tagging Technology: Description, History and Present Status" (Washington, D.C.: Library of Congress, CRS, March 26, 1976), 33 pp.

Means, Howard "Dynamite Lady" 21 Washingtonian (March 1986), pp. 132ff.
A profile of Beth Salamanca, an expert on terrorist bombs.

Newhouser, C. R. "Mail Bombs" (Gaithersburg, Maryland: International Association of Chiefs of Police, n.d.), 32 pp.

"Paris Terror Bombs Tossing Cold Water on Leisure Industry" 322 Variety (February 12, 1986), pp. 1-2.

"Protection Against Mail Bombs" 5, 6 Assets Protection (November-December 1980), pp. 41-42.
Includes a mail bomb recognition checklist.

Rosenberg, Robert "Tick... Tick... Tick...: For the Guys in the Jerusalem Bomb Squad, Business is Booming" 33, 7 Playboy (July 1986), pp. 86, 110, 131, 158-163.

Salamanca, Beth A. "Vehicle Bombs: Death on Wheels" in Neil C. Livingstone and Terrell E. Arnold, eds. Fighting Back: Winning the War Against Terrorism (Lexington: Lexington Books, 1986), pp. 35-48.

Spencer, Joseph Frank Target: San Francisco; An Analysis of Bombing Incidents in San Francisco, and an Assessment of the San Francisco Police Response (Golden Gate University, D.P.A. dissertation 1979), 155 pp.

"Terrorist Bombings" 1, 9 Executive Risk Assessment (July 1979), pp. 1-6.

SKYJACKINGS

Adams, Nathan M. "Destination Teheran: Anatomy of a Hijacking" 126 Reader's Digest (October 1985), pp. 71-80.
A review of the Islamic Jihad Organization's hijacking of a Trans World Airlines plane.

Amster, Robin and Jane Levere "Industry Reports Minimal Impact from Latest Terrorism Incident" 45 Travel Weekly (September 15, 1986), pp. 1-2.
A discussion of the effects of the attack on the Pan Am jet in Pakistan.

Ashley, Steven "Can Technology Stop Terror in the Air?" 227 Popular Science (November 1985), pp. 68-73.

Bogan, J. A., J. D. Truby and M. Monday "Passenger Screening: An Impractical Joke" 1, 5 TVI Journal (1980), pp. 10-16.

Butman, Hillel From Leningrad to Jerusalem (1981).
The leader of the 1970 unsuccessful hijacking out of Russia by Jewish refuseniks tells of the hijack plan and his years in prison.

Carlson, Kurt One American Must Die: A Hostage's Personal Account of the Hijacking of Flight 847 (New York: Congden and Weed, 1986).

Channing, Rory "Iranian Threat Raises Specter of Tanker Hijackings: Saudi Arabia, Kuwait Could be Targets" Oil Daily (March 4, 1986), p. 6.

Cooper, H. H. Anthony "Skyjacking: The Threat to Corporate Aviation" 1, 5 TVI Journal ((1980), pp. 2-6.

Derickson, Uli and Jim Gallo "I'm No Heroine" 127 Reader's Digest (November 1985), pp. 131-136.
A personal narrative by a TWA flight attendant involved in a hijacking.

"Deterring Airport Terrorist Attacks and Compensating the Victims" 125 <u>University of Pennsylvania Law Review</u> (May 1977), pp. 1134-1165.

Dupin, Chris, Craig Dunlap, Tom McNiff, Jr., Joseph Bonney and Thomas Taylor "Seajack Spotlights Cruise Security" 366 <u>Journal of Commerce</u> (October 9, 1985), pp. 1Aff.
A discussion of the effects of the Achille Lauro hijacking.

Feazel, Michael "Pilots May Boycott Nations That Encourage Terrorism" 124 <u>Aviation Week</u> (April 14, 1986), p. 34.
Discussions by the International Federation of Air Line Pilots Associations.

Feiler, Stuart I. "Terrorism: Is It Winning?" 20 <u>Hotels and Restaurants International</u> (September 1986), pp. 71-72.
The article includes charts on percentage of terrorist acts by region, and number of hijackings by geographic region.

Finger, Seymour Maxwell "Security of International Civil Aviation: The Role of the International Civil Aviation Organization" 6, 4 <u>Terrorism: An International Journal</u> (1983), pp. 519-527.
ICAO agreements have helped reduce air hijackings from 245 in 1969-1971 to 147 in 1978-1980.

Fingerman, Mark E. "Skyjacking and the Bonn Declaration of 1978: Sanctions Applicable to Recalcitrant Nations" 10, 1 <u>California Western International Law Journal</u> (Winter, 1980), pp. 123-152.

"Freedom of the Airways" 154 <u>America</u> (February 22, 1986), pp. 130-131.
An editorial regarding counter-terrorist searches.

Hartzman, Richard "Airport Terrorism and Airline Hijackings" 21 <u>Meetings and Conventions</u> (July 1986), p. 145.

"Hijackers' Choice" <u>Parade Magazine</u> (September 8, 1985), p. 20.
Statistics on the frequency of hijackings in 11 top US airports. Miami led the way with 24 hijackings, followed by New York JFK (20), Los Angeles (14), Chicago O'Hare (13).

Horvitz, J. F. "Arab Terrorism and International Aviation: Deterrence Versus the Political Act" 24 <u>Chitty's Law Journal</u> (May 1976), pp. 145-154.

Hubbard, David G. <u>Winning Back the Sky: A Tactical Analysis of Terrorism</u> (Dallas: Saybrook, 1986), 141 pp.
Reviewed by George James 91 <u>New York Times Book Review</u> (February 16, 1986), p. 17; and Richard B. Finnegan 111 <u>Library Journal</u> (January 1986), p. 69.

Leonard, Edward "Hijacked: When his Wife and Son Died Aboard EgyptAir Flight 648, a Calgary Man Channelled his Rage into a Campaign to Protect Air Travellers from Terrorism" 101 <u>Saturday Night</u> (June 1986), pp. 44-49.

Levere, Jane "Shein: Security is Key to El Al's Success" 45 Travel Weekly (March 10, 1986), pp. 1-4.

Leich, Marian Nash "Contemporary Practice of the United States Relating to International Law" 77, 4 American Journal of International Law (1983), pp. 875-877.
A look at the problem of obtaining information on the fate of persons who hijack airplanes to Cuba.

Murphy, Harry "Prevention of Aerial Piracy to the US, 1972-1978" (Gaithersburg, Maryland: International Association of Chiefs of Police, 1979).

Nestlebaum, Karen "Airports Buckle Up: Heightened Concern and Tightened Controls Follow in Wake of Last Summer's Terrorism" 20 Meetings and Conventions (November 1985), pp. 41-43.

North, David M. "Terrorist Actions Boost Sales of Corporate Jets" 123 Aviation Week (July 8, 1985), pp. 27-28.

Quandt, Richard "Some Statistical Characterizations of Aircraft Hijacking" 6 Accident Analysis and Prevention (1975), pp. 115ff.

Rosenfield, Stanley B. "Air Piracy: Is It Time to Relax Our Security?" in Jon S. Schultz and Jon P. Thomas, eds. Criminal Justice Systems Review (Buffalo: William S. Hein, 1974), pp. 67-94.

Schroth, Raymond A. "'These People are Fighting for my Mind'-Reflections on Hijackings and the Press" 154 America (February 1, 1986), pp. 65-67.

"Skyjacking and the Bonn Declaration of 1978: Sanctions Applicable to Recalcitrant Nations" 10 California Western International Law Journal (1980), pp. 123ff.

"STAG Topics: Terrorism, Travel Costs" 45 Travel Weekly (March 3, 1986), p. 6.
Discussions regarding economic aspects of terrorism at conferences of the Society of Travel Agents in Government.

Sturken, Barbara "Pilot Assails Government Training Against Terrorism" 45 Travel Weekly (April 24, 1986), p. 4.
Pilot Edward Parise calls airport security inadequate.

"Terrorism in the Terminal: Airline Liability Under Article 17 of the Warsaw Convention" 52 New York University Law Review (May 1977), pp. 283-305.
The author argues for a limited construction of the convention, which would not impose liability on the carrier.

"Terrorists Seize Cruise Ship in Mediterranean" 85 Department of State Bulletin (December 1985), pp. 74-81.
Transcripts of speeches regarding the Achille Lauro hijacking.

Thackrah, John Richard "Hijacking in the Middle East in the Sixties" 62 War in Peace (March 1984).

US Senate "Aircraft Sabotage Act: S.2623: A Bill to Implement the Montreal Convention for the Suppression of Unlawful Acts Against the Safety of Civil Aviation, and for other purposes" (Washington, D.C.: 98th Congress, 2nd session, May 2, 1984), 10 pp.
Proposed by Senators Thurmond and Denton.

Virtanen, Michael "Legislators Address Terrorism, Insurance; Industry Lobbyists Meet Key Officials" 45 Travel Weekly (March 3, 1986), p. 4.

"Worldwide Significant Criminal Acts Involving Civil Aviation, January-December 1980" (Washington, D.C.: Department of Transportation, Federal Aviation Administration, 1981).

"You Can Run But You Can't Hide" 128 Reader's Digest (February 1986), pp. 54-59.
A discussion of the hijacking of the Achille Lauro.

HOSTAGE-TAKING

"Agreement on the Release of the American Hostages" Department of State Bulletin (February 1981), pp. 1-22.

"America in Captivity: Points of Decision in the Hostage Crisis; An Inquiry by the New York Times" New York Times Magazine (May 1981), entire issue.
Includes articles on "Why Carter Admitted the Shah", "The Shah's Health: A Political Gamble", "How a Sit-In Turned Into a Siege", "Putting the Hostages' Lives First", "Going the Military Route", and "Epilogue: For America, a Painful Reawakening."

Andrew, R. J. "The Siege at Princess Gate: Attack on the Iranian Embassy" in Brian Michael Jenkins, conference director Terrorism and Beyond: An International Conference on Terrorism and Low-Level Conflict (Santa Monica: The Rand Corporation, R-2714-DOE/DOJ/DOS/RC, December 1982), pp. 243-246.

Asencio, Diego and Nancy Asencio with Ron Tobias Our Man is Inside (Boston: Little, Brown, 1983), 244 pp.
A US Ambassador recalls his role as one of the hostages inside during an Embassy takeover in Latin America. Reviewed by Karen DeYoung "Terrorists and Diplomats: The Siege in Bogata (sic)" Washington Post Book World (February 13, 1983), p. 5.

Aston, Clive C. and Adrian Cocayne A Contemporary Crisis: Political Hostage-Taking and the Experience of Western Europe (Westport, Conn.: Greenwood, 1982), 217 pp.

Aston, Clive C. Governments to Ransom: The Emergence of Political Hostage-Taking as a Form of Crisis (Westport, Conn.: Greenwood, 1982).

Aston, Clive C. "Hostage-Taking: An Overview" in David Carlton and Carlo Schaerf, eds. The Age of Terror (London: Macmillan, 1980).

Aston, Clive C. "Political Hostage-Taking in Western Europe" 157 Conflict Studies (1984), 21 pp.

Aston, Clive C. "Restrictions Encountered in Responding to Terrorist Sieges: An Analysis" in Richard Shultz and Steven Sloan, eds. Responding to the Terrorist Threat: Security and Crisis Management (New York: Pergamon, 1980), pp. 59-92.

Aston, Clive C. "The United Nations Convention Against the Taking of Hostages: Realistic or Rhetoric?" in Paul Wilkinson, Guest Editor "British Perspectives on Terrorism 5, 1-2 Terrorism (1981), pp. pp. 139-160.
Compromises which had to be made to ensure passage in the UN will hinder and possibly prevent the convention's general ratification.

Atkinson, Scott E., Todd Sandler and John Tschirhart "On Terrorism: Theoretical and Empirical Aspects" (unpublished ms., 1984).

Atkinson, Scott E., Todd Sandler and John Tschirhart "Terrorism in a Bargaining Framework" 30 Journal of Law and Economics (1987).
The authors use ITERATE data to test several hypotheses, and found that terrorists receive greater ransoms when they demand more initially, get higher ransoms for seizing hostages from several nationalities, and attempt to decrease their own costs. Certain types of targets, such as foreign embassies and international flights, may be more lucrative for terrorists. Bluffing does not pay.

Bahn, Charles "Hostage Taking: The Takers, the Taken, and the Context: Discussion" 347 Annals of the New York Academy of Sciences (June 20, 1980), pp. 151-156.

Bassiouni, M. Cherif "Protection of Diplomats Under Islamic Law" 74, 3 American Journal of International Law (July 1980), pp. 609-633.

Benjamin, Charles M. "The Iranian Hostage Negotiations: A Metagame Analysis" paper presented to the 23rd annual convention of the International Studies Association, Cincinnati, Ohio, March 24-27, 1982.

Bracey, Dorothy Heid "Forensic Psychology and Hostage Negotiation: Introductory Remarks" 347 Annals of the New York Academy of Sciences (June 20, 1980), pp. 109-112.

Brock, G. R. Lusti, L. Marks, et al. Siege: Six Days at the Iranian Embassy (London: Macmillan, 1980).
A discussion of the occupation of the Iranian Embassy in London.

Brody, Alan E., Roger T. Castonguay and Paul E. Versaw Policy Options in Offshore Crisis Situations: A Case Study (Washington: U.S. State Department Foreign Service Institute, 1983), 29 pp.

Bucheli, Fausto with Robin Maxson <u>Hostage: The True Story of an American's 47 Days of Terrorist Captivity in Latin America</u> (Grand Rapids, Michigan: Zondervan, 1982), 293 pp.

Clutterbuck, Richard "Management of the Kidnap Risk" in Paul Wilkinson, Guest Editor "British Perspectives on Terrorism" 5, 1-2 <u>Terrorism</u> (1981), pp. 125-138.

Cole, Richard B. <u>Executive Security: A Corporate Guide to Effective Response to Abduction and Terrorism</u> (New York: Wiley, 1980).

Conover, Pamela Johnston and Lee Sigelman "Presidential Influence and Public Opinion: The Case of the Iranian Hostage Crisis" 63, 2 <u>Social Science Quarterly</u> (1982), pp. 249-264.

Cooper, H. H. Anthony "Hostage Negotiations: Options and Alternatives" 2 <u>Clandestine Tactics and Technology</u> (Gaithersburg, Maryland: International Association of Chiefs of Police, 1977), 68 pp.

Cooper, H. H. Anthony <u>The Hostage-Takers</u> (Boulder: Paladin Press, 1981), 100 pp.

Cooper, H. H. Anthony "Kidnapping: How to Avoid It; How to Survive It" 5 <u>Clandestine Tactics and Technology</u> (Gaithersburg, Maryland: International Association of Chiefs of Police, 1979).

Corsi, Jerome R. "Terrorism as a Desperate Game: Fear, Bargaining and Communication in the Terrorist Event" paper presented at the Third Biennial Meeting of the International Society for Research on Aggression, Washington, D.C., September 23, 1978, published in 25, 1 <u>Journal of Conflict Resolution</u> (March 1981), pp. 47-86.

Cramer, Chris and Sim Harris <u>Hostage</u> (London: J. Clare Books, 1982), 213 pp.

Danto, B.M. and R. W. Kobetz "Psychological Advice for Potential Kidnap and Hostage-Taking Victims" (1980), 6 pp.

Davidson, G. Paul "Anxiety and Authority: Psychological Aspects for Police in Hostage Negotiation Situations" 9, 1 <u>Journal of Police Science and Administration</u> (March 1981), pp. 35-38.
    Davidson points out that hostage-takers might interpret being presented with a psychologist as a negotiator as indicating that the authorities believe him to be insane.

Des Pres, Terrence <u>The Survivor: An Anatomy of Life in the Death Camps</u> (New York: Oxford, 1980), 230 pp.

Dreyfuss, Robert with Thierry LeMarc <u>Hostage to Khomeini</u> (New York: New Benjamin Franklin House, 1980), 241 pp.

Engelmayer, Sheldon D. and Robert J. Wagman <u>Hostage</u> (Ottawa, Illinois: Caroline House, 1981), 128 pp.
    A look at the Iranian hostage crisis.

Epstein, David G. and William Megathlin "The Seven Hour Siege and the Pucker Principle" Law and Order (March 1979), pp. 18-23.

Fleming, Diana and Kellogg Fleming "Siege at Larnaca: A Cruising Couple's Brush with Terrorism" 11 Cruising World (December 1985), pp. 94-97.
A personal narrative of a hostage crisis.

Frankel, Norman "The Terrorist Attack Against Israel at the 1972 Munich Olympics: A Schematic Model" paper presented to the International Studies Association/Midwest annual meeting, Loyola University of Chicago, October 16-18, 1980.

Free: The Pictorial Saga of 444 Days of Rage, Hope, and Heroism, with a commentary by Eric Sevareid (New York: Bonanza, 1981), 96 pp.

Freifeld, Sidney A. "Diplomatic Hostage-Taking: A Retrospective Look at Bogota" International Perspectives (September-October 1980), pp. 13-18.

Friedlander, Robert A. "Iran: The Hostage Seizure, The Media, and International Law" in Abraham H. Miller, ed. Terrorism: The Media and the Law (Dobbs Ferry, New York: Transnational Publishers, 1982), pp. 51-66.

Glad, Betty "Jimmy Carter's Management of the Iranian Hostage Crisis: A Bargaining Perspective" paper presented to the annual convention of the American Political Science Association, New York City, September 3-6, 1981.

Gladis, S. D. "Hostage/Terrorist Situation and the Media" 48, 9 FBI Law Enforcement Bulletin (September 19790), pp. 10-15.

Glasgow, Matt "If You are Taken Hostage..." 35 Soldiers (May 1980), pp. 11-14.
What to expect and what to do.

Graves, B., and Thomas Strentz The Kidnapper: His Crime and His Background (Quantico, Virginia: FBI Academy, Special Operations and Research Staff, Research Paper, 1977).

Gruhier, Fabien Les Temps des Otages (France: Moreau, 1979), 319 pp.

Hamilton, Lawrence "Political Kidnapping as a Deadly Game" Simulation and Games (December 1980).

"Hostage Incidents: Examples in Modern History" 81 Department of State Bulletin (March 1981), pp. 23-28.

"Hostage Tips" 272 Harpers (February 1986), p. 16.

"Human Rights Commission Condemns Hostage-Taking, Launches Study on Religious Freedom, Reviews First Report on Torture" 23 UN Monthly Chronicle (April 1986), pp. 72-79.

"International Convention Against the Taking of Hostages" 5, 3 Terrorism (1981), pp. 293-300.
A reprint of the December 17, 1979 20-article UNGA convention.

Jaros, Dean, Lee Sigelman and Pamela Johnston Conover "Sophistication and Foreign Policy Preferences: The Iranian Hostage Crisis" 15, 1 Polity (1982), pp. 151-155.
A telephone survey of Kentuckians established that a definite foreign policy stance produced a less sophisticated response from all of those surveyed.

Jenkins, Brian Michael "Embassies Under Siege: A Review of 48 Embassy Takeovers, 1971-1980" (Santa Monica: The Rand Corporation, R-2651-RC, January 1981), 38 pp.

Jenkins, Brian Michael "Talking to Terrorists" (Santa Monica: The Rand Corporation, P-5749, 1981).
The paper looks at the problems of communication during a terrorist kidnapping or hostage incident and offers some general guidelines.

Jenkins, Brian Michael "Terrorists Seize Hostages in Arcadia: Laconia Commandos on Alert: A Scenario for Simulation in Negotiations with Terrorists Holding Hostages" (Santa Monica: The Rand Corporation, P-6339, May 1979), 9 pp.

Jenkins, Brian Michael and Robin Wright "Why Taking Hostages is a Winning Terror Tactic" Washington Post (July 12, 1987), pp. C1-C4.

Katz, Robert Days of Wrath: The Ordeal of Aldo Moro, The Kidnapping, The Execution, The Aftermath (Garden City: Doubleday, 1980), 326 pp.

Kennedy, Moorhead The Ayatollah in the Cathedral (New York: Hill and Wang, 1986), 241 pp.
Reviewed by Jonathan Yardley "A Diplomat's Faith: A Plea for Understanding" Washington Post Book World (July 20, 1986), p. 3. A former hostage argues that the embassy takeover was a result of US ignorance of foreign cultures and history.

Kennedy, Moorhead "The Root Causes of Terrorism" 46 Humanist (September-October 1986), pp. 5-10.
A personal narrative of the Iranian hostage crisis.

Knutson, Jeanne N. "Dynamics of the Hostage Taker: Some Major Variants" 347 Annals of the New York Academy of Sciences (June 20, 1980), pp. 117-128.

Laingen, Bruce "Diplomats and Terrorism: A Former Hostage Looks at the Need for Physical Safety and Multilateral Accords" 58 Foreign Service Journal (September 1981), pp. 19-21.
Laingen, who was held during the Iranian crisis, suggests that physical security requires an understanding of the local political environment.

Lanceley, Frederick J. "The Antisocial Personality as a Hostage-Taker" 9, 1 <u>Journal of Police Science and Administration</u> (March 1981), pp. 28-34.
The author offers an overview of the evolution of this type of personality as it appears in the mentally ill, the criminal, and the terrorist, and offers suggestions for handling bargaining situations.

Larson, David L. "The American Response to the Iranian Hostage Crisis: 444 Days of Decision" 57 3-4 <u>International Social Science Review</u> (1982), pp. 195-209.

Lingo, E. J. "Proaction to the Terrorist Hostage-Taking Challenge: A Training Exercise" 49, 4 <u>Police Chief</u> (1982), pp. 51-53.

Malawer, Stuart S. "Rewarding Terrorism: The U.S.-Iranian Hostage Accords" <u>International Security Review</u> (Winter 1981-1982), pp. 477-496.

Matt, A. R. "Trouble on the Water!" 46, 9 <u>Police Chief</u> (September 19790), pp. 68-70.

McDonald, John <u>Flight From Dhahran: The True Experiences of an American Businessman Held Hostage in Saudi Arabia</u> (Englewood Cliffs, New Jersey: Prentice-Hall, 1981), 260 pp.

McDonald, John W., Jr. "The United Nations Convention Against the Taking of Hostages: The Inside Story" 6, 4 <u>Terrorism</u> (1983), pp. 545-560.
Despite Soviet obstructionism, the UNGA adopted the treaty.

McFadden, Robert D., Joseph B. Treaster, and Maurice Carroll <u>No Hiding Place: The New York Times Inside Report on the Hostage Crisis</u> (New York: Times Books, 1981), 314 pp.

McGeorge, Harvey J., II "Plan Carefully, Rehearse Thoroughly, Execute Violently: The Tactical Response to Hostage Situations" 146, 1 <u>World Affairs</u> (Summer 1983), pp. 59-68.

Mickolus, Edward F. "Comment: Counting Things Versus Things that Count" <u>Journal of Conflict Resolution</u> (March, 1987).
A comment on Sandler and Scott's "Terrorist Success in Hostage-Taking: An Empirical Study" in the same issue of <u>JCR</u>. The author points out problems in using his ITERATE II dataset to study hostage-taking behavior.

Miller, Abraham H. <u>Terrorism and Hostage Negotiations</u> (Boulder: Westview, 1980), 134 pp.
Reviewed by James P. Bennett 95, 4 <u>Political Science Quarterly</u> (Winter 1980-81), pp. 680-681.

Moody, Sid <u>444 Days: The American Hostage Story</u> (New York: Rutledge, 1981).

Moorehead, Caroline <u>Fortune's Hostages: A Study of Kidnapping in the World Today</u> (London: H. Hamilton, 1980), 256 pp.

Nanda, Ved P. "Progress Report on the United Nations' Attempt to Draft an 'International' Convention against the Taking of Hostages" 6 Ohio Northern University Law Review (1979), pp. 89-108.
Nanda reviews other international conventions on terrorism, notes the debates in the UN on the hostages convention, and analyzes the provisions of the convention as it was reported out of its drafting committee. At the time of writing, it had not yet been debated in the General Assembly's Sixth (Legal) Committee.

Niehous, William "Hostage Survival: A Firsthand Look" Security Management (November 1979), pp. 6-54.
An American business executive whose kidnapping in Venezuela set a longevity record recounts his techniques for maintaining personal dignity.

Ochberg, Francis M. "Terrorism--Is There An Answer? Practical Suggestions to Potential Hostages and to Those Working to Rescue Victims: How to Lead from Strength" (London: Institute of Psychiatry, 1978, unpublished paper).

Paen, Alex Embassy (New York: New American Library, 1981).
A look at the takeover of the US Embassy in Tehran.

Pelletier, Jean and Claude Adams The Canadian Caper (New York: Morrow, 1981), 239 pp.
Reviewed by Richard Dudman "The Embassy and the Escape" Washington Post Book World (August 25, 1981), p. B4. An account of how the Canadian Embassy in Tehran helped 6 Americans escape.

Phillips, David Attlee "On Looking Into the Barrel of a Gun" Washingtonian (April 1980), pp. 114-117.
The CIA's former Latin America Division Chief discusses the experiences of several Americans previously held hostage by terrorists, and suggests that the American hostages in Tehran will exhibit many of their symptoms upon release.

Platz, Klaus Wilhelm "International Convention Against the Taking of Hostages" 40, 2 Zeitschrift fur auslandisches offentiliches Recht und Volkerrecht (1980), pp. 276-311.

Porter, Richard E. "Military Hostages: What They Need to Know and Don't: A Code of Conduct for United States Military Personnel Who are Victims of Hostile Peacetime Detention" 33 Air University Review (January-February, 1982), pp. 94-101.

Queen, Richard with Patricia Hass Inside and Out: Hostage to Iran, Hostage to Myself (New York: G.P. Putnam's Sons, 1981).
Queen was released early during the Iranian hostage crisis because of his multiple sclerosis.

"Report of the Ad Hoc Committee on the Drafting of an International Convention Against the Taking of Hostages" 32 United Nations General Assembly Official Records Supplement 39 (U.N. Doc. A/32/39 1977), and 33 UNGAOR Supplement 39 (UN Doc. A/33/39 1978).

Ressler, R. K. "Army Hostage Negotiations: An Insight into Army Regulations" 7, 3 Detective (Summer 1979), pp. 6-13.

Rodman, Peter W. "The Hostage Crisis: How Not to Negotiate" 4, 3 Washington Quarterly (Summer 1981), pp. 9-24.

Ronhovde, Kent "Federal Criminal Statutes Which May have Application to the Taking of Hostages" (Washington, D.C.: Library of Congress, CRS, March 18, 1977), 7 pp.

Rosen, Barbara and Barry Rosen, with George Feifer The Destined Hour: The Hostage Crisis and One Family's Ordeal (New York: Doubleday, 1982), 328 pp.
Reviewed by Diane Cole "One Family's 444-Day Nightmare" Washington Post (September 7, 1982), p. B-4.

Roukis, George S. "Negotiating with Terrorists" in Patrick J. Montana and George S. Roukis, eds. Managing Terrorism: Strategies for the Corporate Executive (Westport, Conn.: Quorum Books, 1983), pp. 109-122.

Rovner, Sandy "Hostages and Hostility" Washington Post Health (November 4, 1986), p. 7.

Salinger, Pierre America Held Hostage: The Secret Negotiations (Garden City: Doubleday, 1981), 360 pp.

Samuels, Jon M. "Hostage Situations" 2 Clandestine Tactics and Technology (Gaithersburg, Maryland: International Association of Chiefs of Police, n.d.).

Sandler, Todd, Scott Atkinson, Jon Cauley, Eric Ik Soon Im, John L. Scott and John Tschirhart "Economic Methods and the Study of Terrorism" paper presented at the conference on Research and Terrorism, University of Aberdeen, Scotland, April 15-17, 1986, 24 pp.

Sandler, Todd, and John L. Scott "Terrorist Success in Hostage-Taking Incidents: An Empirical Study" Journal of Conflict Resolution (March, 1987).
The article uses probit analysis to explain terrorist logistical and negotiation success in hostage situations using ITERATE II data.

Schlossberg, H. "Values and Organization in Hostage and Crisis Negotiation Teams" 347 Annals of the New York Academy of Sciences (June 20, 1980), pp. 113-116.

Scott, Charles W. Pieces of the Game (1984).
The author is profiled by Carla Hall "Hostage: Pieces of the Pain: Col. Charles Scott's Memories of 444 Days Captive in Iran" Washington Post (May 26, 1984), pp. C1-2.

Segal, J., et al. "Universal Consequences of Captivity: Stress Reactions Among Divergent Populations of Prisoners of War and Their Families" 28, 3 International Social Science Journal (1976).

Shamwell, Horace F., Jr. "Implementing the Convention on the Prevention and Punishment of Crimes Against Internationally Protected Persons, Including Diplomatic Agents" 6, 4 Terrorism (1983), pp. 529-543.
We have seen little action so far beyond US measures.

Simpson, Anthony E. "The Literature of Criminal Justice: Terrorism and Hostage-Taking" Law Enforcement News (May 7, 1979), pp. 21-22.

Souchon, Henri "Hostage-Taking: Its Evolution and Significance" 299 International Criminal Police Review (June-July 1976), pp. 168-173.

Stimson, Eva "A Conversation with a Former Beirut Hostage: Benjamin Weir" 29 Christianity Today (November 8, 1985), p. 52.

Strentz, Thomas "Law Enforcement Policy and Ego Defenses of the Hostage" 48, 4 FBI Law Enforcement Bulletin (1979), pp. 2-12.

Strentz, Thomas "Stockholm Syndrome: Law Enforcement Policy and Ego Defenses of the Hostage" 347 Annals of the New York Academy of Sciences (June 20, 1980), pp. 137-150.

"The Taking and Killing of Hostages: Coercion and Reprisal in International Law" 54 Notre Dame Lawyer (1978).

Trelford, D., ed. Siege, Six Days at the Iranian Embassy (London: Macmillan, 1980).

"The United Nations Effort to Draft a Convention on the Taking of Hostages" 27 American University Law Review (1978), pp. 433-442.

US Department of State Hostage Seizures (Washington, D.C.: US Department of State, Office for Combatting Terrorism, 1983).

US Senate "Act for the Prevention and Punishment of the Crime of Hostage-Taking: S. 2624: A Bill to Implement the International Convention Against the Taking of Hostages" (Washington, D.C.: 98th Congress, 2nd Session, May 2, 1984), 5 pp.
Sponsored by Senators Thurmond and Denton.

Weir, Rev. Benjamin and Carol Weir Hostage Bound, Hostage Free (1987), 183 pp.
The memoirs of a clergyman held in Lebanon from May 8, 1984 until released in September 1985. Story reported by Joan Mower "Weir Details Ordeal as Beirut Hostage: New Book Describes Captivity, Is Silent on Arms Sale to Iran" Washington Post (May 26, 1987), p. A10.

Wells, Tim 444 Days: The Hostages Remember (New York: Harcourt Brace Jovanovich, 1985), 469 pp.
Reviewed by Anne Chamberlin "Terror in Tehran: Surviving a Nightmare" Washington Post Book World (February 9, 1986), pp. 8-9.

Wolf, John B. "Hostage Extraction: A Comparative Analysis of the Options" (Gaithersburg, Maryland: IACP, 1980).

NUCLEAR AND OTHER FORMS OF HIGH-TECHNOLOGY TERRORISM

Alexander, Yonah "Super-Terrorism" in Yonah Alexander and John M. Gleason, eds. Behavioral and Quantitative Perspectives on Terrorism (New York: Pergamon, 1981), pp. 343-361.

Alexander, Yonah and Charles K. Ebinger Political Terrorism and Energy: The Threat and Response (New York: Praeger, 1982), 258 pp.

America's Hidden Vulnerability: Crisis Management in a Society of Networks (Washington, D.C.: Center for Strategic and International Studies, Panel on Crisis Management, 1984).

Arnold, Ron "Eco-Terrorism" 14 Reason (February 1983), pp. 31-36.
A look at terrorism by environmental extremists.

Ausness, "Putting the Genie Back in the Bottle: U.S. Controls Over Sensitive Nuclear Technology" 16 George Washington Journal of International Law and Economics (1981).

Bass, Gail V. and Brian Michael Jenkins "A Review of Recent Trends in International Terrorism and Nuclear Incidents Abroad" (Santa Monica, The Rand Corporation, N-1979-SL, 1983), 73 pp.

Bass, Gail V., Brian Michael Jenkins and Konrad Kellen "The Appeal of Nuclear Crimes to the Spectrum of Potential Adversaries" (Santa Monica, The Rand Corporation, N-2803-SL, February 1982), 56 pp.

Bass, Gail V., Brian Michael Jenkins, Konrad Kellen, Joseph Krofcheck, G. Petty, R. Reinstedt, and David Ronfeldt "Motivations and Possible Actions of Potential Criminal Adversaries of US Nuclear Programs" (Santa Monica: The Rand Corporation, R-2554-SL, February 1980), 91 pp.

Beadmoore, Michael "Terrorism in the Information Age: A Recipe for Disaster?" 20 Computerworld (July 7, 1986), p. 17.

Bell, J. Bowyer "A Future Free of Surprise" 17, 5 Society (July-August, 1980), pp. 17-18.

Bequai, August "Technocrimes: The Computerization of Crime and Terrorism" 76 Management Review (May 1987), p. 63.

Beres, Louis Rene "Strategies of Counter-Nuclear Terrorism: Theory and Decision on the Frontiers of Law Enforcement and Criminal Justice" in Joel J. Kramer, ed. The Role of Behavioral Science in Physical Security: Proceedings of the Third Annual Symposium, May 2-4, 1978 (Washington, D.C.: National Bureau of Standards Special Publication 480-38, 1979), pp. 29-46.

Bremer, Jan S. "Offshore Energy Terrorism: Perspectives on a Problem" 6, 3 Terrorism (1983), pp. 455-468.

Clark, Richard Charles Technological Terrorism (Old Greenwich, Conn.: Devin-Adair, 1980), 220 pp.
Reviewed by Harold K. Jacobson 454 Annals of the American Academy of Political and Social Science (March 1981), pp. 208-209, and by Bennett Ramberg 96, 1 Political Science Quarterly (Spring 1981), pp. 176-177.

Cobbe, James "The Threat to Mining Coal and Uranium" paper presented at the Conference on Political Terrorism and Energy: The Threat and Response, Washington, D.C., Georgetown University Center for Strategic and International Studies, May 1, 1980, published as "Supply Security of Coal and Uranium", in Yonah Alexander and Charles K. Ebinger, eds. Political Terrorism and Energy: The Threat and Response (New York: Praeger, 1982).

Cohen, Bernard L. "Q & A: Understanding a Trillion-Dollar Question, Interview by Richard Brookhiser" National Review (February 2, 1979), pp. 142-155.
Cohen argues that there is little threat by terrorists re nuclear matters, and believes that it would be preferable for terrorists to waste their time with nuclear bombs, rather than other activities.

Collins, "Combatting Nuclear Terrorism" New York Times Magazine (December 14, 1980), pp. 38ff.

Comptroller General of the United States Key Crude Oil and Products Pipelines are Vulnerable to Disruptions (Report to the Congress, EMD-79-63, August 27, 1979).

Cranston, Alan "The Nuclear Terrorist State" in Benjamin Netanyahu, ed. Terrorism: How the West Can Win (New York: Farrar, Straus, Giroux, 1986), pp. 177-181.

Crenshaw, Martha "The Prospect of Catastrophic Terrorism" 8 Armed Forces and Society (1981). pp. 156ff.

DeWitt, Hugh E. "Has the US Government Disclosed the Secret of the H-Bomb?" 35, 6 Bulletin of the Atomic Scientists (June 1979), pp. 60-62.

Douglass, Joseph D., Jr. CBW: The Poor Man's Atomic Bomb (Cambridge, Mass.: Institute for Foreign Policy Analysis, Inc., 1984).

Dunn, Lewis A. "Nuclear 'Gray Marketeering'" 1 International Security (Winter 1977), pp. 107-118.

Dunn, Lewis A., Paul Bracken and Barry J. Smernoff Routes to Nuclear Weapons: Aspects of Purchase or Theft (Croton-on-Hudson: Hudson Institute, April 1977).

Edelhertz, Herbert and Marilyn Walsh The White-Collar Challenge to Nuclear Safeguards (Lexington: Heath, 1978).

Falk, Richard A. "Inquiry and Morality" 17, 5 <u>Society</u> (July-August, 1980), pp. 18ff.

Feld, Bernard "Nuclear Violence at the Non-Governmental Level" in David Carlton and Carlo Schaerf, eds. <u>Contemporary Terror</u> (London, 1981).

Frank, Forrest R. "Suppressing Nuclear Terrorism: A Modest Proposal" testimony before the US Senate Committee on Government Operations, Export Reorganization Act of 1976, Hearings Before the Committee on S. 1439 (94th Congress, second session, June 1975).
 Frank suggested a treaty to suppress the theft or unlawful use of nuclear weapons or materials.

Frank, J. "On Emotional Responses to Nuclear Issues and Terrorism" in <u>Psychosocial Aspects of Nuclear Developments</u> (Washington, D.C.: American Psychiatric Association, Task Force Report 20, 1982).

Friedlander, Robert A. "Might Can Also Be Right: The Israeli Nuclear Reactor Bombing and International Law" 28 <u>Chitty's Law Journal</u> (December 1980), pp. 352-358.

Friedlander, Robert A. "Terrorism and Nuclear Decisions" 23 <u>Society</u> (January-February 1986), pp. 59-62.

Friedlander, Robert A. "The Ultimate Nightmare: What if Terrorists Go Nuclear?" 12, 1 <u>Denver Journal of International Law and Policy</u> (Fall 1982), pp. 1-11.
 The author argues that the question is not if but when, and notes that the international legal community has yet to establish rules regarding handling nuclear terrorism.

Greenwood, Ted "Discouraging Nuclear Proliferation in the Next Decade and Beyond: Non-State Entities" in Augustus R. Norton and Martin Harry Greenberg, eds. <u>Studies in Nuclear Terrorism</u> (Boston: Hall, 1979), pp. 139-146.
 Although terrorists might be interested in acquiring a weapons capability, most will be dissuaded by threats of retaliation, loss of prestige, and reprisal. Terrorists have not tended to cause mass casualties.

"Handy Woman's Guide: How to Build Your Own Atomic Bomb and Strike a Balance of Power with the Patriarchy" <u>Majority Report</u> (1974).
 An adaptation for a feminist journal of an article which first appeared in <u>Take Over</u> (July 4, 1974).

Herbert, Frank "Frank Herbert on DNA Terrorism" 5 <u>Omni</u> (August 1983), pp. 16-17.

Hirsch, Daniel, Stephanie Murphy and Bennett Ramberg "Protecting Reactors From Terrorists" 42 <u>Bulletin of the Atomic Scientists</u> (March 1986), pp. 22-25.

Howley, John G., LCDR, USN <u>Communications: The Key Element in Protection of Offshore Energy Assets</u> (Maxwell Air Force Base, Alabama, Air University, May 1976, Report No. 1225-76).

Hurwitz, Elliott "Terrorists and Chemical/Biological Weapons" 35 Naval War College Review (May-June 1982), pp. 36-40.

International Task Force on Prevention of Nuclear Terrorism Final Report (Washington, D.C.: Nuclear Control Institute, June 25, 1986), 32 pp.
The task force grew out of a 1985 conference of 150 experts from 13 countries. According to UPI, the report said nuclear terrorism has become more likely because of:
--the growing incidence, sophistication, and lethality of conventional forms of terrorism,
--state support of terrorists,
--an increasing number of potential targets,
--potential black and gray markets for nuclear materials.

Jenkins, Brian Michael "The Consequences of Nuclear Terrorism" (Santa Monica: The Rand Corporation, P-6373, August 1979), 32 pp.; same title appeared in John Kerry King, ed. International Political Effects of the Spread of Nuclear Weapons (Washington, D.C.: US Central Intelligence Agency and US Department of Defense, April, 1979), pp. 79-102.

Jenkins, Brian Michael "High Technology Terrorism and Surrogate War: The Impact of New Technology on Low-Level Violence" 6, 4 Schriftenreihe der Polizei-Fuehrungsakademie (1979), pp. 277-298.

Jenkins, Brian Michael "International Cooperation in Locating and Recovering Stolen Nuclear Materials" 6, 4 Terrorism (1983), pp. 561-575.
Jenkins mentions several thefts since 1966, and notes development of international measures, such as the 1981 UN Convention on the Physical Protection of Nuclear Materials.

Jenkins, Brian Michael "Nuclear Terrorism and Its Consequences" 17, 5 Society (July-August, 1980), pp. 5-15.

Jenkins, Brian Michael "The Potential Criminal Adversaries of Nuclear Programs: A Portrait" (Santa Monica: The Rand Corporation, P-6513, July 1980), 8 pp.

Jenkins, Brian Michael "Will Terrorists Go Nuclear?" 29, 3 Orbis (Fall 1985), pp. 507-516.

Jones, Arthur "Nuclear Terrorism 'More Likely' Than War; Experts Say U.S. Likely Target" 22 National Catholic Reporter (February 7, 1986), p. 5.

Joyner, Christopher C. "Offshore Maritime Terrorism: International Implications and the Legal Response", paper presented to the 24th annual convention of the International Studies Association, Mexico City, April 5-9, 1983, published in 36,4 Naval War College Review (1983), pp. 16-31.
Coastal states must act to protect offshore drilling rigs.

Kessler, J. Christian Potential Threats to Offshore Structures (Center for Naval Analyses, Institute of Naval Studies, March 3, 1976, CNA Paper 1230-75).

Kessler, Richard J. "Terrorism and the Energy Industry", in Yonah Alexander and Charles K. Ebinger, eds. Political Terrorism and Energy: The Threat and Response (New York: Praeger, 1982).

Kirkwood, Craig W., and Stephen M. Pollock "Multiple Attribute Scenarios, Bounded Probabilities, and Threats of Nuclear Theft" 14 Futures (December 1982), pp. 545-553.

Koburger, Charles W. "Oil, Ships and Violence: The Threat to Merchant Shipping in the Persian Gulf" 84 Navy International (December 1979), pp. 5-7.

Kuipers, M. "Nucleair Terrorisme" (Groningen: Polemologisch Instituut, unpublished paper, n.d.), 28 pp.

Kupperman, Robert H. "Countering High Technology Terrorism" paper presented to the annual convention of the International Studies Association, Atlanta, March 27-31, 1984

Kupperman, Robert H. "Technology Threats of Terrorism" paper presented at the Conference on Political Terrorism and Energy: The Threat and Response, Washington, D.C., Georgetown University Center for Strategic and International Studies, May 1, 1980

Lamb, John and James Etheridge "DP: The Target of Terror; Attacks on Computer Centers are Becoming More Common in Countries All Over the World" 32 Datamation (February 1, 1986), pp. 44-46.

Livingstone, Neil C. CBW: The Poor Man's Atomic Bomb (Cambridge, Massachusetts: Institute for Foreign Policy Analysis, 1984).

Livingstone, Neil C. "The Impact of Technological Innovation" in Uri Ra'anan, Robert L. Pfaltzgraff, Jr., Richard H. Shultz, Ernst Halperin, and Igor Lukes Hydra of Carnage: International Linkages of Terrorism: The Witnesses Speak (Lexington, Mass.: Lexington Books, 1986), pp. 137-154

Livingstone, Neil C. "Low-Level Violence and Future Targets" 2, 4 Conflict (1980), pp. 351-382.

Livingstone, Neil C. "Megadeath: Radioactive Terrorism", in Yonah Alexander and Charles K. Ebinger, eds. Political Terrorism and Energy: The Threat and Response (New York: Praeger, 1982).

Lloyd, Andrew "DP: An Easy Target: While Terrorist Attacks Usually Endanger People, Europeans Fear Computers Are Being Threatened as Well" 26 Datamation (June 1980), pp. 99-100.

MacBain, Merle "Will Terrorism Go To Sea?" 23 Sea Power (January 1980), pp. 15-24.

Macdonald, Brian, ed. War in the Eighties: Men Against High Tech (Proceedings, Fall, 1982, Toronto: Canadian Institute of Strategic Studies, 1983).

Macnair, Douglas G. "Terrorism in the Marine Environment" in Brian Michael Jenkins, conference director Terrorism and Beyond: An International Conference on Terrorism and Low-Level Conflict (Santa Monica: The Rand Corporation, R-2714-DOE/DOJ/DOS/RC, December 1982), pp. 273-276.

Maechling, Eugenie "Security Risks to Energy Production and Trade: The Problems of the Middle East" 10 Energy Policy (June 1982), pp. 120-130.
The author concludes that the oil facilities are indefensible.

Maechling, Lisa and Yonah Alexander "Security Risks to Energy Production and Trade", in Yonah Alexander and Charles K. Ebinger, eds. Political Terrorism and Energy: The Threat and Response (New York: Praeger, 1982).

Mark, Clyde "The Threat to Oil and Natural Gas Logistics" paper presented at the Conference on Political Terrorism and Energy: The Threat and Response, Washington, D.C., Georgetown University Center for Strategic and International Studies, May 1, 1980

Matt, A. Robert "Maritime Terrorism: An Unacceptable Risk" Parts 1, 2, and 3   16, nos. 2,3, and 4 Ocean Industry (February, March and April 1981).

Mazur, Allan "Research Note: Bomb Threats Against American Nuclear-Energy Facilities" 11, 1 Journal of Political and Military Sociology (Spring 1983), pp. 109-122.

McGeorge, Harvey J. "Terrorist Use of Chemical and Biological Agents to Attack United States Air Force Facilities" (preliminary analysis prepared for Jaycor, February 27, 1984).

Miller, G. Wayne "Could Someone Blow up Boston?" New England Magazine (September 10, 1978), pp. 10-18.

Mullen, Robert K. "Clandestine Use of Chemical or Biological Weapons" 4 Clandestine Tactics and Technology (Gaithersburg, Maryland: International Association of Chiefs of Police, n.d.).

Mullen, Robert K. "The International Clandestine Nuclear Threat" 2 Clandestine Tactics and Technology (Gaithersburg, Maryland: International Association of Chiefs of Police, n.d.).

Mullen, Robert K. "Subnational Threats to Civil Nuclear Facilities and Safeguards Institutions" in Richard H. Shultz, Jr. and Stephen Sloan, eds. Responding to the Terrorist Threat: Security and Crisis Management (New York: Pergamon, 1980), pp. 134-173.

Nuclear Energy Policy Study Group "Nuclear Terrorism" in Augustus R. Norton and Martin Harry Greenberg, eds. Studies in Nuclear Terrorism (Boston: Hall, 1979), pp. 290-305.
A group hoping to design, plan and construct a nuclear weapon

would need to devote several months of highly technical efforts, with attendant health costs and a risk that the bomb would not work. Far easier would be attacks on a nuclear reactor.

Norton, Augustus R. "Terror by Fission: An Analysis and Critique" Chitty's Law Journal (1980).

Norton, Augustus R. "Terrorists, Atoms and the Future: Understanding the Threat" 32 Naval War College Review (1979), pp. 30-50.

Norton, Augustus R. "The Threat of Nuclear Terrorism" National Defense (October 1980).

Norton, Augustus R. "Understanding the Nuclear Terrorism Problem" 5 Clandestine Tactics and Technology (Gaithersburg, Maryland: International Association of Chiefs of Police, n.d.).

Norton, Augustus R. and Ben-Gal "Terror by Fission: An Analysis and Critique" 27 Chitty's Law Journal (1979).
The authors claim that the efforts of an MIT chemistry major in 1975 (he designed an 800-pound weapon with a 15-pound plutonium core for $10,000) were "a qualified success" and that there would be serious difficulties in translating his design into an actual weapon.

Norton, Augustus R. and Martin Harry Greenberg "Understanding the Nuclear Terrorism Problem" (Bureau of Operations and Research, International Association of Chiefs of Police, 1979).

Office of Technology Assessment of the US Congress "The Non-State Adversary" in Augustus R. Norton and Martin Harry Greenberg, eds. Studies in Nuclear Terrorism (Boston: Hall, 1979), pp. 306-336.
The authors discuss terrorists, criminals, and psychotics, finding that those who are most technically capable of acquiring nuclear weapons are the least likely to wish to do so. The authors also note the impact of nuclear safeguards on civil liberties.

Petrakis, G. "Terrorism: New Weapons Technology and Gun Barrel Philosophy for the Terrorist" 28, 8 Law and Order (August 1980), pp. 20-28.

Phillips, John Aristotle and David Michaelis "How I Designed an A-Bomb in my Junior Year at Princeton" 115, 691 Reader's Digest (November 1979), pp. 121-126.

Pilat, J. F. "Anti-Nuclear Terrorism in the Advanced Industrialized West", in Yonah Alexander and Charles K. Ebinger, eds. Political Terrorism and Energy: The Threat and Response (New York: Praeger, 1982).

Ponte, Lowell "The Dawning Age of Technoterrorism" 1 Next (July-August 1980), pp. 49-54.

Power Technologies, Inc. Power System Vulnerability to Malevolent Attack (PTI report no. R16-81, March 4, 1981).

Radin, D. I. "Weekend Scientist: Let's Make a Thermonuclear Device" 25, 4 Journal of Irreproducible Results (1979), pp. 3-4.
A satire on articles purporting to show the ease of making nuclear explosives.

Ramberg, Bennett Destruction of Nuclear Energy Facilities in War: The Problem and the Implications (Lexington: Lexington Books, 1980), 224 pp.
Ramberg looks at the damage which would result from sabotage or direct attack, and makes suggestions for changes in design, policy, and law.

Ronfeldt, David F. and William Sater The Mindsets of High-Technology Terrorists: Future Implications from an Historical Analog (Santa Monica: The Rand Corporation, 1981), 33 pp.

Russett, Bruce M. "Who Are Terrorists?" 17, 5 Society (July-August, 1980), pp. 16-17.

Salmore, Barbara G. and Douglas W. Wimon "Nuclear Terrorism in Perspective" 17, 5 Society (July-August, 1980).

Sater, William Puerto Rican Terrorists: A Possible Threat to US Energy Installations? (Santa Monica: The Rand Corporation, 1764-SL, October, 1981), 30 pp.

Schelling, Thomas C. "Thinking About Nuclear Terrorism" 6, 4 International Security (Spring 1982), pp. 61-77.

Schelling, Thomas C. "Who Will Have the Bomb?" in Augustus R. Norton and Martin Harry Greenberg, eds. Studies in Nuclear Terrorism (Boston: Hall, 1979), pp. 42-56.
Schelling discusses what it means to have a nuclear weapons capability (not simply possessing a bomb, but having the ability to create one within a given period of time). He believes that states are more likely than terrorists to become nuclear proliferators, due to technical constraints.

Schoenbaum, Steve "Establishing Acceptable Risk Criteria for Countering Terrorism Against Offshore Petroleum Assets" paper presented at the First International Congress on Physical Protection in the Petroleum Installations, n.d.

Science Applications, Inc. State of the Art Report on the Vulnerability to Terrorism of U.S. Resources Systems (SAI 81-237-WA, report prepared for the Federal Emergency Management Agency, December 1, 1980).

Scott, D. Terrorism: The Nuclear Threat (Washington, D.C.: Citizens Energy Project, 1981).

Shemella, Paul Frost and Fire: The Maritime LNG Sabotage Threat (Monterey, California: Naval Postgraduate School, thesis, 1982).

Singer, Fred "The Threat to Energy Industry: An Overview" paper presented at the Conference on Political Terrorism and Energy: The Threat and Response, Washington, D.C., Georgetown University Center for Strategic and International Studies, May 1, 1980

Stewart, John B., Jr., et al. Generic Adversary Characteristics Summary Report (Washington, D.C.: Division of Safeguards, Office of Nuclear Material Safety and Safeguards, US Nuclear Regulatory Commission, 1979, available from National Technical Information Service), 61 pp.

Teller, Edward "The Spectre of Nuclear Terrorism" in Benjamin Netanyahu, ed. International Terrorism: Challenge and Response: Proceedings of the Jerusalem Conference on International Terrorism (1980).

Thompson, W. Scott "Whose Order?" 17, 5 Society (July-August, 1980).

Watson, F. M., Jr. "Terrorists and the Homemade A-Bomb" (Gaithersburg, Maryland: IACP, n.d.), 23 pp.

Watson, Jack D. The Defense of Offshore Structures (Center for Naval Analyses, Institute of Naval Studies, 25 February 1971, CNA Paper 1415).

Wehr, Paul "Nonviolence and Nuclear Terrorism" paper presented to the International Sociological Association, 1978. Available from the author at the University of Colorado at Boulder, 80309.
 Wehr argues that the stockpiling of nuclear weapons--which could be stolen by terrorists--is in itself a form of state terrorism. The nonviolent campaign against these weapons is an effective countermeasure.

Zofka, Z. "Denkbare Motive und Moegliche Aktionsformen eines Nuklear Terrorismus (Thinkable Motives and Possible Forms of Action of Nuclear Terrorism)" (Essen: Auge, 1981), 107 pp.

Philosophical Approaches

Amon, M. "The Unraveling of the Myth of Progress", in David C. Rapoport and Yonah Alexander, eds. The Morality of Terrorism: Religious and Secular Justifications (New York: Pergamon, 1982).

Apter, David E. "Notes on the Underground: Left Violence and the National State" 108, 4 Daedalus (Fall 1979), pp. 155-172. Apter notes that Filippo Michele Buonarotti (1761-1837) and Francois-Noel Babeuf (1760-1797) were prototypes for the modern anarchist and communist terrorists.

Aronson, S. "Nazi Terrorism: The Complete Trap and the Final Solution", in David C. Rapoport and Yonah Alexander, eds. The Morality of Terrorism: Religious and Secular Justifications (New York: Pergamon, 1982).

Aseyevskiy, Aleksandr Ivanovich Kto organizuyet i napravlyayet mezhdunarodnyy terrorizm?: Iz Posluzhnogo Spiska Tsru (Moscow: Politizdat, 1982), 110 pp.

Aseyevskiy, Aleksandr Ivanovich Tsru, shipinazh, terrorizm, zloveshchiye plany (Moscow: Politizdat, 1984), 269 pp.

Bill, James A. "Power and Religion in Revolutionary Iran" 36, 1 Middle East Journal (1982), pp. 22-47.

Burtchaell, James Tunstead "Moral Response to Terrorism" in Neil C. Livingstone and Terrell E. Arnold, eds. Fighting Back: Winning the War Against Terrorism (Lexington: Lexington Books, 1986), pp. 191-212.

Carmichael, D. J. C. "Of Beasts, Gods, and Civilized Men: The Justification of Terrorism and of Counterterrorist Measures" 6, 1 Terrorism (1982), pp. 1-26.

Carter, M. "The French Revolution: 'Jacobin Terror'", in David C. Rapoport and Yonah Alexander, eds. The Morality of Terrorism: Religious and Secular Justifications (New York: Pergamon, 1982).

Congdon, Lee "Lukacs, Camus and the Russian Terrorists" 1 _Continuity_ (1980), pp. 17-36.

Crenshaw, Martha, ed. _Terrorism, Legitimacy, and Power: The Consequences of Political Violence_ (Middletown: Wesleyan, 1983), 162 pp.
Reviewed by J. Bowyer Bell in _Society_ (November-December 1983), pp. 123-125.

Decter, Midge "The Theory of Grievances" in Benjamin Netanyahu, ed. _Terrorism: How the West Can Win_ (New York: Farrar, Straus, Giroux, 1986), pp. pp. 190-192.

Dispot, L. _Le Machine a Terreur_ (Paris: Grasset, 1975). Dutch edition entitled _De Terreur Machine_ (Wereldvenster, 1980), 221 pp.
A discussion of the interrelationship of terror and French history.

"Document on Terror", in David C. Rapoport and Yonah Alexander, eds. _The Morality of Terrorism: Religious and Secular Justifications_ (New York: Pergamon, 1982).

Donnelly, Jack "Natural Law and Right in Aquinas' Political Thought" 33, 4 _Western Political Quarterly_ (December 1980), pp. 520-535.

Dror, Yehezkel "Terrorism as a Challenge to the Democratic Capacity to Govern" in Martha Crenshaw, ed. _Terrorism, Legitimacy, and Power: The Consequences of Political Violence_ (Middletown: Wesleyan, 1983), pp. 65-90.

Dugan, Maire A. "An Assessment of Ideological Positions Justifying Violence and Nonviolence in Terms of the Consequences of Social Change Tactics" paper presented at the 33rd meeting of the New York State Political Science Association, Kiameshu, New York, April 1979.

Dugard, John "International Terrorism and the Just War", in David C. Rapoport and Yonah Alexander, eds. _The Morality of Terrorism: Religious and Secular Justifications_ (New York: Pergamon, 1982).

Efirov, S. A. _Attempt on the Life of the Future_ (Moscow, 1984).

Ferencz, Benjamin "When One Person's Terrorism is Another Person's Heroism" 9, 3 _Human Rights_ (1981), pp. 38-42.

Fetscher, Irving and Guenther Rohrmoser _Ideologien und Strategien: Analysen zum Terrorismus 1_ (Opladen, West Germany: Westdeutscher Verlag, 1981).

Fikentscher, Wolfgang "Terrorism, Marxism, and the Soviet Constitution" in Benjamin Netanyahu, ed. _Terrorism: How the West Can Win_ (New York: Farrar, Straus, Giroux, 1986).

Fischer-Galati, Stephen "Fascist-Communist Convergence" 18, 4 _Society_ (1981), pp. 30-31.

Fleming, Marie The Anarchist Way to Socialism (Totowa: Rowman and Littlefield, 1979).

Fleming, Marie "Propaganda by the Deed: Terrorism and Anarchist Theory in Late Nineteenth-Century Europe" 4, 1-4 Terrorism (1980), pp. 1-24.

Florencio, Rafael Nunez El Terrorismo Anarquista (1888-1909). Reviewed by Antonio Robles Egea 36 Revista de Estudios Politicos (November-December 1983), pp. 286-289.

Gerstein, R. "Do Terrorists Have Rights?", in David C. Rapoport and Yonah Alexander, eds. The Morality of Terrorism: Religious and Secular Justifications (New York: Pergamon, 1982).

Grachev, A. S. Political Extremism (Moscow, 1986).

Greenberg, Joel, and Diarmaid MacDermott "Young People Who Back Violence to Right Wrongs: How Do Terrorists Try to Justify Their Criminal Behavior?" 118 Scholastic Update (May 16, 1986), pp. 4-6.

Gregor, A. James "Fascism's Philosophy of Violence and the Concept of Terror", in David C. Rapoport and Yonah Alexander, eds. The Morality of Terrorism: Religious and Secular Justifications (New York: Pergamon, 1982).

Gregor, A. James "The Socialism of Fools (Left-Wing Fascism)" 18, 4 Society (1981), pp. 36-39.

Hamilton, Michael P. "Terrorism: Its Ethical Implications for the Future" 11 Futurist (December 1977), pp. 351-354.

Henry, Ernst "Lenin on Terrorism" Soviet Life (October 1981), p. 22.

Henry, Ernst "Terroizm i Neofashizm (Terrorism and Neofascism)" 11 Mirovaia Ekonomika i Mezhdunarodnye Otnosheniia (1981), pp. 107-116.
Henry examines alleged fascist activities in Europe and the US during 1977-1981.

Hobe, Konrad Zur Ideologischen Begrundung des Terrorismus: ein Beitrag zur Auseinandersetzung mit der Gesellschaftskritik und der Revolutionstheorie des Terrorismus (Cologne: Bundesanzeiger, 1979), 48 pp.

Holler, Lyman E. "'They Shoot People Don't They?' A Look at Soviet Terrorist Mentality" 32, 6 Air University Review (1981), pp. 83-88.

Horowitz, Irving Louis "Left-Wing Fascism: An Infantile Disorder" 18, 4 Society (1981), pp. 19-24.

Ivianski, Z. "The Moral Issue: Some Aspects of Individual Terror", in David C. Rapoport and Yonah Alexander, eds. The Morality of Terrorism: Religious and Secular Justifications (New York: Pergamon, 1982).

Izzeddin, Ahmed Jalai "Terror and Democracy: Security Through Repression?" 32 World Press Review (September 1985), pp. 37-38.

Joes, Anthony James "Black Shirt, Red Heart" 18, 4 Society (1981), p. 32.

Joffe, Josef "Guilt and Innocence: The Hazards of Empathy" 32 World Press Review (September 1985), pp. 38-39.

Kalinowski, Sharon Ann Leftist Terrorist Motivation (California State University at Long Beach, M.S. thesis, 1979), 109 pp.

Kassis, Vadim Borisovich and Leonid Kalosov Terrorizm Bez Maski (Moscow: Molodaya Gvardiya, 1983), 171 pp.

Kavolis, V. "Models of Rebellion", in David C. Rapoport and Yonah Alexander, eds. The Morality of Terrorism: Religious and Secular Justifications (New York: Pergamon, 1982).

Kemp, Jack "A False Symmetry" in Benjamin Netanyahu, ed. Terrorism: How the West Can Win (New York: Farrar, Straus, Giroux, 1986), pp. 193-195.

Kirkpatrick, Jeane J. "The Totalitarian Confusion" in Benjamin Netanyahu, ed. Terrorism: How the West Can Win (New York: Farrar, Straus, Giroux, 1986), pp. 56-60.

Kolakowski, Leszek "Terrorism and the Concept of Legitimacy" in Benjamin Netanyahu, ed. Terrorism: How the West Can Win (New York: Farrar, Straus, Giroux, 1986), pp. 48-51.

Kucuk, Ejub "Political Terrorism as a Means of Psychological Warfare and Propaganda" 21 Socialist Thought and Practice (August 1981), pp. 76-88.
Kucuk sees terrorism as a means of psychological warfare and the act as a social communication.

Ledeen, Michael "Cultural Terrorism" 255, 1528 Harpers (1977), pp. 99-100.

Lefort, Claude "D'un Doute a L'Autre (From One Doubt to Another)" 6 Esprit (France) (1982), pp. 23-30.
A look at Maurice Merleau-Ponty's views of the Soviets, Marxism, and violence.

Letman, Sloan T. and Francis G. Spranza "Political Alienation and Terrorism" paper presented at the Illinois Sociological Association, 1978, available from the authors at the Chicago campus of Loyola University, 60611.
Terrorism is used when all other methods to solve alienation problems fail.

Levy Bernard-Henri "The War Against All" New Republic (February 11, 1978), pp. 14-18.
A neo-Marxist discussion of the dialectic between state and individual terrorism.

Lopez, George A. "Terrorism and Alternative Worldviews" paper presented at the annual convention of the Southwest International Studies Association, San Antonio, Texas, 1981, 19 pp.

Louch, A. "Terrorism: The Immorality of Belief", in David C. Rapoport and Yonah Alexander, eds. The Morality of Terrorism: Religious and Secular Justifications (New York: Pergamon, 1982).

Lyakhov, Yevgeniy Grigoryevich Problemy sotrudnichestva gosudarstv v bor be s mezhdunarodnym terrorizmom (Moscow: Mezhdunar otnosheniya, 1979), 166 pp.

MacDaniel, J.F. Political Assassination and Mass Execution: Terrorism in Revolutionary Russia: 1878-1938 (Ann Arbor: University of Michigan, Department of History, Ph.D. Dissertation, 1979), 402 pp.

Mahler, Horst Per la Critica del Terrorismo (Bari: De Donato, 1980), 155 pp.

Miller, David "The Use and Abuse of Political Violence" 32, 3 Political Studies (Great Britain) (1984), pp. 401-419.
A look at the ethics of violence within liberal democracy.

Mirsky, Zinovy "Terrorism and the Bourgeoisie" 34 New Times (Moscow) (August 1980), pp. 18-20.

"The Morality of Brutality: Reflections on Dedication in Political Violence" (Cape Town, South Africa: Terrorism Research Centre, 1981).

Mosse, George L. "Retreat to the Status Quo (Left-Wing Fascism)" 18, 4 Society (1981), pp. 39-40.

Murphy, M. D. "Good and Bad Terrorism" 177, 4 New Republic (1977), p. 3.

Nedava, Yosef "Some Aspects of Individual Terrorism: A Case Study of the Schwartzbard Affair" 3, 1-2 Terrorism (1979), pp. 69-80.
Schwartzbard assassinated an individual responsible for pogroms in the Ukraine in 1920. His defence in a French court was that the genocide justified his act, which was accepted by the court. The author looks to the development of municipal and domestic law on the handling of genocide and murders of those responsible for genocide.

Nisbet, Robert "Myths and Mirrors" 18, 4 Society (1981), pp. 27-28.

O'Brien, Conor Cruise "Liberty and Terror: Illusions of Violence, Delusions of Liberation" 49 Encounter (October 1977), pp. 34-41.

O'Brien, Conor Cruise "Thinking about Terrorism" 257 Atlantic (June 1986), pp. 62-66.

O'Brien, Conor Cruise "Virtue and Terror" 32 New York Review of Books (September 26, 1985), pp. 28-31.
A look at Jean-Jacques Rousseau and Maxmilien Robespierre.

Pankov, Yu., ed. Political Terrorism: An Indictment of Imperialism (Moscow: Progress Publishers, 1983), 278 pp.

Pells, Richard "Hunting Embryonic Fascists" 18, 4 Society (1981), pp. 25-27.

Petrakis, G. "Terrorism: Multinational Corporation and the Nation State: The Anarchist's Rationale for Terrorism" 28, 7 Law and Order (July 1980), pp. 14-18.

Phillips, Robert L. "The Roots of Terrorism" 103 Christian Century (April 9, 1986), pp. 355-357.

Plimak, E. G. and V. G. Khoros "People's Will: Its History and Relationship to the Present" 5 Voprosy Filosofii (USSR) (1981), pp. 97-112.

Pottenger, J. R. "Liberation Theology: Its Methodological Foundation for Violence", in David C. Rapoport and Yonah Alexander, eds. The Morality of Terrorism: Religious and Secular Justifications (New York: Pergamon, 1982).

Quester, George "Eliminating the Terrorist Opportunity", in David C. Rapoport and Yonah Alexander, eds. The Morality of Terrorism: Religious and Secular Justifications (New York: Pergamon, 1982).

Rapoport, David C. "Fear and Trembling: Terrorism in Three Religious Traditions" 78 American Political Science Review (September 1984), pp. 658-677.

Rapoport, David C. "Messianism and Terror: The Jerusalem Dialogues" 19 Center Magazine (January-February 1986), pp. 30-39.
Presentations by David Biale, Roger Friedland, Hava Lazarus-Yafeh, Armand L. Mauss, and Ninian Smart.

Rapoport, David C. "Terror and the Messiah: An Ancient Experience and Some Modern Parallels", in David C. Rapoport and Yonah Alexander, eds. The Morality of Terrorism: Religious and Secular Justifications (New York: Pergamon, 1982).

Rapoport, David C. and Yonah Alexander, eds. The Morality of Terrorism: Religious and Secular Justifications (New York: Pergamon, 1982), 388 pp.

Rapoport, David C. and Yonah Alexander, eds. The Rationalization of Terrorism (Frederick, Maryland: University Publications of America, 1982), 233 pp.

Robbins, Thomas "A Peripheral Disorder (Left-Wing Fascism)" 18, 4 Society (1981), pp. 33-36.

Rose, Jonathan "What 19th-Century Terror Tells Us About Today's; What Did Terrorists Hope to Gain from their Deadly Crimes 100 Years Ago?" 118 Scholastic Update (May 16, 1986), pp. 7-9.

Stackhouse, Max L. "Torture, Terrorism, and Theology: The Need for a Universal Ethic" 103 Christian Century (October 8, 1986), pp. 861-863.

Taylor, Stuart, Jr. "When Is a Terrorist Not Necessarily a Terrorist?" New York Times (December 12, 1984), p. 14Y.

Trautman, Frederic The Voice of Terror: A Biography of Johann Most (Westport, Connecticut: Greenwood Press, 1980).

Trent, Darrell M. "New Religion: Terrorism" 4 Human Rights (1980), p. 10.

Tugwell, M. "Guilt Transfer", in David C. Rapoport and Yonah Alexander, eds. The Morality of Terrorism: Religious and Secular Justifications (New York: Pergamon, 1982).

Vityuk, Viktor Under Other People's Banners: The Hypocrisy and Self-Deception of 'Leftist' Terrorism (Moscow: Progress, 1985), 235 pp.

Waugh, William L., Jr. "The Values in Violence: Organizational and Political Objectives of Terrorist Groups" 3, 4 Conflict Quarterly (Summer 1983), pp. 5-19.

Wilkinson, Paul "Fascism Has Never Believed in Waiting for a Democratic Mandate" paper presented at the Council of Europe Conference on the Defence of Democracy Against Terrorism in Europe, November 1980.

Wilkinson, Paul "The Laws of War and Terrorism", in David C. Rapoport and Yonah Alexander, eds. The Morality of Terrorism: Religious and Secular Justifications (New York: Pergamon, 1982).

Wolffers, Arthur "Philosophische Uberlegungen zum Terrorismus" 66 Archiv fur Rechts- und Sozialphilosophie (1980), pp.453-468.

Wolman, B. B. "Futility of Terrorism" 7, 1-2 International Journal of Group Tensions (1977).

Woolf, S. J. "Prototypes and Terrorists" 18, 4 Society (1981), pp. 28-29.

Young, Robert "Revolutionary Terrorism, Crime and Morality" 4 Social Theory and Practice (Fall 1977), pp. 287-302.

Zasulic, Vera and O. Ljubatovic Memorie di Donne Terroriste (Memories of Terrorist Women) (Rome: Savelli, 1979).

Zoppo, Ciro E. "The Moral Factor in Interstate Politics and International Terrorism" in David C. Rapoport and Yonah Alexander, eds. <u>The Rationalization of Terrorism</u> (Frederick, Maryland: University Publications of America, 1982).

Terrorist Infrastructure

LINKS OF TERRORIST GROUPS

Alexander, Yonah "International Network of Terrorism", in Yonah Alexander and Charles K. Ebinger, eds. Political Terrorism and Energy: The Threat and Response (New York: Praeger, 1982).

Alexander, Yonah "Terror International: The PLO-IRA Connection" American Professors for Peace in the Middle East Bulletin (October 1979).

Blaufarb, Douglas S. "Terrorist Trends and Ties" 31, 3 Problems of Communism (May-June 1982), pp. 73-77.
A review of books outlining the network of terrorist links.

Bozeman, Adda B. "Closed Societies and the Resort to Violence" in Uri Ra'anan, Robert L. Pfaltzgraff, Jr., Richard H. Shultz, Ernst Halperin, and Igor Lukes Hydra of Carnage: International Linkages of Terrorism: The Witnesses Speak (Lexington, Mass.: Lexington Books, 1986), pp. 19-48.

"A Brotherhood of Terrorism: A British View" 32 World Press Review (March 1985), pp. 46-47.

Casey, William J. "The International Linkages: What Do We Know?" in Uri Ra'anan, Robert L. Pfaltzgraff, Jr., Richard H. Shultz, Ernst Halperin, and Igor Lukes Hydra of Carnage: International Linkages of Terrorism: The Witnesses Speak (Lexington, Mass.: Lexington Books, 1986), pp. 5-16.

Chapman, Robert D. and M. Lester Chapman The Crimson Web of Terrorism (Boulder: Paladin, 1980), 155 pp.

Doherty, Daniel A. "Carlos From 1970 to 1976: A Lesson in Transnational Terrorism" 2 Joint Perspectives (Summer 1981), pp. 70-79.

Gaucher, Roland Le Reseau Curiel ou la Subversion Humanitaire (Paris: Editions J. Picollec, 1981), 433 pp.

Goulden, Joseph with Alexander W. Raffio The Death Merchant: The Rise and Fall of Edwin P. Wilson (New York: Simon and Schuster, 1984), 455 pp.
 The story of a former CIA employee who used his connections to set up contracts to sell explosives used by terrorists supported by Libyan leader Muammar Qadhafi. Reviewed by Patrick Brogan "The Gang That Couldn't Shoot Straight" Washington Post Book World (August 19, 1984), pp. 4-5.

Hunter, J. D. The Terror Alliance (London: Seven House, 1981), 318 pp.

"Jerusalem Conference Outlines 'Terror International'" 23, 28 Near East Report (July 11, 1979), pp. 128-129.

Kupperman, Robert H. and Darrell M. Trent "The Terrorist International: The Past is Prologue and America is Vulnerable" 17 Across the Board (February 1980), pp. 50-68.
 Excerpts from their book Terrorism: Threat, Reality and Response.

Livingstone, Neil C. "Terrorism: The International Connection" 30 Army (December 1980), pp. 14-17, 20-21.

Lloyd, Richard Beyond the CIA: The Frank Terpil Story (Seaver Books, 1983), 256 pp.
 The story of an individual accused of supplying weapons to terrorists.

Maas, Peter Manhunt (New York: Random House, 1986), 301 pp.
 Reviewed by Patrick Brogan in Washington Post Book World (April 27, 1986), p. 7. The story of Edwin P. Wilson, a corrupt former CIA employee who sold explosives to Libyan leader Muammar Qadhafi.

Maas, Peter "Selling Out: How an Ex-C.I.A. Agent Made Millions Working for Qaddafi" New York Times Magazine (April 13, 1986), pp. 26-41.

Merari, Ariel "The Internationalisation of Political Terrorism: Causes, Scope and Treatment" paper presented to the Council of Europe Conference on Defence of Democracy Against Terrorism in Europe, Tasks and Problems, Strasbourg, November 12-14, 1980.

Perry, Victor "Terrorism Incorporated" 28, 2 Midstream (1982), pp. 7-10.
 A look at PLO-Baader Meinhof links.

Pilgrim, Michael K. "Financing International Terrorism" 7 International Security Review (Spring 1982).

Ra'anan, Uri "Vulnerabilities of the International Support Apparatus" in Uri Ra'anan, Robert L. Pfaltzgraff, Jr., Richard H. Shultz, Ernst Halperin, and Igor Lukes Hydra of Carnage: International Linkages of Terrorism: The Witnesses Speak (Lexington, Mass.: Lexington Books, 1986), pp. 221-230.

Ra'anan, Uri, Roger L. Pfaltzgraff, Jr., Richard H. Shultz, Ernst Halperin, and Igor Lukes, eds. Hydra of Carnage: International Linkages of Terrorism: The Witnesses Speak (Lexington: Lexington Books, 1986), 656 pp.
Noted experts from US enforcement agencies give their analyses, juxtaposed with testimonies of former foreign intelligence officers from socialist states.

Sheff, David "An Authority on Terrorism Offers a Chilling New Theory on the Shooting of the Pope" 15 People (June 1, 1981), pp. 32-34.

Sterling, Claire "Network of Terror" 118 Reader's Digest (May 1981), pp. 243-271.
A condensation of Sterling's book: The Terror Network.

Sterling, Claire "The State of the Art" in Uri Ra'anan, Robert L. Pfaltzgraff, Jr., Richard H. Shultz, Ernst Halperin, and Igor Lukes Hydra of Carnage: International Linkages of Terrorism: The Witnesses Speak (Lexington, Mass.: Lexington Books, 1986), pp. 49-56.

Sterling, Claire "The Strange Case of Henri Curiel" Washington Post Magazine (March 15, 1981), pp. 26-30, 38-39.

Sterling, Claire "Terrorism: Tracing the International Network" 130 New York Times Magazine (March 1, 1981), pp. 16-60.

Sterling, Claire "Threat From Left and Right" 19, 3 Society (March-April 1982), pp. 82ff.

Stohl, Michael "Review Essay: The International Network of Terrorism" 20, 1 Journal of Peace Research (1983), pp. 87ff.
This review essay compares Claire Sterling's The Terror Network and Edward Herman's The Real Terror Network. It argues that Sterling's work suffers from sloppy argument and questionable evidence, while Herman's deserves far more attention than it has thus far received.

Zawodny, J. K. "Infrastructures of Terrorist Organizations" 1 Conflict Quarterly (Spring 1981), pp. 24-31.

STATE SUPPORT FOR TERRORISM

Adelman, Jonathan R., ed. Terror and Communist Politics: The Role of the Secret Police in Communist States (Boulder: Westview, 1984), 292 pp.
The chapters cover the nature and extent of internal terror and repression, the range of external intelligence functions, and the effect of secret police interference in internal politics. Chapters are devoted to the Soviet Union, China, Poland, Hungary, Czechoslovakia, Romania, East Germany, and Cambodia.

Alexander, Yonah "Some Perspectives on Terrorism and the Soviet Union" 7 International Security Review (Spring 1982).

Alexander, Yonah "Some Soviet-PLO Linkages" 14 Middle East Review (Spring-Summer, 1982), pp. 65ff.

Alexiev, Alex "The Kremlin and the Pope" 39, 4 Ukrainian Quarterly (1983), pp. 378-388.
Pope John Paul II's impact on Eastern European Catholics is linked to apparent Soviet support of the Bulgarian-led attempted assassination.

Arens, Moshe "Terrorist States" in Benjamin Netanyahu, ed. Terrorism: How the West Can Win (New York: Farrar, Straus, Giroux, 1986), pp. 93-97.

Arguelles, L. "The United States National Security State: The CIA and Cuban Emigre Terrorism" 23, 4 Race and Class (1982).

Ascher, Abraham "Lessons of Russian Terrorism" 29 Problems of Communism (November-December 1980), pp. 70-74.

Aseevskii, A. Who Organizes and Directs International Terrorism? (Moscow: Political LIterature, 1982).

Barron, John The KGB Today: The Hidden Hand (London: Coronet, 1985).

Becker, Jillian The Soviet Connection: State Sponsorship of Terrorism (London: Institute for European Defence and Strategic Studies Occasional paper no. 13, 1985), 55 pp.
Becker examines charges of the US Department of State, and countercharges by the Soviets, and notes Bulgarian involvement in the attempted assassination of the Pope, Soviet intervention in Afghanistan, and Soviet support of self-described national liberation movements.

Bensi, Giovanni La Pista Sovietica: Terrorismo, Violenza, Guerra e Propaganda nella teoria e nella prassi di Mosca (Milan: SugarCo Edizioni, 1983), 159 pp.

Bittman, Ladislav "The Role of the Soviet Bloc Intelligence in International Terrorism: The View from Inside" paper presented to the conference of the International Security Studies Program of the Fletcher School of Law and Diplomacy, April 1985.
Bittman served in the Czechoslovak Intelligence Service for 14 years before defecting to the West.

Blaufarb, Douglas S. "Terrorist Trends and Ties" 31, 3 Problems of Communism (1982), pp. 73-77.
A review of several books which examine Soviet support for terrorism.

Blishchenko, Igor Pavlovich and N. V. Zhdanov "Sotrudnichestvo Gosudarstv v Bor'be Protiv Terroristicheskikh Aktov Mezhdunarodnogo Kharaktera (The Cooperation of States in the Struggle Against International Acts of Terrorism)" 8 Sovetskoe Gosudarstvo i Pravo (1981), pp. 110-119.
Notes the definitional and emotional issues involved in combatting terrorism, and criticizes the US portrayal of the Soviets as a patron state.

Boiter, Albert "Terrorism and Linkage: Moscow's Reaction" 1, 3 Political Communication and Persuasion (1981), pp. 301-305.

Bol'shakov, Vladimir Viktorovich Terrorizm po-Amerikanski (Moscow: Mezhdunar otnosheniya, 1983), 148 pp.

Brenchly, Frank "Diplomatic Immunities and State-Sponsored Terrorism" 164 Conflict Studies (1984), 24 pp.

Browne, Marjorie "Acts and Countries that 'Aid and Abet' International Terrorism" (Washington, D.C.: Library of Congress, CRS, January 13, 1978), 22 pp.

Carnes, Colland F., Commander, USNR "Soviet Intelligence Support to International Terrorism" American Intelligence Journal (January 1986), pp. 18-23.

Chapman, Robert D. "State Terrorism" 3, 4 Conflict (1982), pp. 283-298.
Dialogue summary reasons "State terrorism, or the killing of political opposition figures and dissidents, is an official policy in Libya, Iran, and Syria. Incidents of state-sponsored murders by these governments are described, as well as occurrences in Liberia, Nicaragua, and the US. Colonel Mu'ammar al-Qaddafi instigated a campaign of murders of Libyan political exiles in Europe and the US, confident that Western need for Libyan oil would forestall protest. Political killings have successfully intimidated exile groups. Terrorism in the US can only be fought if present restrictions on police and intelligence procedures are repealed. This would reduce civil rights, but a free society cannot long endure terrorism."

Chapman, Robert D. and M. Lester Chapman The Crimson Web of Terror (Boulder: Paladin, 1980), 155 pp.

Charny, Israel W. How Can We Commit the Unthinkable? Genocide: The Human Cancer (Boulder: Westview, 1982).

Cline, Ray S. "Terrorism: Seedbed for Soviet Influence" 26 Midstream (May 1980), pp. 5-8.

Cline, Ray S. and Yonah Alexander State Sponsored Terrorism Report prepared for the Subcommittee on Security and Terrorism for the Use of the Committee on the Judiciary, US Senate (Washington, D.C.: US Government Printing Office, 1985), 186 pp.

Cline, Ray S. and Yonah Alexander Terrorism as State-Sponsored Covert Warfare (Fairfax, Virginia: Hero Books, 1986), 118 pp.

Cline, Ray S. and Yonah Alexander Terrorism: The Soviet Connection (New York: Crane, Russak and Company, 1984), 165 pp.
The authors center on PLO-Soviet ties, showing how the Soviets aid terrorist organizations worldwide. Appendices include a transcript of a meeting between Yasser Arafat and Soviet Foreign Minister Andrei Gromyko, a copy of a report from the Palestinian delegation to Moscow, and photographs and

certificates of the graduation of Palestinians from Soviet military schools. Reviewed in 62 Foreign Affairs (Spring 1984), p. 1006.

Conquest, Robert Kolyma: The Arctic Death Camps (New York: Oxford, 1979), 254 pp.

deBorchgrave, Arnaud "Unspiking Soviet Terrorism" 7 International Security Review (Spring 1982).

Deriabin, Peter Watchdogs of Terror, 2nd edition (Frederick, Maryland: University Publications of America, 1984).

Deutsch, Richard "Dealing with Qaddafy" 27 Africa Report (March-April 1982), pp. 47-53.
Includes a discussion of Libyan support for terrorists.

Duvall, Raymond D., et al "From Coercion to Insurgency and Back Again" paper presented at the Twelfth World Congress, International Political Science Association, Rio de Janeiro, August, 1982.

Duvall, Raymond D. and Michael Stohl "Governance by Terror", Chapter 6 in Michael Stohl, ed. The Politics of Terrorism (New York: Marcel Dekker, 1983).

Duvall, Raymond D., Michael Stohl, and James Austin "Terrorism as Foreign Policy" (unpublished ms., 1983).

Dziak, John "Soviet Intelligence and Security Services in the 1980s: The Paramilitary Dimension" in Intelligence Requirements for the 1980s: Counterintelligence (New York: National Strategy Information Center, 1980), pp. 95-112.

Efremov, V. "Mezhdunarodnyi Terrorizm: Orudie Imperializma i Reaktsii ('International Terrorism' is the Weapon of Imperialism and Reaction)" 7 Aziia i Afrika Segodnia (1981), pp. 24-26.
The Soviets believe that the US has been supporting terrorism.

Elad, Shlomi and Ariel Merari The Soviet Bloc and World Terrorism (Tel Aviv University: Jaffee Center for Strategic Studies, 1984), 81 pp.

Enders, Thomas "Cuban Support for Terrorism and Insurgency in the Western Hemisphere: Statement Before Subcommittee of Senate Judiciary Committee, March 12, 1982" 376 Current Policy (1982), 3 pp., also available in 82 Department of State Bulletin (August 1982), pp. 73-75.

"Exposing the Libyan Links: Part 2, The Qaddafi Connection" 130 New York Times Magazine (June 21, 1981), pp. 32-42.

Fein, Helen "A Formula for Genocide: Comparison of the Turkish Genocide (1915) and the German Holocaust (1939-1945)" 1 Comparative Studies in Sociology (1978).

Ferencz, Benjamin B. Less Than Slaves (Cambridge: Harvard, 1979).
The author looks at the cooperation between the Nazi SS and German industrial firms in using slave labor.

Francis, Samuel T. "Latin American Terrorism: The Cuban Connection" 104 Heritage Foundation Backgrounder (November 9, 1979), 23 pp.
Francis surveys the major Latin guerrilla and terrorist formations, and finds Cuban support for virtually all of them. He suggests that this indicates tacit Soviet support, and probably direction.

Francis, Samuel T. The Soviet Strategy of Terror (Washington, D.C.: The Heritage Foundation, 1981), 78 pp.

Friedlander, Robert A. "A Riddle Inside a Mystery Wrapped in an Enigma: Terrorism and the 'Soviet Connection'" 8, 11 Update Report (Gaithersburg, Maryland: International Association of Chiefs of Police, 1982), 10 pp.

Garza, Roberto M. "Militarism and Repression in Latin America: A Quantitative Appraisal" paper presented at the annual convention of the International Studies Association/Midwest, Chicago, November 1985.

Goldberg, Arthur J. "London's Libyan Embassy Shootout: A Case of International Terrorism" in Benjamin Netanyahu, ed. Terrorism: How the West Can Win (New York: Farrar, Straus, Giroux, 1986), pp. 139-145.

Goldberg, Arthur J. "The Shoot-Out at the Libyan Self-Styled People's Bureau: A Case of State-Supported International Terrorism" 30 South Dakota Law Review (Winter 1984), pp. 1-7.

Goren, Roberta Soviet Attitude and Policy to International Terrorism, 1967-1977 (University of London: Ph.D. dissertation).
Goren died before the dissertation was published. This is one of the first detailed discussions of Soviet support for terrorism. A posthumous version was published as Goren, Roberta, edited by Jillian Becker The Soviet Union and Terrorism (Boston: Allen and Unwin, 1984), 232 pp.

Gorokhov, A. "State Terrorism: Instrument of US Imperial Policy" 3 International Affairs (USSR) (March 1984), pp. 92-99.

Graber, G. S. The History of the SS (New York: McKay, 1978).

Haggman, Bertil Moskva och Terrorist-Internationalen (Stockholm: Contra Forlag & Company, K. B., 1984)
Reviewed by William F. Sater TVI Journal (Summer 1985), p. 63. Haggman looks at the role of the Soviets and their allies in aiding the PLO, Baader-Meinhof Group, the Red Brigades, the ETA, the IRA, and the Armenian terrorist groups.

Halperin, Ernst "Central America: The Role of Cuba and of the Soviet Union" in Uri Ra'anan, Robert L. Pfaltzgraff, Jr., Richard H. Shultz, Ernst Halperin, and Igor Lukes Hydra of Carnage: International Linkages of Terrorism: The Witnesses Speak (Lexington, Mass.: Lexington Books, 1986), pp. 125-134.

Halperin, Ernst "Terrorism: Moscow's Motive" 7 International Security Review (Spring 1982).

Harden, Blaine "Terrorism" Washington Post Magazine (March 15, 1981), pp. 14-16, 18-22.
The author wonders if the Soviets are behind international terrorism to the extent claimed by Claire Sterling.

Harff, Barbara "The Etiology of Genocides" paper presented to the American Political Science Association annual convention, Washington, D.C., August 1984, 27 pp.

Harff, Barbara Genocide and Human Rights: International Legal and Political Issues (University of Denver Monograph Series in World Affairs, 1984).

Harff, Barbara "Genocide as State Terrorism", paper presented to the annual convention of the International Studies Association, Atlanta, March 27-31, 1984

Henri, Ernst Stop Terrorism! (Moscow: Novosti Press Agency Publishing House, 1982), 200 pp.; also available as Protiv Terrorizma (Moscow: Izd-vo Agentstva pechati Novosti, 1981), 155 pp.

Henze, Paul B. Goal: Destabilization, Soviet Agitational Propaganda, Instability and Terrorism in NATO South (Marina del Rey, California: European American Institute for Security Research, 1981).

Henze, Paul B. "Mehmet Ali Agca--Whose Agent?" Reader's Digest (September 1981).

Henze, Paul B. "Origins of the Plot to Kill the Pope" 6, 4 Washington Quarterly (Autumn, 1983), pp. 3-20.

Henze, Paul B. "The Plot to Kill the Pope" 27, 118/119 Survey (Autumn-Winter 1983), pp. 2-21..

Henze, Paul B. The Plot to Kill the Pope (New York: Charles Scribner's Sons, 1983), 216 pp.
Reviewed by Luigi Barzini "The Gunman in Saint Peter's Square" Washington Post Book World (December 11, 1983), pp. 4, 11.

Herman, Edward S. The Real Terror Network: Terrorism in Fact and Propaganda (Boston: South End Press, 1982), 252 pp.
Reviewed by Miles D. Wolpin in 35 Monthly Review (October 1983), pp. 59-60.

"Historical Antecedents of Soviet Terrorism" (Washington, D.C.: 97th Congress, Hearings of the Subcommittee on Security and Terrorism, Committee on the Judiciary, June 11-12, 1981).

Holland, Carolsue "The Black, the Red, and the Orange: System Terrorism versus Regime Terror" (available from Box 6837, New York, New York 09633, 1978 paper).
Includes case studies of the Black Hand, Red Hand, Ulster Defense Association, Saiqa.

Horner, Charles "The Facts About Terrorism" 69, 6 Commentary (June 1980), pp. 40-45.
Discusses Soviet and other governments' training and arming terrorists.

Implementation of the Helsinki Accords: Hearing Before the Commission on Security and Cooperation in Europe, Ninety-Seventh Congress, Second Session, The Assassination Attempt on Pope John Paul II, September 23, 1982 (Washington, D.C.: US Government Printing Office, 1983), 29 pp.

Iviansky, Zeev "Provocation at the Center: A Study in the History of Counter-Terror" 4, 1-4 Terrorism (1980), pp. 53-88.
A look at the origins of the Russian secret police.

Johnson, R. W. and Patrick Forbes "Who's Afraid of the State?" 112 New Statesman (November 28, 1986), pp. 8-9.

Kaiser, Charles "A Plague of Libyans" 336 Rolling Stone (February 5, 1981), pp. 24-26.
A look at the attempted assassination of Faisal Zagallai, a Libyan student at Colorado State University for his anti-Qadhafi activities.

"The KGB Abroad: 'Murder International, Inc.'" 27 Survey (Great Britain) (1983), pp. 80-87.
Documents, charts, and interviews regarding KGB "wet affairs."

"The KGB Abroad: 'Wet Affairs': Soviet Use of Assassination and Kidnapping" 27 Survey (Great Britain) (1983), pp. 68-79.

Kiracofe, Clifford A. "The Soviet Network in Central America" 27 Midstream (May 1981), pp. 3-6.
Argues that the PLO has initiated terrorist acts in Central America with Soviet aid.

Kovalev, Eduard The St. Peter's Square Attack (Moscow: Novosti, 1985).
A Soviet journalist gives the Bulgarian view of the papal assassination attempt.

Kuper, Leo Genocide: Its Political Use in the Twentieth Century (London and New Haven: Yale University Press, 1981).

Laipson, Ellen "Iraqi Support for Terrorism 1980-82" (Washington, D.C.: Library of Congress, CRS, March 16, 1982), 2 pp.

Ledeen, Michael A. "Intelligence, Training and Support Components" in Uri Ra'anan, Robert L. Pfaltzgraff, Jr., Richard H. Shultz, Ernst Halperin, and Igor Lukes Hydra of

Carnage: International Linkages of Terrorism: The Witnesses Speak (Lexington, Mass.: Lexington Books, 1986), pp. 155-168.

Ledeen, Michael A. "Soviet Sponsorship: The Will to Disbelieve" in Benjamin Netanyahu, ed. Terrorism: How the West Can Win (New York: Farrar, Straus, Giroux, 1986), pp. 87-92.

Leskovsek, Valentin "Libya and al-Wadhdhafi: Selected References, 1976-1982" (Washington, D.C.: Library of Congress, CRS, January 27, 1982), 3 pp.

Levy, Rudolf "Terrorism and Communism: A History and Profile: Conclusion" Military Intelligence (October-December 1980), pp. 26-28.

Livingstone, Neil C. "Death Squads" 146, 3 World Affairs (1983-84), pp. 239-248.
A look at Latin American anti-Communist terrorism, which is frequently linked with local conservative regimes.

Livingstone, Neil C. "States in Opposition: The War Against Terrorism" 3, 2-3 Conflict (1981), pp. 83-142.

Livingstone, Neil C. and Terrell E. Arnold "The Rise of State-Sponsored Terrorism" in Neil C. Livingstone and Terrell E. Arnold, eds. Fighting Back: Winning the War Against Terrorism (Lexington: Lexington Books, 1986), pp. 11-24.

Lopez, George A. "A Scheme for the Analysis of Governments as Terrorists" paper presented to the annual convention of the Midwest Political Science Association, Milwaukee, Wisconsin, 1982.

Lopez, George A. and Michael Stohl eds. Development, Dependence and State Repression (Westport, Connecticut: Greenwood, 1987).
The essays in this volume cautions researchers that the context of repression resides very much in the local culture and decisional settings of elites within particular states. It also provides ample evidence of the linkage between repression and those larger economic and political factors which bind states together in international affairs.

Maksudov, L. "The True Organizers of 'International Terrorism'" 11 International Affairs (USSR) (November 1981), pp. 30-36.

McCamant, John F. "Governance Without Blood: Social Science's Antiseptic View of Rule: or, The Neglect of Political Repression" paper presented to the annual convention of the Midwest Political Science Association, Milwaukee, Wisconsin, 1982, 57 pp., published in Michael Stohl and George A. Lopez, eds. The State as Terrorist: The Dynamics of Governmental Violence and Repression (Westport: Greenwood, 1984).

Merari, Ariel A Data Base on International Terrorism in 1979: Terrorist Groups, Terrorist Activities, and Countries: Attitudes to Terrorism (Tel Aviv: Center for Strategic Studies, 1980), 198 pp. in Hebrew

Mickolus, Edward F. "Types of State Support for International Terrorism: A Proposed Continuum" (in preparation, 1987).

Mitchell, Christopher, Michael Stohl, David Carleton and George Lopez "State Terrorism: Issues of Concept and Measurement" in Michael Stohl and George Lopez eds. Government Violence and Repression: An Agenda for Research (Westport, Connecticut: Greenwood, 1986), pp. 1-27.

Murphy, John F. State Support for International Terrorists (American Bar Association Standing Committee on Law and National Security, in preparation).

NBC "The Man Who Shot the Pope--A Study in Terrorism" (September 21, 1982).

Newell, David Allen The Russian Marxist Response to Terrorism: 1978-1917 (Stanford University, Ph.D. dissertation, 1981), 514 pp.

Orlow, Dietrich "Comments on Weisberg's 'Avoiding Central Realities' and Richard's 'Terror and the Law'" 5, 2 Human Rights Quarterly (May 1983), pp. 186-190.

Oruka, H. Odera "Legal Terrorism and Human Rights" Praxis International (January 1982), pp. 376-385.

Paltchev, Ivan L'Attentat Contre le Pape et Les Racines du Terrorisme (Sofia: Presse, 1985), 122 pp.
Paltchev claims that the Bulgarians were not involved in the assassination attempt against the Pope.

Petrakis, G. "Terrorism: The Terrorist as a Surrogate Soldier" 28, 9 Law and Order (September 1980), pp. 31-38.

Pierre-Charles, Gerard "Dominacion Politica y Terrorismo de Estado (Political Domination and State Terrorism)" 40, 3 Restiva Mexicana de Socilogia (July-September 1978), pp. 929-945.

Pincher, Chapman The Secret Offensive: Active Measures, A Saga of Deception, Disinformation, Subversion, Terrorism, Sabotage and Assassination (London: Sidgwick and Jackson, 1985), 314 pp.
Reviewed by James R. Kuhlman 111 Library Journal (April 15, 1986), p. 86.

Pisano, Vittorfranco "Clandestine Operations in Italy: The Bulgarian Connection" Journal of Conflict Studies (University of New Brunswick) (Winter, 1984), pp. 28-38.

Pisano, Vittorfranco S. "Libya's Foothold in Italy" 5 Washington Quarterly (Spring 1982), pp. 179-182.
The author looks at the Libyan use of Italian territory in supporting terrorism, and Libyan support for domestic Italian terrorists.

Plate, Thomas and Andrea Darvi Secret Police: The Inside Story of a Network of Terror (Garden City: Doubleday, 1981), 458 pp.

"The PLO, The Soviet Union, and International Terrorism" (Jerusalem: Israel Information Center, August 30, 1981).

Raine, Linnea P., ed. The International Implications of the Papal Assassination Attempt: A Case of State-Sponsored Terrorism (Washington, D.C.: Georgetown University Center for Strategic and International Studies, 1985), 23 pp.

Randle, M. Militarism and Repression (1980), 156 pp.
A discussion of third world state terrorism.

Randle, M. "Militarism and Repression" 7, 1 Alternatives (1981), pp. 61-144.

Reagan, Ronald "The New Network of Terrorist States: President Reagan's Address Before the American Bar Association" 85 Department of State Bulletin (August 1985), pp. 7-10.

Richards, David A. J. "Terror and the Law" 5, 2 Human Rights Quarterly (May 1983), pp. 171-185.

"The Role of Cuba in International Terrorism and Subversion: Intelligence Activities of the DGI" (Washington, D.C.: 97th Congress, Hearings of the Subcommittee on Security and Terrorism, Committee on the Judiciary, February 26, 1982).

"The Role of Cuba in International Terrorism and Subversion: Terrorist and Subversive Activities of the Cuban Government in Latin America" (Washington, D.C.: 97th Congress, Hearings of the Subcommittee on Security and Terrorism, Committee on the Judiciary, March 11, 1982).

"The Role of Cuba in International Terrorism and Subversion: Terrorist and Subversive Activities of the Cuban Government in Latin America and Puerto Rico" (Washington, D.C.: 97th Congress, Hearings of the Subcommittee on Security and Terrorism, Committee on the Judiciary, March 12, 1982).

"The Role of Cuba in International Terrorism and Subversion: Terrorist and Intelligence Activities of the Cuban Government in South Florida" (Washington, D.C.: 97th Congress, Hearings of the Subcommittee on Security and Terrorism, Committee on the Judiciary, March 4, 1982).

Romerstein, Herbert Soviet Support for International Terrorism (Washington: Foundation for Democratic Education, 1981), 40 pp.

Roulette, Christian The John Paul II-Antonov-Agca Connection (Paris: Sorbier, 1984), 315 pp.
A French lawyer claims there was no Bulgarian Connection.

Sanders, Sol W. "The Growing Debate over Soviet Ties to Terrorism" Business Week (June 1, 1981), pp. 51-52.

Sanguinetti, Gianfranco On Terrorism and the State: The Theory and Practice of Terrorism Divulged for the First Time (London: B. M. Chronos, 1982), 101 pp.

Scherer, John L. "The Plot to Kill the Pope" 7, 4 Terrorism (1985), pp. 351-366.

Scuka, Dario "A Preliminary Assessment of the Effects of a US Policy Introducing Economic Sanctions Against Libya, Iraq, South Yemen and Somalia for Granting Asylum to Terrorists" (Washington, D.C.: Library of Congress, CRS, September 6, 1978), 26 pp.

Shultz, Richard "The Role of External Forces in Third World Conflicts" 4 Comparative Strategy (1984).

Shultz, Richard H. "Soviet Global Strategy and Support for International Terrorist Groups" in The 1980s: Decade of Confrontation? Proceedings of the Eighth Annual National Security Affairs Conference 13-15 July 1981, cosponsored by the National Defense University and the Under Secretary of Defense for Policy (Washington, D.C.: National Defense University Press, Fort Lesley J. McNair, 1981), pp. 243-264.

"Soviet, East German, and Cuban Involvement in Fomenting Terrorism in Southern Africa" 50, 2 Rivista di Studi Politici Internazionali (April-June 1983), pp. 283-288.

Sterling, Claire "The Great Bulgarian Cover-Up: Betrayals, False Alibis, and Bungling by the Pope's Would-Be Assassins" 192 New Republic (May 27, 1985), pp. 16-20.

Sterling, Claire "The Plot to Murder the Pope" 121 Reader's Digest (September 1982), pp. 71-84.

Sterling, Claire The Terror Network: The Secret War of International Terrorism (London: Weidenfeld and Nicholson, and New York: Holt, Rinehart and Winston 1981), 357 pp. Reviewed by Leo Raditsa "The Source of World Terrorism" 27, 10 Midstream (1981), pp. 42-48. Sterling looks at links of international terrorists, and finds extensive Soviet support of these activities.

Sterling, Claire The Time of the Assassins (London: Angus and Robertson, 1984, and New York: Holt, Rinehart and Winston, 1983), 264 pp. Reviewed by Allan E. Goodman "Margin for Terror" Washington Post Book World (February 12, 1984), p. 9.

Sterling, Claire "Unraveling the Riddle" in Benjamin Netanyahu, ed. Terrorism: How the West Can Win (New York: Farrar, Straus, Giroux, 1986), pp. 103-105.

Stewart, Bernard L., ed. "Conference Report: State-Sponsored Terrorism: The Threat and Possible Countermeasures" 8, 3 Terrorism (1986), pp. 253ff.

Stohl, Michael "International Dimensions of State Terrorism" in Michael Stohl and George A. Lopez, eds. The State as Terrorist: The Dynamics of Governmental Violence and Repression (Westport, Connecticut: Greenwood, 1984).

Stohl, Michael "National Interest and State Terrorism" (West Lafayette: Purdue University, March 1982), 28 pp.

Stohl, Michael "National Interests and State Terrorism" 36 Political Science (July 1984), pp. 37-52.
This article is interested in the effects insurgent terrorism has on our understanding of terrorism in general and its impact on the study of state terrorism in particular.

Stohl, Michael "States, Terrorism and State Terrorism: The Role of the Superpowers" in Robert O. Slater and Michael Stohl, eds. Current Perspectives on International Terrorism (London: Macmillan, 1987).

Stohl, Michael "The Superpowers and International Terrorism", paper presented to the annual convention of the International Studies Association, Atlanta, March 27-31, 1984

Stohl, Michael "The Superpowers and International Terrorism" in Michael Stohl and George A. Lopez, eds. Government Violence and Repression: An Agenda for Research (Westport, Connecticut: Greenwood Press, 1986), pp. 207-228.

Stohl, Michael and Raymond Duvall "Terrorism as Foreign Policy", paper presented to the 24th annual convention of the International Studies Association, Mexico City, April 5-9, 1983.

Stohl, Michael and George A. Lopez, eds. Government Violence and Repression: An Agenda for Research (Westport, Connecticut: Greenwood Press, 1986), 278 pp.
This volume deals with human rights abuses on the part of individual states. This study written by specialists from several countries attempts to define the parameters of state terrorism, analyze its causes, and identify the types of data and methods needed for policy relevant research. It focuses on state use of acts of terror to intimidate, "pacify", coerce, or destroy whole populations, groups, or classes of citizens.

Stohl, Michael and George A. Lopez, eds. The State as Terrorist: The Dynamics of Governmental Violence and Repression (Westport: Greenwood, 1984), 202 pp.
Reviewed in 17 New York University Journal of International Law and Politics (Spring 1985), pp. 809-810.

Stohl, Michael and George A. Lopez, eds. Terrible Beyond Endurance?: The Foreign Policy of State Terrorism (Westport, Connecticut: Greenwood, 1987), 341 pp.
This book argues that technological development has helped to promote state terrorism and the use of surrogates for carrying out aggressive aims. The essays in this volume analyze the different forms of terrorism in terms of the differential costs and benefits associated with them. They serve as a framework for examining the questions of why countries act or support terrorists; what can be done to raise the costs and decrease the benefits of terrorism; and what the role of the United States in response to terrorist acts should be.

Stohl Michael and George A. Lopez "Terror and the State: From Robespierre to 1984" Chitty's Law Journal (forthcoming).

"Surrogate Actors in Africa " in Uri Ra'anan, Robert L. Pfaltzgraff, Jr., Richard H. Shultz, Ernst Halperin, and Igor Lukes Hydra of Carnage: International Linkages of Terrorism: The Witnesses Speak (Lexington, Mass.: Lexington Books, 1986), pp. 587-508.

"Surrogate Actors in the Caribbean: Central America" in Uri Ra'anan, Robert L. Pfaltzgraff, Jr., Richard H. Shultz, Ernst Halperin, and Igor Lukes Hydra of Carnage: International Linkages of Terrorism: The Witnesses Speak (Lexington, Mass.: Lexington Books, 1986), pp. 307-360.
Documents on support to terrorists by communist regimes.

"Surrogate Actors in the Caribbean: Grenada" in Uri Ra'anan, Robert L. Pfaltzgraff, Jr., Richard H. Shultz, Ernst Halperin, and Igor Lukes Hydra of Carnage: International Linkages of Terrorism: The Witnesses Speak (Lexington, Mass.: Lexington Books, 1986), pp. 361-430.

"Surrogate Actors in Europe" in Uri Ra'anan, Robert L. Pfaltzgraff, Jr., Richard H. Shultz, Ernst Halperin, and Igor Lukes Hydra of Carnage: International Linkages of Terrorism: The Witnesses Speak (Lexington, Mass.: Lexington Books, 1986), pp. 569-586.

"Surrogate Actors in the Middle East" in Uri Ra'anan, Robert L. Pfaltzgraff, Jr., Richard H. Shultz, Ernst Halperin, and Igor Lukes Hydra of Carnage: International Linkages of Terrorism: The Witnesses Speak (Lexington, Mass.: Lexington Books, 1986), pp. 477-568.

Svetov, B. and O. Tarin Mezhdunarodnyy terrorizm i Tsru: dokumenty, svidetel'stva, fakty (Moscow: Progress, 1981), 142 pp.

Tarabochia, Alfonso L. "Cuba: The Technocracy of Subversion, Espionage, and Terrorism" 3 Clandestine Tactics and Technology (Gaithersburg, Maryland: International Association of Chiefs of Police, 1976), 45 pp.

"Terrorism: The Role of Moscow and its Subcontractors" (Washington, D.C.: 97th Congress, Hearings of the Subcommittee on Security and Terrorism, Committee on the Judiciary, June 26, 1981).

Terry, J. P. "State Terrorism: A Juridical Examination in Terms of Existing International Law" 10, 1 Journal of Palestine Studies (1980), pp. 94-117.

Timmerman, Jacobo Prisoner Without a Name, Cell Without a Number (New York: Alfred A. Knopf, 1981).
Written by a Jewish victim of Argentinian state terrorism.

Tumarkin, Nina "Political Ritual and the Cult of Lenin" 5, 2 Human Rights Quarterly (May 1983), pp. 203-206.
Paper given to the Symposium on Terror in the Modern Age: The Vision of Literature, the Response of Law.

Unger, Leopold "Widziane z Brukseli (The View from Brussels)" 3 Kultura (France) (1983), pp. 70-81.
A look at Soviet and Bulgarian support for assassination attempts in the West.

US House of Representatives, Committee on Foreign Affairs, Subcommittee on Human Rights and International Organizations "Political Killings by Governments of Their Citizens: Hearings" (Washington, D.C.: November 16 and 17, 1983), 306 pp.

US House of Representatives, Committee on Foreign Affairs, Subcommittee on Inter-American Affairs "Review of the Presidential Certification of Nicaragua's Connection to Terrorism: Hearing" (Washington, D.C.: USGPO, September 30, 1980), 50 pp.

US Senate "S.2626: A Bill to Prohibit the Training, Supporting, or Inducing of Terrorism, and for other purposes" (Washington, D.C.: 98th Congress, 2nd session, May 2, 1984), 9 pp.
Sponsored by Senators Thurmond and Denton.

US Senate Committee on the Judiciary, Subcommittee on Security and Terrorism Firearm Felonies by Foreign Diplomats (Washington, D.C.: USGPO, 98th Congress, Second Session, July 24 and September 21, 1984), 150 pp.

US Senate Committee on the Judiciary, Subcommittee on Security and Terrorism "Historical Antecedents of Soviet Terrorism: Hearings" (Washington, D.C.: 97th Congress, First Session, June 11-12-1981.

US Senate Committee on the Judiciary, Subcommittee on Security and Terrorism "The Role of the Soviet Union, Cuba and East Germany in Fomenting Terrorism in Southern Africa"(Washington, D.C.: 97th Congress, 2nd session, March 22, 24, 25, 29, 31, 1982), 902 pp.

US Senate Committee on the Judiciary, Subcommittee on Security and Terrorism "Soviet, East German, and Cuban Involvement in Fomenting Terrorism in Southern Africa: Report of the Chairman" (Washington, D.C.: US Government Printing Office, 1982), 28 pp.
A report on hearings held on March 22, 24, 25, 29, and 31, 1982.

US Senate Committee on the Judiciary, Subcommittee on Security and Terrorism "The Role of Cuba in International Terrorism and Subversion: Hearings: February 26, March 4, 11, and 12, 1982" (Washington, D.C.: US Government Printing Office, 1982), 273 pp.

US Senate Committee on the Judiciary, Subcommittee on Security and Terrorism "Terrorism: The Role of Moscow and Its Subcontractors: Hearing, June 26, 1981" (Washington: US Government Printing Office, 1982), 55 pp.

Vanhecke, Charles "Argentina's 'Nuremberg Trial'" 32 World Press Review (September 1985), pp.47-48.
A review of the status of the torture cases from the "dirty war" against terrorists.

Vernisy, Jacques de "The New International Terrorism: Militant Regimes Develop a Deadly Alternative to Traditional Diplomacy" 27 World Press Review (November 1980), pp. 23-25.

Weisberg, Richard "Avoiding Central Realities: Narrative Terror and the Failure of French Culture under the Occupation" 5, 2 Human Rights Quarterly (May 1983), pp. 151-170.
A discussion of French behavior during the Holocaust.

Wilkinson, Paul "Can a State be 'Terrorist'?" 57, 3 International Affairs (Great Britain) (Summer 1981), pp. 467-472.

Wilkinson, Paul "State-Sponsored International Terrorism: The Problems of Response" The World Today (Summer 1984), 7 pp.

Wilkinson, Paul "Support Mechanisms in International Terrorism" in Robert O. Slater and Michael Stohl, eds. Current Perspectives on International Terrorism (London: Macmillan, 1987).

Wilkinson, Paul "Uncomfortable Truths About International Terrorism" 19 Across the Board (January 1982), pp. 78-84.
Wilkinson shows how difficult it is to establish the extent of Soviet involvement with terrorists.

Wolf, John B. "Enforcement Terrorism" 3 Police Studies (Winter 1981), pp. 45-54.

NARCOTICS TRAFFICKING AND TERRORISM

Abrams, Elliott "Drug Wars: The New Alliances Against Traffickers and Terrorists" 792 Current Policy (Washington, D.C.: US Department of State, Bureau of Public Affairs, February 10, 1986), 4 pp.
A reprint of an address given by the Assistant Secretary for Inter-American Affairs before the Council on Foreign Relations in New York City.

Adams, Nathan M. "Drugs for Guns" Readers Digest (November 1983), pp. 88ff.

Blum, Yehuda Z. "Extradition: A Common Approach to the Control of International Terrorism and Traffic in Narcotic Drugs" 13, 2 Israel Law Review (April 1978), pp. 194-202.
Castro and the Narcotics Connection: Special Report (Washington, D.C.: Cuban American National Foundation, 1983), 88 pp.

Chao Hermida, Francisco Terrorismo y Drogas: Hijos Mellizos de la Subversion (Caracas, Venezuela: Editorial Arte, 1984), 103 pp.

Clarke, Philip C. "Drugs and Terrorism: The Deadly Alliance" 121 American Legion (August 1986), pp. 16-19.

The Cuban Government's Involvement in Facilitating International Drug Traffic (Washington, D.C.: Joint Hearing before the Subcommittee on Security and Terrorism of the Committee on the Judiciary and the Subcommittee on Western Hemisphere Affairs of the Foreign Relations Committee and the Senate Drug Enforcement Caucus, United States Senate, 98th Congress, First Session, Miami, Florida, April 30, 1983), 687 pp.

Diaz, Tom "Terrorism" 9 Nuestro (June-July 1985), pp. 19-22.

Drugs and Terrorism, 1984: Record of Hearings before the Subcommittee on Alcoholism and Drug Abuse of the Committee on Labor and Human Resources (Washington, D.C.: US Senate, 98th Congress, 2nd session, August 2, 1984).

Frost, Charles C. "Drug Trafficking, Organized Crime and Terrorism: The International Cash Connection" in Uri Ra'anan, Robert L. Pfaltzgraff, Jr., Richard H. Shultz, Ernst Halperin, and Igor Lukes Hydra of Carnage: International Linkages of Terrorism: The Witnesses Speak (Lexington, Mass.: Lexington Books, 1986), pp. 189-198.

Henze, Paul B."Organized Crime and Drug Linkages" in Uri Ra'anan, Robert L. Pfaltzgraff, Jr., Richard H. Shultz, Ernst Halperin, and Igor Lukes Hydra of Carnage: International Linkages of Terrorism: The Witnesses Speak (Lexington, Mass.: Lexington Books, 1986), pp. 171-188.

Hume, Ellen "'Narco-Terrorism,' Other Dramatic Media Topics Make Congress's Oversight Hearings Political Art" Wall Street Journal (November 1, 1985), pp. 48, 62.

International Terrorism and the Drug Connection (Ankara: The University of Ankara, 1984), 294 pp. also published in French as Le Terrorisme Internationale et le Trafic de Stupefiants.
Reviewed by William F. Sater TVI Journal (Summer 1985), p. 63. The book concentrates on the Armenian Secret Army for the Liberation of Armenia, and its possible connections with drug traffickers and the Soviets. Alternate title is Armenian Terrorism, Its Supporters, The Narcotic Connection, the Distortion of History: Symposium on International Terrorism, 17-18 April 1984, Rectorate Conference Hall.

Marshall, Jonathan "The Business of Terrorism" 3 Dial (January 1982), pp. 48-51.
A look at how drug traffickers and organized crime finance terrorism.

McKinnon, Raymond J. "Terrorism and DEA Foreign Operations" 12 Drug Enforcement (Summer 1985), p. 28.

Oakley, Robert B. "Combatting International Terrorism" 12 <u>Drug Enforcement</u> (Summer 1985), pp. 25-32.

Richey, Warren "Links Grow Between Drug Runners and Terrorist Groups: Exchange of Profits for Guns Impairs Enforcement Effort" 77 <u>Christian Science Monitor</u> (May 22, 1985), p. 3.

Somer, Tarik "Armenian Terrorism and the Narcotic Traffic" paper presented at the Symposium on International Terrorism, Ankara University, Turkey, April 17, 1984.

Steinitz, Mark S. "Insurgents, Terrorists, and the Drug Trade" 8, 4 <u>Washington Quarterly</u> (Fall 1985), pp. 57-69.

"Surrogate Actors: Nark-Intern (Narcotics International)" in Uri Ra'anan, Robert L. Pfaltzgraff, Jr., Richard H. Shultz, Ernst Halperin, and Igor Lukes <u>Hydra of Carnage: International Linkages of Terrorism: The Witnesses Speak</u> (Lexington, Mass.: Lexington Books, 1986), pp. 431-476.
Includes interviews with Carlos Lehder Rivas, a major Colombian trafficker, Mario Estevez Gonzales, a former Cuban DGI agent, Antonio Farach, a former Sandinista diplomat, former smugglers Crump and Perez, and a DEA report on Bulgarian Involvement in Drug Trafficking.

Taylor, Clyde D. "Links Between International Narcotics Trafficking and Terrorism" 85 <u>Department of State Bulletin</u> (August 1985), pp. 69-75.

"UN Report Links Traffic in Narcotics to Latin Terrorism" 135 <u>New York Times</u> (January 3, 1986), p. A4.

US Senate, <u>International Terrorism, Insurgency, and Drug Trafficking: Present Trends in Terrorist Activity</u> (Washington, D.C.: Joint Hearings before the Committee on Foreign Relations and the Committee on the Judiciary, 99th Congress, First Session, May 13, 14 and 15, 1985), 426 pp.

Warner, John "Terrorists and Drug Traffickers Develop Working Alliances: Trend Expected to Continue" <u>Narcotics Control Digest</u> (October 12, 1983).

Westrate, David L. "Drug Trafficking and Terrorism" 12 <u>Drug Enforcement</u> (Summer 1985), pp. 19-24.

Terrorism
by Geographic Area

EUROPE AND CANADA

Acquaviva, Sabino S. Guerriglia e Guerra Rivoluzionaria in Italia (Italy: Rizzoli, 1979), 175 pp.

Acquaviva, Sabino S., ed. Terrorismo e Guerriglia in Italia: La Cultura Della Violenza (Italy: Citta Nuova, 1979), 222 pp. Essays and documents on the Red Brigades.

Adolph, Robert B., Jr. "Terrorism: The Causal Factors" 8 Military Intelligence (July-September 1982), pp. 49-57. A look at the Red Brigades and the Baader-Meinhof Gang.

Agostini, Piero Mara Cagol (Venezia: Marsilio Trento, TEMI, 1980), 163 pp.

Al di la del 7 Aprile (Brescia: Shakespeare and Company, 1980), 44 pp.

Alexander, Shana "The Patriot Game" 15 New York (November 22, 1982), pp. 58-68. The case of 5 New Yorkers charged with IRA gunrunning.

Alexander, Yonah and Kenneth A. Myers, eds. Terrorism in Europe (New York: St. Martin's, and London: Croom Helm, 1982), 216 pp.

Alexander, Yonah and Alan O'Day, eds. Terrorism in Ireland (London: Croom Helm and New York: St. Martin's Press, 1984), 227 pp.

Anti-Terrorist Legislation in the Federal Republic of Germany (Washington, D.C.: Library of Congress Law Library, March 1979), 143 pp.

Anttila, Inkeri "Finland: A Country with No Terrorism or Skyjacking" in Ronald D. Crelinsten, Danielle Laberge-Altmejd and Denis Szabo, eds. Terrorism and Criminal Justice (Toronto: Lexington, 1978).

Arbatova, N. K. "Terrorizm v Sovremennoi Italii (Terrorism in Modern Italy)" 12 Voprosy Istorii (USSR) (1981), pp. 176-181.
A look at the rise of left- and right-wing terrorism in response to Italian Communist Party electoral fortunes.

Ascari, O. Accusa: Reato di Strage. La Storia di Piazza Fontana (Charge: Mass Murder. The Story of Piazza Fontana) (Milan: Editoriale Nuova, 1979).

Ascher, Abraham "Lessons of Russian Terrorism" 29, 6 Problems of Communism (November-December 1980), pp. 70-74.

Auseinandersetzung mit dem Terrorismus, Moglichkeiten der Politischen Bildungsarbeit (Bonn: Das Bundesministerium, 1981), 229 pp.

Baker, Blake The Far Left: An Expose of the Extreme Left in Britain (London: Weidenfeld and Nicolson, 1981), 182 pp.

Ballard, Bea and Nick Anning "The Elusive Firebombers" 102 New Statesman (August 28, 1981), pp. 6-7.
A discussion of the Southwark National Front in the United Kingdom.

Barbato, T. Il Terrorismo in Italia: Cronaca e Documentazione (Milan: Editrice Bibliografica, 1980).

Barker, Ralph Not Here but in Another Place (New York, 1980).
A diary of events surrounding the Moluccan train hijackings.

Basaglia, F., and F. Fornari La Violenza (Florence: Vallecchi, 1978).

Basso, L. Socialismo e Rivoluzione (Milan: Feltrinelli, 1980).

Becker, Jillian "Another Final Battle on the Stage of History" in Paul Wilkinson, Guest Editor "British Perspectives on Terrorism" 5, 1-2 Terrorism (1981), pp. pp. 89-106.

Becker, K. E. and H. P. Schreiner, eds. Anti-Politik: Terrorismus, Gewalt, Gegengewalt (West Germany: Fackeltrager, 1979), 262 pp.

Bell, J. Bowyer "The Chroniclers of Violence in Northern Ireland: An Analysis of Tragedy" 36, 4 Review of Politics (October 1974), pp. 421-443.

Benda, R. "Austria: No Place for Terrorists" 4 Kriminalistik (1980), pp. 172-175.

Benda, R. "Austria: Country for Terrorists" 6 Kriminalistik (1980), pp. 254-258.

Bereciartu, G. Jauregui Ideologia y Estrategia Politica de ETA 1959-1968 (Madrid, 1981).

Bergman, Jay "Vera Zasulich, the Shooting of Trepov and the Growth of Political Terrorism in Russia, 1878-1881" 4, 1-4 Terrorism (1980), pp. 25-51.

Bertini, B. P. Franchi and U. Spagnoli Extremismo, Terrorismo, Ordine Democratico (Rome: Editori Riuniti, 1978).

Besancon, Alain "The First European Terrorists" in Benjamin Netanyahu, ed. Terrorism: How the West Can Win (New York: Farrar, Straus, Giroux, 1986), pp. 44-47.

Bew, Paul and Henry Patterson "The Protestant-Catholic Conflict in Ulster" 36 Journal of International Affairs (Fall-Winter 1982-83), pp. 223-234.

Bibes, Genevieve "Le Terrorisme Italien: Essai D'Explication (Italian Terrorism: Attempt at an Explanation)" 357, 4 Etudes (France) (1982), pp. 293-306.
Bibes explains it as growing out of sociocultural factors.

Billig, Michael and Raymond Cochrane "The National Front and Youth 15, 4 Patterns of Prejudice (Great Britain) (1981), pp. 3-15.
A 1970s anti-Semitic racist group in England.

Blackstone Associates "Documents--Italy: Threat Assessment" 2, 3-4 Terrorism (1979), pp. 283-296.

Blankenburg, E., ed. Politik der Inneren Sicherheit (Frankfurt A.M., 1980).
On West German anti-terrorism policies.

Blinken, Anthony J. "The New Terrorism: A Coalition of Violence in Europe" 192 New Republic (April 1, 1985), pp. 12ff.

Bloomfield, Lincoln P., Jr. "Anarchy in Turkey: The Growing Pains of a Young Democracy" 2, 1 Conflict (1980), pp. 31-56.

Blutspur der Gewalt: Bilanz eines Jahrzehnts des Terrorismus (Zurich: Verlag Neue Zurcher Zeitung, 1980), 187 pp.
A reprint of a series of articles which appeared in the Neue Zurcher Zeitung in 1978.

Bobbio, L. Lotta Continua, Storia di Una Organizzazione Rivoluzionaria (Rome: Savelli, 1979).

Bocca, Giorgio Il Caso 7 Aprile (Milan: Feltrinelli, 1980).

Bocca, Giorgio Dalle Origini all'eta' Contemporanea (From the Origins to Now) (Bologna: Zanichelli, 1980).

Bocca, Giorgio Il Terrorismo Italiano 1970/1980 (Milan: Biblioteca Universale Rizzoli, 1981).

Bonanate, Luigi, C. Marletti, L. Migliorino, et al. Dimensioni del Terrorismo Politico (Milan: Franco Angeli, 1979).

Bonanno, Alfredo Maria Del Terrorismo, di Alcuni Imbecilli e di Altre Cose (Catania: Edizioni di Anarchismo, 1979), 36 pp.

"Booklet Giving History of ASALA's Existence Gives New Insight into the Revolutionary Movement" The Armenian Reporter (January 31, 1985), p. 12.

de Boor, W., R. Brossarth-Maticek, C. Meves, E. Mueller-Luckmann, Reinhard Rupprecht, H. Schwind, and L. Veelken, eds. Causes of Terrorism in the Federal Republic of Germany (Berlin: Walter de Gruyter, 1978), 174 pp.

Bossi Fedrigotti, I. Amore Mio Uccidi Garibaldi (My Love, Kill Garibaldi (Milan: Longanesi, 1980).

Botstein, Leon "German Terrorism from Afar" 46, 2 Partisan Review (1979), pp. 188-204.

Bowden, Tom The Breakdown of Public Security: The Case of Ireland 1916-1921 and Palestine 1936-1939 (Beverly Hills: Sage, 1977), 342 pp.
Bowden argues that the breakdown of public security is a necessary prerequisite for any successful revolutionary war. The first step is to blind governments by attacking their intelligence network.

Boyle, Kevin, Tom Hadden, and Paddy Hillyard "The Facts on Internment in Northern Ireland" in Ronald D. Crelinsten, Danielle Laberge-Altmejd and Denis Szabo, eds. Terrorism and Criminal Justice (Toronto: Lexington, 1978).

Boyle, Kevin, Tom Hadden and Paddy Hillyard Ten Years on in Northern Ireland (Nottingham: Cobden Trust, 1980), 119 pp.

Boyle, Kevin and Paddy Hillyard Law and State: The Case of Northern Ireland (London: Martin Robertson, 1975).

Bradshaw, Jon "The Dream of Terror" 90 Esquire (July 18, 1987), pp. 24-45, 47-50.
A look at Andreas Baader and Ulrike Meinhof.

Breindel, E. "Terrorism Does Not Avenge a Tragic Past: Armenians and Turks" 186, 22 New Republic (1982), pp. 9-10.

Brodeur, J. P. "October Crisis and the Commissions of Inquiry" 13, 2 Criminologie (1980), pp. 79-98.

Browne, William Huffaker Morning Coat, Spats, and Pistol-- Boris V. Savinkov, The Terrorist, As Politician and Diplomat, 1917-1925 (Washington, D.C.: George Washington University, Ph.D., 1980).

Brunn, Gerhard "Nationalist Violence and Terror in the Spanish Border Provinces: ETA" in Wolfgang J. Mommsen and Gerhard Hirschfeld, eds. Social Protest, Violence and Terror in Nineteenth and Twentieth Century Europe (New York: St. Martin's, 1982).

Bundesjugendkuratorium Jugend und Terrorismus (Munchen: Juventa-Verlag, 1979), 128 pp.

Burton, Frank The Politics of Legitimacy: Struggles in a Belfast Community (London: Routledge and Kegan Paul, 1978).

Bush, Margaret A. "Kill the Tsar! Youth and Terrorism in Old Russia" 63 Horn Book (January-February, 1987), pp. 77-78.

Cameron Commission Report: Disturbances in Northern Ireland (London: H. R. Stationery Office, #532, 1969).

Cappadocia, Ezio "Terrorism in Italy: A Commentary" 89, 4 Queen's Quarterly (Canada) (1982), pp. 770-782.

Carroll, Terrance G. "Northern Ireland" in Astri Suhrke and Lela Garner Noble Ethnic Conflict in International Relations (New York: Praeger, 1977), pp. 21-42.

Carroll, Terrance G. "Regulating Conflicts: The Case of Ulster" 51 Political Quarterly (October-December 1980), pp. 451-463.

Cattani, Alfred "Germany: From Student Protest to Criminal Violence" 28 Swiss Review of World Affairs (January 1979), pp. 17-31.

Cavallini, M. Il Terrorismo in Fabbrica (Terrorism in the Factory) (Rome: Editori Riuniti, Interventi, 1978).

Cervone, Vittorio Ho Fatto di Tutto per Salvare Moro (Torino: Marietti, 1979), 191 pp.

Chaliand, Gerard and Yves Ternon The Armenians: From Genocide to Resistance (London: Zed Press, 1983).

Chelazzi, Gabriele La Dissociazione dal Terrorismo (Milan: Giuffre, 1981), 154 pp.

Chiesa, G. "Pokushenie na Ital'ianskuiu Demokratiiu: Delo Ob Ubiistve Al'do Moro (The Attack on Italian Democracy: The Murder of Aldo Moro)" 8 Sovetskoe Gosudarstvo i Pravo (USSR) (1983), pp. 104-110.
Chiesa claims that the reactionary wing of the Christian Democrats made more political capital out of the incident than did the Red Brigade's murderers.

Chodos, Robert and Nick Auf der Maur Quebec: A Chronicle 1968-1972 (Toronto: Canadian Journalism Foundation, 1972)

Christie, Stuart Stefano Delle Chaiae (London: Anarchy Magazine/Refract Publications, 1984), 182 pp.

"A Chronology: Euroterrorist Actions 1984--April 1985" 5, 4 TVI: Terrorism Violence Insurgency Journal (Spring 1985), pp. 18-21.

Clark, Robert P. The Basque Insurgents: ETA, 1952-1980 (Madison: University of Wisconsin Press, 1984), 328 pp.
Reviewed by Goldie Shabad in 6, 1 TVI: Terrorism Violence Insurgency Journal (Summer 1985), pp. 59-62.

Clark, Robert P. "Basque Resistance and ETA" paper presented at the spring conference of the National Capital Area Political Science Association and the International Studies Association-D.C. Chapter, Mount Vernon College, Washington, D.C., February 27, 1982.

Clark, Robert P. "The Basque Resistance: Violent and Non-Violent" paper presented to the panel on the Role of Terrorism in Ethnic Nationalism at the annual convention of the International Studies Association/South, University of Florida, October 29-31, 1981.

Clark, Robert P. The Basques: The Franco Years and Beyond (Reno: University of Nevada Press, 1980).

Clark, Robert P. "Patterns in the Lives of ETA Members" 6, 3 Terrorism (1983), pp. 423-454.
A look at 48 case histories and data on 447 other individuals.

Clutterbuck, Richard "Terrorism and the Security Forces in Europe" 111, 1 Army Quarterly and Defence Journal (January 1981), pp. 12-29.
A look at antiterrorist doctrine in the UK, West Germany, and Italy.

Clutterbuck, Richard "Threats to Public Order in Britain" 107 Army Quarterly (July 1977), pp. 279-290.

Conference on the Defence of Democracy Against Terrorism in Europe Compendium of Documents (Strasbourg, France: Council of Europe, Parliamentary Assembly, 1981).

Conference on the Defence of Democracy Against Terrorism in Europe Tasks and Problems (Strasbourg, France: Council of Europe, Parliamentary Assembly, 1980).

Connell, D. "U.K.: Prevention of Terrorism Act" 3 Index on Censorship (1980).

Consiglio Regionale Piemonte Una Regione Contro Il Terrorismo 1969-1978, Dati e Cronache (A Region Against Terrorism, 1969-1978, Facts and History) (Savigliano: Nuove Arti Grafiche, S.p.A., 1979).

Contemporary Italian Terrorism: Analysis and Countermeasures (Washington, D.C.: Library of Congress Law Library, May 1979), 185 pp.

Contro Il Terrorismo per la Liberta (Against Terrorism, for Freedom) (Venice: Marsilio, 1979).

Convegno Per un Impegno Comune e Democratico Contro l'Eversione e il Terrorismo e Contro Ogni Attentato alla Convivenza Civile (Milano: Grafica Giuliani, 1978), 79 pp.

Coogan, Tim Pat The IRA (London: Fontana, 1980).

Corea, Gena "Northern Ireland: The Violence Isn't All in the Street" 8 Ms. (July 1979), pp. 94-99.
Argues that violence against women is the key question for Ulster, and that it is connected to the street violence issue.

Cordes, Bonnie "Action Directe Comes of Age" 5, 4 TVI: Terrorism Violence Insurgency Journal (Spring 1985), pp. 6-7.

Corso internazionale di alta specializzazione per le forze di polizia (Messina: Centro Internzaionale di Ricerche e Studi Sociologici, Penali Penitenziari, 1979), 95 pp.

Corsun, Andrew "Armenian Terrorism: A Profile" 82 US Department of State Bulletin (August 1982), pp. 31-35.

Cowan, S. "Terrorism and the Italian Left" in C. Boggs and D. Plotke, eds. The Politics of Eurocommunism, Socialism in Transition (London: Macmillan, 1980).

Coyle, Dominick J. Minorities in Revolt: Political Violence in Ireland, Italy, and Cyprus (London: Associated University Press, and Rutherford, New Jersey: Fairleigh Dickinson University Press, 1983), 253 pp.

Cronin, Sean IRA Ideology and the Roots of Conflict in Northern Ireland, 1956-1962 (New School for Social Research, Department of Political Science, Ph.D. dissertation, 1979).

Cronin, Sean Irish Nationalism: A History of its Roots and Ideology (New York: Continuum, 1981), 391 pp.

Cuperus, J. and R. Klijnsma Onderhandelen of Bestormen: Het Beleid Van de Nederlandse Overheid Inzake Terroristische Acties (Negotiate or Storm: The Dutch Government's Policy During Terroristic Actions) (Groningen: Polemologisch Instituut, 1980), 98 pp.

Dasnabedian, Hratch "The Armenian Revolutionary Federation Record: The Balance Sheet of Ninety Years" 34, 2 Armenian Review (1981), pp. 115-126.
Discusses ARF terrorism in 1890-1895.

The Day of the S.A.S. (London: Express Newspapers, 1980), 64 pp.

Demi, Ahmet "Ngjarje te Jetuara ne Vitin 1924 (Events of 1924)" 38, 2 Studime Hist. (Albania) (1984), pp. 207-213.
A look at the failed plot to kill King Zog I and the democratic revolution which followed.

DeRidder, Martine M. "Basque Terrorism: Evaluating Governmental Responses to ETA", paper presented to the 24th annual convention of the International Studies Association, Mexico City, April 5-9, 1983.

Devlin, Paddy The Fall of the Northern Irish Executive (Belfast, Paddy Devlin, 1975).

"A Document Published Recently by the Red Army Faction: West Germany's Leading Terrorist Organization" 5, 4 TVI: Terrorism Violence Insurgency Journal (Spring 1985), p. 17.

Documenti Arces Il PCI e la Violenza (The PCI and Violence) (Milan: Donati, 1978).

Donahue, Deirdre E. "Human Rights in Northern Ireland: Ireland v. the United Kingdom" 3 Boston College International and Comparative Law Review (Summer 1980), pp. 377-432.

Dornberg, John "West Germany's Embattled Democracy: The Antiterrorist Menace from the Right" 5 Saturday Review (June 10, 1978), pp. 18-21.

Dossier sul Terrorismo 1980 (Torino: F.ili Scravaglio & C., 1981), 63 pp.

Dowling, Kathryn "Civil Rights, Human Rights, and Terrorism in Northern Ireland" 7, 4 Journal of Intergroup Relations (1979-1980), pp. 3-23.

Drake, Richard "The Red and the Black: Terrorism in Contemporary Italy" 5, 3 International Political Science Review (1984), pp. 279-298.

Drake, Richard "The Red Brigades and the Italian Political Tradition" in Yonah Alexander and K. A. Myers, eds. Terrorism in Europe (London: Croom Helm, 1982).

Duhamel, Luc "Lenine, La Violence et L'Eurocommunisme" 13, 1 Canadian Journal of Political Science (1980), pp. 97-120.

Dutter, Lee E. "Northern Ireland and Theories of Ethnic Politics" 24, 4 Journal of Conflict Resolution (December 1980), pp. 613-640.

Edwards, Rob "Instant Punditry" 109 New Statesman (June 28, 1985), pp. 10-11.
A look at the research on terrorism and hijacking by Paul Wilkinson of the University of Aberdeen.

Enzensberger, M.H. Politica e Terrore (Rome: Savelli, 1978).

Faligot, Roger Nous avons tue Mountbatten! L'IRA (Irish Republican Army) Parle (France: Picollec, 1981), 227 pp.
Interviews with IRA commanders involved with the assassination of Lord Mountbatten.

Fare, Ida and Franca Spiritto Mara e le Altre (Mara and the Others) (Milan: Feltrinelli, 1979).

Fay, James R. "Terrorism in Turkey: Threat to NATO's Troubled Ally" 61, 4 Military Review (April 1981), pp. 16-26.

Ferrarotti, Franco Alle Radici Della Violenza: Criminalita Comune, Terrorismo, Violenza Quotidiana alla Luce di Un'Esplosiva Analisi Sociologica (At the Roots of Violence) (Italy: Rizzoli, 1979), 187 pp.

Collection of articles which appeared in <u>Corriere della Sera</u>, <u>La Critica Sociologica</u> and <u>Citta e Regione</u>, with concentration on Italian terrorism.

Ferrarotti, Franco "Una Tragedia Italiana: Il Sacrificio di Aldo Moro" <u>Critica Sociologica</u> (July-December 1980), pp. 63-72.

Ferrarotti, Franco <u>La Ypnosi Della Violenza</u> (Milan: Rizzoli 1980).

Fields, Rona M. <u>Northern Ireland: Society Under Siege</u> (New Brunswick: Transaction, 1980), 267 pp.

Fiorillo, Ernesto "Terrorism in Italy: Analysis of a Problem" 2, 3-4 <u>Terrorism</u> (1979), pp. 261-270.

Flechtheim, Ossip K. "Die politische Kultur der Bundesrepublik und der Terrorismus" 18, 4-5 <u>Vorgange</u> (1979), pp. 71-82.

Flemming, Peter A. "International Terrorism in Western Europe" paper presented at the annual convention of the International Studies Association/Midwest, Indianapolis, November 1986.

Fortier, David H. "Brittany: 'Briez Atao'" in Charles R. Foster, ed. <u>Nations Without a State: Ethnic Minorities in Western Europe</u> (New York: Praeger, 1980), pp. 136-152 Breiz Atao (Brittany Forever) is a Breton nationalist journal.

Foss, Yvind <u>Blant Terrorister og Syndere</u> (Oslo: Ansgar, 1978), 125 pp.

"The Francesco Piperno Case" 4 <u>Terrorism</u> (1980), pp. 293-310.

Francis, Samuel T. "Terrorist Renaissance: France, 1980-1983" 146, 1 <u>World Affairs</u> (Summer 1983), pp. 54-68.

Fraser, John "The Inner Contradictions of Marxism and Political Violence: The Case of the Italian Left" 48, 1 <u>Social Research</u> (1981), pp. 21-44.

Freund, J., M. Maffesoli and C. Rath <u>Il Luogo Della Violenza: La Violenza e la Citta (The Site of Violence: Violence and the City)</u> (Bologna: Cappelli, 1979).

de Gaay Fortman, Wilhelm Friedrich <u>Rechtsstaat en Terrorisme</u> (Alphen aan den Rijn: Samsom, 1979), 26 pp.

Galleni, Mauro <u>Rapporto sul Terrorismo: Le Stragi, gli Agguati, i Sequestri, Le Sigle, 1969-1980</u> (Milan, Rissoli Editore, 1981).

Garmendia, Jose Mari <u>Historia de ETA</u> 2 volumes (San Sebastian: L. Haranburu, 1980).

Garrett, J. Brian "Ten Years of British Troops in Northern Ireland" 4 <u>International Security</u> (Winter 1979-1980), pp. 80-104.

Geistig-politische Auseinandersetzung mit dem Terrorismus (Bonn: Arbeitsstab Offentlichkeitsarbeit gegen Terrorismus im Bundesministerium d. Innern, 1979), 157 pp.

Gerber, Rudolf "Materiellrechtliche Probleme der Bekampfung des Terrorismus" 33, 2 Kriminalistik (1979), pp. 71-80.

Gerogel, Jacques "Un An Apres l'Affaire Moro: L'Italie Entre Terrorisme et Politique, ou: Un Art de Survivre" 80 Revue Politique et Parlementaire (March-April 1979), pp. 54-74.

Gilbert, Sari "The Terrorist Grip on Italy" Boston Globe Magazine (May 31, 1981), pp. 10-11, 16-18.
Gilbert notes that Italians are beginning to react against the violence that has claimed 220 dead and 700 wounded in the last 12 years.

Glandon, Virginia E. "The Irish Press and Revolutionary Irish Nationalism" 16, 1 Eire-Ireland (1981), pp. 21-33.
A look at the Irish nationalist newspapers from 1896-1922.

Govea, Rodger "The European Response to Terrorism" in Leon Hurwitz, ed. The Harmonization of European Public Policy: Regional Responses to Transnational Challenges (Westport: Greenwood, 1983).

Greer, Herb "Ulster: In the Empty House of the Stare" 73 Commentary (January 1982), pp. 55-64.
A history of the 800-year-old problem.

Gregory, F. E. C. "The British Police and Terrorism" in Paul Wilkinson, Guest Editor "British Perspectives on Terrorism" 5, 1-2 Terrorism (1981), pp. 107-124.

Gribin, Nikolai Petrovich Tragediia Olstera (Ulster Tragedy) (Moscow: Mezhdunarodnye Otnoseheniia, 1980), 190 pp.

Grishaev, Pavel Ivanovich Rezhim Terrora i Bezzakoniia (Moscow: Mezhdunar Otnosheniia, 1979), 255 pp.

Guiso, G. La Condanna di Aldo Moro (The Sentence of Aldo Moro) (Milan: SugarCo, 1979).

Gunter, Michael M. "The Armenian Terrorist Campaign Against Turkey", paper presented to the 24th annual convention of the International Studies Association, Mexico City, April 5-9, 1983, published in 27, 2 Orbis (Summer 1983), pp. 447-477.

Gunter, Michael M. "Contemporary Armenian Terrorism" 8, 3 Terrorism (1986), pp. 213-252.

Gunter, Michael M. "Contemporary Aspects of Armenian Terrorism" in International Terrorism and the Drug Connection (Ankara University Press, 1984), pp. 103-144.

Gurkan, Ihsan, Lt. Gen. "Conflict: A Turkish View" in Brian Michael Jenkins, conference director Terrorism and Beyond: An International Conference on Terrorism and Low-Level Conflict

(Santa Monica: The Rand Corporation, R-2714-DOE/DOJ/DOS/RC, December 1982), pp. 101-114.

Haden-Guest, Anthony "The King of Fiat: Living with Terrorism" 11 New York (May 1, 1978), pp. 40-44.

Harmon, Christopher C. "Left Meets Right in Terrorism: A Focus on Italy" Strategic Review (Winter 1985).

Harmon, Christopher C. "The Red and the Black: Left-Right Terrorist Collusion in Italy, Germany, and France" paper presented to the annual convention of the American Political Science Association, September 1, 1984, 66 pp.

Harris, George S. "The Left in Turkey" 29, 4 Problems of Communism (July/August 1980), pp. 25-41.

Hart, W. "Ulster's Prison Guards: 'A Different Kind of Fear'" 6, 3 Corrections Magazine (June 1980), pp. 20-27.

Hart, W. "Waging Peace in Northern Ireland" 3, 3 Police Magazine (May 1980), pp. 22-32.

Haugseng, Magne "Violent Deaths as an Indicator of Denominational Conflict in Northern Ireland" paper presented to the Fifth Annual United Kingdom Politics Work Group Conference, University of Wales, Cardiff, September 16-19, 1980.

Hayes, B. "The Effects of Terrorism in Society: An Analysis, with Particular Reference to the UK and the European Economic Community" 2, 3 Police Studies (Fall 1979), pp. 4-10.

Hayes, Richard E. and Thomas S. Schiller The Impact of Government Behavior on the Frequency, Type, and Targets of Terrorist Group Activity: The Italian Experience, 1968-1982 (McLean, Va.: Defense Systems, Inc. 1983), 142 pp.

Hayes, Richard E. and Melvin Y. Shibuya The Impact of Government Behavior on the Frequency, Type, and Targets of Terrorist Group Activity: The Spanish Experience, 1968-1982 (McLean, Va: Defense Systems, Inc., 1983), 123 pp.

Haynal, A. Il Senso Della Disperazione (The Meaning of Desperation) (Milan: Feltrinelli, 1980).

Hedlund, Ingvar Ska Sverige Utbilda Terrorister? (Stockholm: Forlags AB Marieberg, 1980), 120 pp.

Herman, Valentine and Rob Van Der Laan Bouma "Martyrs, Murderers or Something Else? Terrorism in the Netherlands, the United Kingdom and the Federal Republic of Germany" (Rotterdam: Erasmus University, 1979).
Public opinion towards terrorist groups is discussed.

Herman, Valentine and Rob Van Der Laan Bouma "Nationalists Without a Nation: South Moluccan Terrorism in the Netherlands" 4, 1-4 Terrorism (1980), pp. 223-257.

Hess, H. Angriff auf das Herz des Staates: Soziale Hintergruende des Terrorismus in Italien (1982).

Hewitt, Christopher "Violence in Northern Ireland: Ethnic Conflict and Radicalization in an International Setting" paper presented at the spring conference of the National Capital Area Political Science Association and the International Studies Association-D.C. Chapter, Mount Vernon College, Washington, D.C., February 27, 1982.

Hildermeier, Manfred "The Terrorist Strategies of the Social-Revolutionary Party before 1914" in Wolfgang J. Mommsen and Gerhard Hirschfeld, eds. Social Protest, Violence and Terror in Nineteenth and Twentieth Century Europe (New York: St. Martin's, 1982), pp. 80-87.

Hoffman, Bruce "The International Symposium on the Rehabilitation of Terrorists in Turkey" 6, 1 TVI: Terrorism Violence Insurgency Journal (Summer 1985), pp. 44-50.

Hoffman, Bruce "Right-Wing Terrorism in Europe" (Santa Monica: The Rand Corporation, N-1856-AF, March 1982), 31 pp., also appeared in 5, 3 Conflict (1984), pp. 185-210, and in 28, 1 Orbis (Spring 1984), pp. 16-26.
The Note examines rightwing organizations in Italy, West Germany, and France.

Horchem, Hans Josef "The Development of West German Terrorism After 1969: An Overview" 5, 4 TVI: Terrorism Violence Insurgency Journal (Spring 1985), pp. 10-16.

Horchem, Hans Josef "European Terrorism: A German Perspective" 6, 1 Terrorism (1982), pp. 27-51.

Horchem, Hans Josef "Rightist Extremism in the Federal Republic of Germany, 1977" 1, 3 Conflict (1979), pp. 171-190.

Horchem, Hans Josef "Terrorism and Government Response: The German Experience" 4, 3 Jerusalem Journal of International Relations (1980) pp. 43-55.

Houston, John "The Northern Ireland Economy: A Special Case?" 16 Politics Today (August 16, 1976), pp. 274-288.

Hume, John "The Irish Question: A British Problem" 58 Foreign Affairs (Winter 1979-80), pp. 300-313.

Ingraham, Barton L. Political Crime in Europe: A Comparative Study of France, Germany and England (Berkeley: University of California, 1979), 380 pp.
Reviewed by Hilliard A. Gardiner, 75, 1 American Political Science Review (March 1981), pp. 237-239.

"Inside the IRA: How Ireland's Outlaws Fight Their Endless War: Special Report" 8 Life (October 1985), pp. 40-46.

Invernizzi, Gabriele "Belgium's Two Faces" 33 World Press Review (February 1986), pp. 55-56.

Itil, Turan "Terrorism in Turkey with Special Consideration of Armenian Terrorism" in International Terrorism and the Drug Connection (Ankara: Ankara University Press, 1984), pp. 29-48.

Janke, Peter "Spanish Separatism: ETA's Threat to Basque Democracy" 123 Conflict Studies (October 1980).

Jarach, A. Terrorismo Internazionale (Florence: Vallecchi, 1979).

Jeschke, Axel and Wolfgang Malanowski, eds. Der Minister und der Terrorist: Gesprache zwischen Gerhart Baum und Horst Mahler (West Germany: Spiegel-Verlag Rudolf Augstein BmbH, 1980), 224 pp.
Discussions conducted by Der Spiegel with Minister of the Interior Gerhart Baum and Horst Mahler, a member of the Red Army Faction who was sentenced to 12 years for terrorist activities.

Jesi, F. Cultura di Destra (Right Wing Culture) (Milan: Garzanti, 1979).

Johnston, A. "Britain, Ireland and Ulster" 7, 3 Review of International Studies (Great Britain) (1981), pp. 187-198.
A review of six books published between 1975-1978.

Jones, Mervyn "Verdict in London: Terrorists on Trial" 10, 4 Present Tense (1983), pp. 25-28.
The trial of Arab terrorists held for the shooting of Israel's Ambassador in London in 1982.

Jorgensen, Birthe "Defending the Terrorists: Queen's Counsel Before the Courts of Northern Ireland" 9, 1 Journal of Law and Society (Great Britain) (1982), pp. 115-126.

Katz, R. Day of Wrath: The Ordeal of Aldo Moro: The Kidnapping, The Execution, The Aftermath (Garden City: Doubleday, 1980), 326 pp.
Reviewed by Godfrey Hodgson "Aldo Moro's Communiques and Italy's Great Schism" Washington Post (May 27, 1980), p. B-7.

Kearney, Richard "Terrorisme et Sacrifice, Le Cas de L'Irlande Du Nord" 4 Esprit (France) (1979), pp. 29-44.

Kellen, Konrad "The New Challenge: Euroterrorism Against NATO" 5, 4 TVI: Terrorism Violence Insurgency Journal (Spring 1985), pp. 3-5.

Kellen, Konrad "The Road to Terrorism: Confessions of a German Terrorist" 5, 2 TVI Journal (Fall 1984), pp. 36-38.

Kelley, Kevin The Longest War: Northern Ireland and the IRA (Dingle, Co. Kelly, Ireland: Brandon and Westport, Conn.: L. Hill, 1982), 364 pp.

Kelly, Keith J. "The Survival of the IRA" 142 America (May 24, 1980), pp. 440-443.
The Provos did not start the 'Troubles', but they have exploited them.

Kelly, Michael J. and Thomas H. Mitchell "Post-Referendum Quebec: The Potential for Conflict" 1 Conflict Quarterly (Summer 1980), pp. 15-19.
The absence of Rene Levesque might unleash the Parti Quebecois's militant extremists, as might the government's mishandling of constitutional reform. A resurgence in terrorism would not be of the 1960s symbolic form, and might be more indiscriminate.

Kirkaldy, John "English Cartoonists: Ulster Realities" 16, 3 Eire-Ireland (1981), pp. 27-42.
The cartoons tend to magnify anti-Irish sentiment.

Klein, Hans-Joachim Ruckkehr in Die Menschlichket (Return to Humanity: Appeal from a Terrorist Who Defected) (Reinbeck bei Hamburg: Aktvell Vowohlt Verlag, 1979).

Komolova, N. P. "Gibel' Al'do Moro (Death of Aldo Moro)" 3 Novaia i Noveishaia Istoriia (USSR) (1981), pp. 140-160.

Kopkind, Andrew "Euro-Terror: Fear Eats the Soul" New Times (June 12, 1978), pp. 28-36, 61-62, 66.

Kovalev, Eduard and Vladimir Malyshev Terror, vdokhnovitel i ispolniteli: ocherki o podryvnoy deyatel nosti Tsru v Zapadnoy Yevrope (Moscow: Politizdat, 1984), 222 pp.

Krahenbuhl, Margaret "Political Kidnapping in Turkey, 1971-1972" (Santa Monica: The Rand Corporation, R-2105-DOS/ARPA, July 1977).

Krieger, Wolfgang "Worrying about West German Democracy" 50 Political Quarterly (April-June 1979), pp. 192-204.

Lagorio, Lelio Appunti, 1978-1981 (Firenze: Le Monnier, 1981), 253 pp.

Lang, David Marshall The Armenians: A People in Exile (London: G. Allen and Unwin, 1981), 203 pp.

Lawlor, S. M. "Ireland from Truce to Treaty: War or Peace? July to October 1921" 22, 85 Irish Historical Studies (Ireland) (1980), pp. 49-64.

Ledeen, Michael "Inside the Red Brigades: An Exclusive Report" 11 New York (May 1, 1978), pp. 36-38.

Lee, Alfred McClung "The Dynamics of Terrorism in Northern Ireland, 1968-1980" 48, 1 Social Research (Spring 1981), pp. 100-134.

Lee, Alfred McClung Terrorism in Northern Ireland (Bayside, New York: General Hall, 1983), 253 pp.

Legault, Albert "The Dynamics of Terrorism: The Case of the Red Brigades" 14, 4 Etudes Internationales (Canada) (December 1983), pp. 639-682.

Lespart, Michel <u>Les Oustachis, Terroristes de l'Ideal</u> (Paris: Editions de la Pensee Moderne, 1976), 282 pp.

<u>Libro Bianco Sul Terrorismo Tedesco da Schleyer a Mogadiscio (White paper on German Terrorism from Schleyer to Mogadishu)</u> (Rome: Giarrapico, 1978), 223 pp.

Linnel, Mark and Robert Collins "The Terror and the Tears" 122 <u>Reader's Digest (Canada)</u> (January 1983), pp. 149-176.
A personal account of social conditions in Northern Ireland during the guerrilla war.

Lochte, Christian "Fighting Terrorism in the Federal Republic of Germany" in Benjamin Netanyahu, ed. <u>Terrorism: How the West Can Win</u> (New York: Farrar, Straus, Giroux, 1986), pp. 171-174.

Lodge, Juliet, ed. <u>Terrorism: A New Challenge to the State</u> (New York: St. Martin's, 1981), 247 pp.
Reviewed by William L. Waugh, 76, 3 <u>American Political Science Revew</u> (September 1982), pp.691-692. A study by Europeans of terrorism in Europe.

Lord Longford and Anne McHardy <u>Ulster</u> (London: Weidenfeld and Nicolson, 1981), 260 pp.

Lotringer, Sylvere and Christian Marazzi, eds. <u>Italy: Autonomia</u> (New York: Columbia University Press, 1980).

Lowry, Heath "Nineteenth and Twentieth Century Armenian Terrorism: Threads of Continuity" <u>Turkish Daily News</u> (May 4-10, 1984), p. 2.

Mairowitz, David Z. "Scissors in the Head: West Germany's Extreme Reaction to Extremism" <u>Harper's</u> (May 1978), pp. 28-31.

Mallowe, Mike "The Rising of the Moon" 69 <u>Philadelphia Magazine</u> (march 1978), pp. 122-138.
A look at Irish Americans in Philadelphia politics as they attempt to promote the anti-British viewpoint re Northern Ireland.

Mancini, Federico <u>Terroristi e Riformisti</u> (Bologna: Il Mulino, 1981), 168 pp.

Manconi, Luigi <u>La Violenza e la Politica</u> (Italy: Savelli, 1979), 144 pp.

Manconi, Luigi <u>Vivere con il Terrorismo</u> (Milan: Mondadori, 1980), 202 pp.

Manderino, E. <u>55 Giorni: W la Morte, W la Vita (55 Days: Long Live Death, Long Live Life)</u> (Verona: Bertani, 1978).

Manor, F. S. "Liberal Terror" <u>American Spectator</u> (October 1978), pp. 19-21.
Manor defends the FRG's antiterrorism policy by citing the communist threat to democracy.

Manzini, G. Indagine su un Brigatista Rosse (Investigation of a Red Brigades Member) (Turin: Einaudi, 1978).

Marrus, Michael R. "French Antisemitism in the 1980s" 17, 2 Patterns of Prejudice (Great Britain) (1983), pp. 3-20.

Martinelli, R., and A. Padellaro Il Delitto Moro (The Moro Crime) (Milan: Rizzoli, n.d.).

Martino, Antonio "Making Democracy Unsafe for Italy" American Spectator (June-July, 1978), pp. 15-16.
Martino argues that the PCI benefits from Red Brigades activity.

Maslic, Andjelko "Terrorism by Fascist Emigration of Yugoslav Origin" 21 Socialist Thought and Practice (March 1981), pp. 49-64.

Massari, R. Marxismo e Critica del Terrorismo (Marxism and Critique of Terrorism) (Rome: Newton Compton, 1978), 304 pp.

Mayer, Margit "The German October of 1977" 13 New German Critique (Winter 1978), pp. 155-163.

Mazzei, Giuseppe Utopia e Terrore (Firenze: Le Monnier, 1981), 165 pp.

Mazzetti, R. Genesi e Sviluppo del Terrorismo in Italia: Il Maggio Troppo Lungo (Genesis and Development of Terrorism in Italy: The Too Long May) (Rome: Armando, 1979).

McFate, Katherine M. Politics of Popular Insurrection: The Irish Land League (Yale University, Department of Political Science, Ph.D. dissertation).

McNee, Sir David "Keeping the Queen's Peace" 69, 3 Canadian Police Chief (July 1980), pp. 20-24.

Melucci, A., ed. Movimenti di Rivolta (Revolt Movements) (Milan: Etas Libri, 1976).

Melucci, A. "New Movements, Terrorism, and the Political System: Reflections on the Italian Case" 56 Socialist Review (1981), pp. 97-136.

Merritt, Richard L. "From Munich to Mogadishu" American Spectator (June-July 1978), pp. 17-19.
Merritt worries that the FRG could experience a rightwing reaction to terrorism.

van der Meulen, E. I. Dossier Ambon 1950 de Houding van Nederland ten Opzichte van Ambon en de Rms. (Den Haag: Staatsuitgeverij, 1981), 327 pp.
A history of the South Moluccan terrorists.

Meyer, T. An Ende der Gewalt? Der Deutsche Terrorismus: Protokol Eines Jahrzehnts (Frankfurt, Berlin, Wien: Ullstein, 1980), 203 pp.

Minimanual of the Irish Guerrilla originally published by Irish Freedom Fighters Publications, now available in 2 Clandestine Tactics and Technology (Gaithersburg, Maryland: International Association of Chiefs of Police, n.d.).

Minucci, A. Terrirsmo e Crisi Italiana, Intervista di Jochen Kreimer (Terrorism and Italian Crisis, The Interview with Jochen Kreimer) (Rome: Riuniti, 1978).

Mommsen, Wolfgang J. and Gerhard Hirschfeld, eds. Social Protest, Violence and Terror in Nineteenth and Twentieth Century Europe (New York: St. Martin's, 1982).

Moran, Sue "The Case of Terrorist Patrizio Peci: A Character Sketch" 5, 2 TVI Journal (Fall 1984), pp. 34-35.

Moran, Sue "The Red Brigades' Assassination of Economist Ezio Tarantelli" 5, 4 TVI Journal (Spring, 1985), pp. 8-9.

Mori, A. M. Il Silenzio delle Donne e il Caso Moro (The Silence of Women and the Moro Case) (Cosenza: Lerici, 1978).

Morra, G. La Cultura Cattolica e Il Nichilismo Contemporaneo (Catholic Culture and Contemporary Nihilism) (Milan: Rusconi, 1979).

Moss, David "The Kidnapping and Murder of Aldo Moro" 22, 2 European Journal of Sociology (Great Britain) (1981), pp. 265-295.

Moxon-Browne, Edward "Terrorism in France" 144 Conflict Studies (1983), 26 pp.

Moxon-Browne, Edward "The Water and the Fish: Public Opinion and the Provisional IRA in Northern Ireland" 5, 1-2 Terrorism (1981), pp. 41-72, also available in Paul Wilkinson, ed. British Perspectives on Terrorism (London: George Allen and Unwin, 1981), pp. 47-53.
The IRA's longevity suggests that it has public support.

Mulgannon, Terry "The Animal Liberation Front" 5, 4 TVI: Terrorism Violence Insurgency Journal (Spring 1985), pp. 39-40.

Mumcu, Ugur Agca Dosyasi (Istanbul: Tekin Yayinevi, 1982).

Mumcu, Ugur Papa, Agca, Mafya (Istanbul: Tekin Yayinevi, 1984).

Mumcu, Ugur Silah Kacakciligi ve Teror (Weapons Smuggling and Terror) (Istanbul: Tekin Yayinevi, 1981).

Munoz Alonso, Alejandro El Terrorismo en Espana (Barcelona: Planeta/Instituto de Estudios Economicos, 1982), 280 pp.

Naimark, Norman M. Terrorists and Social Democrats: The Russian Revolutionary Movement Under Alexander III (Cambridge: Harvard University Press, 1983), 308 pp.

Neeler, V. E. "Falsifikatory Istorii 'Ishchut' Korni Terrorizma (The Falsifiers of History 'in Search' of the Roots of Terrorism)" 6 Novaia i Noveishaia Istoriia (USSR) (1981), pp. 158-160.
A discussion of Italian terrorism, back to Mazzini and Garibaldi's actions.

Negri, Antonio Il Comunismo e la Guerra (Milan: Feltrinelli, 1980).

Negri, Antonio Il Diminio e il Sabotaggio: Sul Metodo Marxista della Trasformazione Sociale (Dominion and Sabotage: On the Marxist Method of Social Transformation) (Milan: Feltrinelli, 1978).

Negt, Oskar "Terrorism and the German State's Absorption of Conflicts" 12 New German Critique (Fall 1977), pp. 15-27.

Nello, Paolo "La Violenza Fascista Ovvero Dello Squadrismo Nazionalrivoluzionario (Fascist Violence or the Problem of National Revolutionary Squadristi)" 13, 6 Sotira Contemporanea (Italy) (1981), pp. 1009-1025.
Fascism's appeal is laid to the failure of socialism's myth of violent revolution.

"Neo-Nazis in Austria" 16, 1 Patterns of Prejudice (UK) (1982), pp. 13-18.

Nese, M. Terrorismo (Rome: La Tipografica, 1978).

Neuberg, A. L'Insurrezione Armata (Armed Insurrection) (Milan: Feltrinelli, 1970).

Newsinger, John "Revolution and Catholicism in Ireland" 9, 4 European Studies Review (Great Britain) (1979), pp. 457-480.
Excommunication of IRA terrorists has not diminished the group's appeal to Catholics.

Noli, Jean "Imposimato, a Man of Great Courage" 127 Reader's Digest (Canada) (August 1985), pp. 69-73.
Franco Imposimato is an Italian judge combatting crime and terrorism in Italy.

"North Atlantic Council Meets in Rome" 81 Department of State Bulletin (July 1981), pp. 37-41.
The article covers Secretary of State Haig's press conference, extracts from the minutes of the Council, the declaration on terrorism, and the final communique issued after the May 4-5, 1981 meeting.

"Northern Ireland: Problems and Perspectives" 135 Conflict Studies (1982), 48 pp.

"Northern Ireland's Economic Mess" 118 Dun's Business Month (October 1981), pp. 98-99.

Nowak, Jan "Zamach na Papieza (The Attempt on the Pope's Life)" 5 Kultura (France) (1983), pp. 53-66.

O'Ballance, Edgar "IRA Leadership Problems" in Paul Wilkinson, Guest Editor "British Perspectives on Terrorism 5, 1-2 Terrorism (1981), pp. 73-82.

O'Ballance, Edgar Terror in Ireland: The Heritage of Hate (Novato, California: Presidio Press, 1981), 287 pp.

O'Brien, Conor Cruise "The Longest War" paper presented to the Sesquicentennial Symposium on Terrorism: The Challenge to the State, Wesleyan University, January 28-30, 1982, 16 pp.

O'Brien, Conor Cruise States of Ireland (St. Albans: Panther, 1974).

O'Dowd, Liam, Bill Rolston, and Mike Tomlinson Northern Ireland: Between Civil Rights and Civil War (London: CSE Books, 1980), 224 pp.

Oldani, Alberto La Violenza Politica nel Mondo Contemporaneo (Milan: Angeli, 1979), 253 pp.

Orlando, Federico Siamo in Guerra (Rome: A. Armando, 1980), 215 pp.

Orlow, Dietrich "Comments on Weisberg's 'Avoiding Central Realities' and Richards' 'Terror and the Law'" 5, 2 Human Rights Quarterly (1983), pp. 186-190.

Orlow, Dietrich "Political Violence in Pre-Coup Turkey" 6, 1 Terrorism (1982), pp. 53-71.

Orrantia, Mikel Euskadi, Pacificacion? (Madrid: Ediciones Libertarias, 1980), 239 pp.

Ors, Ibrahim, ed. Turkiye'de Teror (Istanbul, May 1980). Proceedings of a conference organized to commemorate Abdi Impekci, a journalist who was assassinated by terrorists.

Ottone, P. Come Finira'? (How will it End?) (Garzanti, 1979).

Padovani, Marcelle Vivre Avec le Terrorisme: Le Modele Italien (Paris: Calmann-Levy, 1982), 250 pp.

Pallotta, G. Aldo Moro, L'Uomo, La Vita, La Fede (Aldo Moro, The Man, His Life, His Faith) (Milan: Massimo, 1978).

Pansa, Giampaolo Storie Italiane di Violenza e Terrorismo (Roma Bari: Laterza, 1980), 279 pp.

Papazian, Sato "Sept Annees de Lutte Armee" Hay Baykar (Paris: Mouvement National Armenien Pour L'ASALA, December 22, 1982), pp. 8-9.

"Paris Terror Bombs Tossing Cold Water on Leisure Industry" 322 Variety (February 12, 1986), pp. 1-2.

Parizeau, A. "Army and the October Crisis" 13, 2 Criminologie (1980), pp. 47-78.

Parizeau, A., ed. "October 1970 - Ten Years After" 13, 2 Criminologie (1980), 113 pp.
A look at Canada a decade after the FLQ terrorist campaign.

Patrick, Derrick Fetch Felix: The Fight Against the Ulster Bombers, 1976-1977 (London: Hamish Hamilton, 1981), 184 pp.

Payne, Stanley G. "Terrorism and Democratic Stability in Spain" 77 Current History (1979), pp. 167-171.

Pengelley, R. B. "Ulster: The Name of the Internal Security Game" 11, 8 International Defense Review (1978), pp. 1297-1301.

Pepper, Curtis Bill "The Possessed" New York Times Magazine (February 18, 1979), pp. 29-43.
A look at the Red Brigades.

Perelli, Luciano Il Terrorismo e lo Stato nel I Secolo a.C. (Palermo: Palumbo, 1981), 132 pp.

Perino, M. Lotta Continua: Sei Militanti Dop Dieci Anni (Lotta Continua: Six Militants Ten Years Later) (Turin: Rosenberg & Sellier, 1979).

Peroff, Kathleen and Christopher Hewitt "Rioting in Northern Ireland" 24, 4 Journal of Conflict Resolution (December 1980), pp. 593-612.
An assessment of the reformist, repressive, and constitutional approaches--none was singularly effective.

Petersen, Jens "Il Problema della Violenza nel Fascismo Italiano (The Problem of Violence in Italian Fascism)" 13, 6 Storia Contemporanea (Italy) (1982), pp. 985-1008.

"Phenomenological and Dynamic Aspects of Terrorism in Italy" 2, 3-4 Terrorism (1979), pp. 159-170.

Philipp, Udo "Combatting Terrorism in Federal Germany" 12, 6 International Defense Review (1979), pp. 999-1001.

Pilat, J. F. "Euroright Extremism" 53/4 Wiener Library Bulletin (1981), pp. 48-63.

Pisano, Vittorfranco S. "The Italian Terrorism Problem" Clandestine Tactics and Technology (Gaithersburg, Maryland: International Association of Chiefs of Police, n.d.).

Pisano, Vittorfranco S. "The Red Brigades: A Challenge to Italian Democracy" 120 Conflict Studies (London: Institute for the Study of Conflict, July 1980), 19 pp.

Pisano, Vittorfranco S. "Spain Faces the Extremists: Cannons to the Left and Cannons to the Right" 2 TVI Journal (1981), pp 10-12.

Pisano, Vittorfranco S. "A Survey of Terrorism of the Left in Italy: 1970-1978" 2, 3-4 Terrorism (1979), pp. 171-212.

Pisano, Vittorfranco S. "Terrorism and Security: The Italian Experience" in US Senate, Committee on the Judiciary, Report of the Subcommittee on Terrorism and Security (Washington, D.C.: 98th Congress, Second Session (November 1984), 94 pp.

Pisano, Vittorfranco S. "Terrorism in Italy: The Dozier Affair" 49, 4 Police Chief (1982), pp. 38-41.

Pisano, Vittorfranco S. "Terrorism of the Right in Italy: Facts and Allegations" 6, 1 TVI: Terrorism Violence Insurgency Journal (Summer 1985), pp. 20-22.

Pisano, Vittorfranco S. "Terrorist Organizations and Tactics" 9 Detective (Spring 1982), pp. 14-17.
An overview of terrorist groups in Italy, France and Spain.

Pluchinsky, Dennis "Political Terrorism in Western Europe: Some Themes and Variations" in Yonah Alexander and Kenneth Myers, eds. Terrorism in Europe (New York: St. Martin's Press, 1982).

"Political Violence and Civil Disobedience in Western Europe, 1982: Introductory Survey, Challenges to Public Order, Chronologies of Events" (London: Institute for the Study of Conflict, 1983), 31 pp.

Portell, Jose Maria Los Hombres de ETA (Barcelona: DOPESA, 1974).

Porter, Paul "Terrorism and the Victorians" 36 History Today (December 1986), pp. 6-7.

Powers, Paul "Violence in Northern Ireland: Ethnic Conflict and Radicalization in an International Setting" paper presented to the panel on the Role of High Risk Violence in Ethnic Nationalism at the annual meeting of the International Studies Association/South, University of Florida at Gainesville, October 29-31, 1981.

Preston, Paul "Walking the Terrorist Tightrope" 234 Contemporary Review (March 1979), pp. 119-123.
A look at ETA terrorism.

Pridham, Geoffrey "Terrorism and the State in West Germany During the 1970s: A Threat to Stability or a Case of Political Over-reaction?" in Juliet Lodge, ed. Terrorism: A Challenge to the State (New York: St. Martin's Press, 1981).

Puaux, Francois "Il y a Cinq Ans, Aldo Moro... (Five Years ago Aldo Moro...)" 6 Review des Deux Mondes (France) (1983), pp. 646-657.
Terrorism in Italy from 1978 through 1981.

RAF: La Guerriglia nella Metropoli (Metropolitan Guerrilla) (Verona: Bertani, 1979).

Ramsay, Robert The Corsican Time-Bomb (Manchester; Dover, New Hampshire: Manchester University Press, 1983), 245 pp.

Raufer, Xavier Terrorisme Maintenant, La France? (Paris, 1982).
Includes a discussion of Direct Action.

Raymond, Raymond James "Irish-America and Northern Ireland: An End to Romanticism?" 39 World Today (March 1983), pp. 106-113.

Reed, David "Northern Ireland's Agony Without End" 120 Reader's Digest (January 1982), pp. 91-95.

Rees, Merlyn "Terror in Ireland--and Britain's Response" in Paul Wilkinson, Guest Editor "British Perspectives on Terrorism" 5, 1-2 Terrorism (1981), pp. 83-88.

"Revolution, Reform and Subversion in West European Countries" 2, 5 World Opinion Update (September 1978), pp. 114-117.

Richards, David A. J. "Terror and the Law" 5, 2 Human Rights Quarterly (1983), pp. 171-185.
A look at Nazi terrorism.

Rico, J. M. "Events of October 1970 and the Administration of Penal Justice in Quebec" 13, 2 Criminologie (1980), pp. 7-45.

Roberts, Julian "Terrorism and German Intellectuals" 3 Journal of Area Studies (Spring 1981), pp. 21-25.

"The Rolf Pohle Extradition Case" (Washington, D.C.: Library of Congress, Law Library, February 16, 1977), 19 pp.

Rosenthal, U. Governmental Decision-Making in Crises: Cases of South Moluccan Terrorism (Alphen A. D. Rijn: Samson, 1984), in Dutch.

Rossetti, C. G. "La Politica Della Violenza e la Crisi Della Legittimita Razionale dello Stat" 18, 3 Studi de Soziologia (July 1980).

Rupprecht, Reinhard "Conditions of Social Revolutionary Terrorism in the Federal Republic of Germany" 9 Kriminalistik (1981), pp. 386-390.

Rupprecht, Reinhard "Entwickelt sich in der Bundesreupblik ein Rechtsextremistischer Terrorismus?" 33, 6 Kriminalistik (1979), pp. 285-290.

Russell, Charles A. "Europe: Regional Review" 3, 1-2 Terrorism (1979), pp. 157-171.
Russell gives Risks International statistics on the types of terrorism seen in Europe in the last decade.

Russell, Charles A. "Statistics Italy, 1978" 2, 3-4 Terrorism (1979), pp. 297-300.

Rutherford, Ward "Options for Ulster" 36 World Today (August 1980), pp. 319-325.
The author argues that there are only 3 solutions: devolution, unification, and independence.

Salierno, Giulio _La Violenza in Italia_ (Milan: Mondadori, 1980).

Salvioni, Daniela and Anders Stephanson "Reflections on the Red Brigades" 29, 3 _Orbis_ (Fall 1985), pp. 489-506.

Savigear, Peter "Corsican Nationalism and the Uses of Violence" paper presented to the panel on the Role of High Risk Violence in Ethnic Nationalism at the annual meeting of the International Studies Association/South, University of Florida at Gainesville, October 29-31, 1981.

Savigear, Peter "Separatism and Centralism in Corsica" 36 _World Today_ (September 1980), pp. 351-355.

Savigear, Peter "Terrorist Activity in Western Europe" (Occasional Paper; Braamfontein: South African Institute of International Affairs, Jan Smuts House, PO Box 31596, Braamfontein, 2071, South Africa, 1982), 14 pp.

Sayari, Sabri "Generational Changes in Terrorist Movements: The Turkish Case" (Santa Monica: The Rand Corporation, P-7124, 1985).

Sayari, Sabri "Patterns of Political Terrorism in Turkey" 6, 1 _TVI: Terrorism Violence Insurgency Journal_ (Summer 1985), pp. 39-43.

Schaap "Germany's Terrifying Witch Hunt" _Mother Jones_ (February-March 1979).

Scheerer, Sebastian "The Crime of Klaus Croissant" 4, 3 _Contemporary Crises: Crime, Law and Social Policy_ (July 1980), pp. 341-349.

Schiller, David Th. "The Current Campaign Against Animal Laboratory Tests in West Germany" 5, 4 _TVI: Terrorism Violence Insurgency Journal_ (Spring 1985), pp. 36-38.

Schmitt, David "Violence in Northern Ireland: Ethnic Conflict and Radicalization in an International Setting" paper presented to the panel on the Role of Terrorism in Ethnic Nationalism at the annual convention of the International Studies Association/South, University of Florida, October 29-31, 1981.

Schofberger, Rudolf und Gotthart Schwarz "Neonazismus in der Bundesrepublik" in Hermann Vinke, ed. _Mit zweierlei Mass: die deutsche Reaktion auf den Terror von Rechts_ (Rowohlt, 1981).

Scorer, C. and P. Hewitt _The Prevention of Terrorism Act: The Case for Repeal_ (London: National Council for Civil Liberties, 1981).

Shannon, Kristin and Peter Regenstreif "Hanging Together" 6, 3 _Wilson Quarterly_ (1982), pp. 44-59.
A look at terrorism in Canada in the early 1970s.

Shanor, Donald R. "Proletarian Monopoly" 28 World Press Review (April 1981), p. 13
A description of the Italian board game The Red Brigade Game.

Sheehan, Thomas "Italy: Terror on the Right" New York Review of Books (January 22, 1981), p. 25.

Shirley, John "The IRA: Portrait in Terror" 8 Penthouse (July 1977), pp. 65-66, 70, 74, 98.

Shivers, Lynne and David Bowman More than the Troubles: A Common Sense View of the Northern Ireland Conflict (Philadelphia: New Society, 1984), 244 pp.

Siltala, Juha "Lapuan Liike ja Kyyditykset 1930 (The Lapua Movement and the Kidnappings of 1930)" 80, 2 Hist. Aikakauskirja (Finland) (1982), pp. 105-123.

Simard, Francis The Last Word on October (Montreal, Canada: Editions Stanke, 1982).
Quebec separatists who kidnapped and murdered provincial Labor Minister Pierre Laporte in October 1970 tell their story. Covered by Paul Majendie "Canadians Decry Profits From Assassins Book" Washington Post (November 26, 1982), p. D8.

Smith, G. Davidson "Issue Group Terrorism: Animal Rights Militancy in Britain" 5, 4 TVI: Terrorism Violence Insurgency Journal (Spring 1985), pp. 44-47.

Smith, William Beattie "Terrorism: The Lessons of Northern Ireland" 5 Journal of Contemporary Studies (Winter 1982), pp. 29-50.

Social Protest, Violence, and Terror in Nineteenth- and Twentieth-Century Europe (New York: St. Martin's, published for the German Historical Institute, London, 1982), 411 pp.

Sole, Robert Le Defi Terroriste: Lecons Italiennes a L'Usasge de L'Europe (France: Seuil, 1979), 282 pp.

Solinas, Stenio Macondo e P38 i.e. Trentotto (Milan: Il Falco, 1980), 99 pp.

"Spanish Journalist, Victim of ASALA Bombing, Becomes Expert on Armenian Cause" The Armenian Reporter (November 15, 1984), p. 2.

Starchenkov, G. "Terrorism in Turkey" 11 Aziia i Afrika Segodnia (USSR) (1981), pp. 39-41.

"Statement by Turkish Terrorists" 6, 1 TVI: Terrorism Violence Insurgency Journal (Summer 1985), p. 51.

Stein, Torsten "Die Bekampfung des Terrorismus im Rahmen der Mitgliedstaaten der Europaischen" 40, 2 Zeitschrift fur auslandisches offentliches Recht und Volkerrecht (1980), pp. 312-321.

Sterling, Claire "Italian Terrorists: Life and Death in a Violent Generation" 57, 1 Encounter (1981), pp. 18-31.

Stoppa, Paolo "Revolutionary Culture Italian-Style" 4 Washington Quarterly (Spring 1981), pp. 100-113.

Sundberg, Jacob W. F. "Operation Leo: Description and Analysis of a European Terrorist Operation" 5, 3 Terrorism (1981), pp. 197-232, also available in Brian M. Jenkins, ed. Terrorism and Beyond: An International Conference on Terrorism and Low-Level Conflict (Santa Monica: The Rand Corporation, R-2714, 1982), pp. 174-202.
A look at Norbert Kroecher, the leader of an aborted terrorist attack scheduled to take place in Stockholm in 1977.

Suny, Ronald Grigor Armenia in the Twentieth Century (Chico, California: Scholars Press, 1983).

Sweden, Arbetsmarknadsdepartementet Handlaggning av arenden angaende avlaggnande av presumtiva terrorister (Stockholm: Arbetsmarknadsdepartementet, LiberForlag, 1981), 28 pp.

Szaz, Z. Michael "Armenian Terrorists and the East-West Conflict" 8, 4 Journal of Social, Political and Economic Studies (Winter 1983), pp. 387-394.

Taylor, Peter Beating the Terrorists? Interrogation at Omagh, Gough, and Castlereagh (Harmondsworth, Middlesex, England and New York: Penguin, 1980), 347 pp.

Ternon, Yves The Armenian Cause (Delmar, New York: Caravan Books, 1985).

Terror im Baskenland, Gefahr fur Spaniens Demokratie? (Reinbek bei Hamburg: Rowohlt, 1979), 139 pp.

"Terrorism in Italy: An Update Report, 1983-1985" Report of the Subcommittee on Security and Terrorism for the use of the Committee on the Judiciary, United States Senate (Washington, D.C.: US Government Printing Office, 1985), 36 pp.

"Terrorism: The Turkish Experience" (Washington, D.C.: 97th Congress, Hearings of the Subcommittee on Security and Terrorism, Committee on the Judiciary, June 25, 1981).

Terrorismo (Torino: Stampatori, 1980), 147 pp.

Theolleyre, Jean Marc Les Neo-Nazis (Paris: Actuel, 1982).

Thompkins, Thomas C. "Terrorist Innovation--The Ingenuity of the Irish" 5, 4 TVI: Terrorism Violence Insurgency Journal (Spring 1985), pp. 52-53.

Tomasevski, K. The Challenge of Terrorism (Rijeka, 1981).

Townshend, Charles Political Violence in Ireland: Government and Resistance Since 1848 (Oxford: Clarendon, 1983), 445 pp.

Tugwell, Maurice "Politics and Propaganda of the Provisional IRA" in Paul Wilkinson, Guest Editor "British Perspectives on Terrorism 5, 1-2 Terrorism (1981), pp. 13-40.

Ulam, Adam B. In the Name of the People (New York: Viking, 1977), 418 pp.
Reviewed by David C. Rapoport 3, 1-2 Terrorism (1979), pp. 173-176. Ulam examines terrorism in Russia in the 19th century, giving material allowing for comparisons with contemporary issues.

US Senate, Committee on the Judiciary, Subcommittee on Security and Terrorism "Terrorism: The Turkish Experience: Hearing" (Washington, D.C.: June 25, 1981), 38 pp.

van Kamm, Ben The South Moluccans: Background to the Train Hijackings (London, 1980).

Van Voris, W. H. "The Provisional IRA and the Limits of Terrorism" 16, 3 Massachusetts Review (1975), pp. 413-428.

Vasale, Claudio Terrorismo e Ideologia in Italia (Rome: A. Armando, 1980), 102 pp.

Ventura, Angelo "Il Problema Storico del Terrorismo Italiano (The Historical Context of Terrorism in Italy" 92, 1 Rivsta Storica Italiana (1980), pp. 125-151.

Vigna, Piero Luigi La Finalita di Terrorismo ed Eversione (Milan: Giuffre, 1981), 278 pp.

Vinci, Piero "Some Considerations of Contemporary Terrorism" 2, 3-4 Terrorism (1979), pp. 149-158.

Virtanen, Michael "U.K. is well guarded against terrorism, Britons tell Senate Panel" 45 Travel Weekly (May 1, 1986), p. 12.
David Gilroy Revan and Roger Gala, two members of the British Parliament, inform the US Senate Subcommittee on Tourism that precautions catch most terrorist attempts.

Wagner, Joachim Missionare der Gewalt (Heidelberg: Kriminalistik Verlag, 1980), 147 pp.

Wagner, Joachim Politischer Terrorismus und Strafrecht im Deutschen Kaiserreich von 1971 (Heidelberg, Hamburg: Decker, 1981), 448 pp.

Wagner-Pacifici, Robin "Negotiation in the Aldo Moro Affair: The Suppressed Alternative in a Case of Symbolic Politics" 12, 4 Politics and Society (1983), pp. 487-517.

Wainstein, Eleanor S. "The Cross and Laporte Kidnappings, Montreal, October 1970" (Santa Monica: The Rand Corporation, R-1986/1-DOS/ARPA, February 1977).

Waldmann, P. "Mitgliederstruktur, Sozialisationsmedien und Gesellschaftlicher Rueckhalt. der Baskischen ETA" 1 Politische Vierteljahres-Schriften (1981), pp. 45-66.

Walker, Christopher <u>Armenia: The Survival of a Nation</u> (New York: St. Martin's Press, 1980).

Walker, Clive "Prevention of Terrorism (Temporary Provisions) Act 1984, Great Britain" 47 <u>Modern Law Review</u> (November 1984), pp. 704-713.

Walsh, Barbara "The Shamrock and the Maple Leaf" 17, 4 <u>Canadian Dimension</u> (1983), pp. 14-19, 40.
A look at hostile Canadian public opinion toward the IRA.

Ward, James J. "Terror, Revolution, or Control? The KPD's Secret Apparat During the Weimar Republic" 7, 3 <u>Terrorism</u> (1984), pp. 257-298.

Wasmund, Klaus "The Political Socialization of Terrorist Groups in West Germany" 11, 2 <u>Journal of Political and Military Sociology</u> (Fall 1983), pp. 223-239.

Wehner, B. "Dissolution of the Special Anti-Terrorism Forces: Pacification of the Population or Criticism of the Bundeskriminalamt" 6 <u>Kriminalistik</u> (1980), pp. 252-253.

Weinberg, Leonard "Patterns of Neo-Fascist Violence in Italian Politics" 2, 3-4 <u>Terrorism</u> (1979), pp. 231-260.

Weisberg, Richard "Avoiding Central Realities: Narrative Terror and the Failure of French Culture Under the Occupation" 5, 2 <u>Human Rights Quarterly</u> (1983), pp. 151-170.

Wesseling, H. L. "Post-Imperial Holland" 15, 1 <u>Journal of Contemporary History (UK)</u> (1980), pp. 125-142.
Includes a discussion of South Moluccan terrorism.

"The West German Guerrilla: Interviews with Jans Josef Klein and Members of the June Second Group" (Orkney: Cienfuegos, 1981).

Whyte, John H. "Recent Writing on Northern Ireland" 70, 2 <u>American Political Science Review</u> (June 1976), pp. 592-596.

Whyte, John H. "Why is the Northern Ireland Problem so Intractable?" 34 <u>Parliamentary Affairs</u> (Autumn 1981), pp. 422-435.
The author argues that the actors (unionists, nationalists, and British) tend to prolong the crisis and political and psychological pressures prevent them from changing course.

Wilamowski, Jacek and Szczepanik, Krysztof "Ustasze i Separatyzm Chorwacki: Przyczynek do Badan nad Chorwackim Ruchem Nacjonalistycznym (The Ustase and Croatian Separatism: A contribution to the Study of the Croatian Nationalist Movement)" 74, 1 <u>Przeglad Hist. (Poland)</u> (1983), pp. 75-94.

Wilkinson, Paul "Armenian Terrorism" 39, 9 <u>World Today</u> (September 1983), pp. 344-350.

Wilkinson, Paul, ed. <u>British Perspectives on Terrorism</u> (Boston: Allen and Unwin, 1981), 193 pp.

Wilkinson, Paul "Introduction to Special Issue on Europe" 5, 1-2 Terrorism (1981), pp. 1-12.

Wilkinson, Paul "The Provisional IRA in the Wake of the 1981 Hunger Strike" 17, 2 Government and Opposition (Spring 1982), pp. 140-156.

Wilkinson, Paul "Still Working 'for the Extinction of Mankind': An Assessment of the Significance of the Resurgence of Fascist Terrorism in Western Europe" 18 Across the Board (January 1981), pp. 27-30.

Wilkinson, Paul "Terrorism's Challenge to Democracy: The Case of the Provisional IRA and Orange Extremism" paper presented to the Sesquicentennial Symposium on Terrorism: The Challenge to the State, Wesleyan University, January 28-30, 1982, 30 pp.

Winn, Gregory F. T. "Terrorism, Alienation and German Society" in Yonah Alexander and John M. Gleason, eds. Terrorism: Quantitative and Behavioral Perspectives (New York: Pergamon, 1981), pp. 256-282.

Winn, Gregory F. T. and George W. Witt "German Terrorists: A Profile" (University of Southern California, unpublished manuscript, 1980).

Wolf, John B. "Agitational Terrorism in Europe: January 1980-February 1981" 7, 2 Update Report (Gaithersburg, Maryland: International Association of Chiefs of Police, 1981).

Wolf, John B. "Appraising the Performance of Terrorist Organizations (selected European Separatist Groups; Fall 78 to Summer 79) 5 Clandestine Tactics and Technology (Gaithersburg, Maryland: International Association of Chiefs of Police, 1980).

Wolf, John B. "European Neo-Fascist Groups" 6, 6 Update Report (Gaithersburg, Maryland: International Association of Chiefs of Police, 1980).

Woolf, S. J. "Prototypes and Terrorists" 18, 4 Society (May/June, 1981), pp. 28-29.
The author looks at European fascism, critiquing an article of Irving Louis Horowitz.

Wright, Steve "A Multivariate Time Series Analysis of the Northern Irish Conflict 1969-1976" in Yonah Alexander and John M. Gleason, eds. Behavioral and Quantitative Perspectives on Terrorism (New York: Pergamon, 1981), pp. 283-328.

Wright, Steve "The State and Terrorism in Northern Ireland", paper presented to the 24th annual convention of the International Studies Association, Mexico City, April 5-9, 1983.

Wright, Steve "A Time Series Analysis of the Northern Irish Conflict 1969-78" (University of Lancaster, United Kingdom, Ph.D. dissertation, 1980).

Yerbury, J. C. "The 'Sons of Freedom' Doukhobors and the Canadian State" 16, 2 Canadian Ethnic Studies (1984), pp. 47-70.

Yermakov, N. "Italy: Terrorism on the Rampage" 12 International Affairs (USSR) (December 1981), pp. 133-135.

Yodfat, Aryeh Y. "Turkey: Policy, Problems, and Conflicts" 19, 3-4 International Problems (Israel) (1980), pp. 8-18. Includes a discussion of terrorism in Turkey.

Zimmermann, Ekkart "Terrorist Violence in West Germany: Some Reflections on Recent Literature" paper read to the 13th World Congress of the International Political Science Association, Paris, July 1985.

Zoppo, Ciro E. "Never Again Without a Rifle" 2, 3-4 Terrorism (1979), pp. 271-282.

MIDDLE EAST

Abraham, Sameer "The PLO at the Crossroads" 9 Middle East Research and Information Project (September 1979), pp. 5-13.

Adams, Nathan "Iran's Ayatollahs of Terror" 126 Reader's Digest (January 1985), pp. 36ff.

Ajami, Fouad The Vanished Imam: Musa Sadr and the Shia of Lebanon (Ithaca: Cornell, 1986).

Akhtar, Shameem "PLO In-Fighting" 36, Pakistan Horizon (1983).

Al-Dajani, Ahmad Sidqi "The PLO and the Euro-Arab Dialogue" 9, 3 Journal of Palestine Studies (1980), pp. 81-124.

Alekseev, A. "Livan: Strashnye Dni (Lebanon: Days of Terror)" 12 Aziia i Afrika Segodnia (USSR) (1982), pp. 22-24. A biography of Talal Naji, a PLO Executive Committee member.

Alexander, Nathan "The Foreign Policy of Libya: Inflexibility Amid Change" 24, 4 Orbis (Winter, 1981), pp. 819-846. Alexander's overview includes the reasons for Qadhafi's support of international terrorists.

Alexander, Yonah "The Nature of the PLO: Some International Implications" 3 Middle East Review (1980), pp. 42-49.

Alexander, Yonah and Alan Nanes, eds. The United States and Iran: A Documentary History (Frederick, Maryland: University Publications of America, 1980).

Alon, Hanan Countering Palestinian Terrorism in Israel: Toward a Policy Analysis of Countermeasures (Santa Monica: Rand Graduate Institute of Policy Studies, Ph.D. dissertation, N-1567-FF, August 1980), 271 pp.

Alpher, Joseph "The Khomeini International" 3, 4 Washington Quarterly (Autumn, 1980), pp. 54-74.

Amos, John W. Palestinian Resistance: Organization of a Nationalist Movement (Elmsford, New York: Pergamon, 1980), 472 pp.

Banji, Ghorbanali The Correlates of Civil Strife in the Middle East, 1955-1973 (North Texas State University, Department of Political Science, Ph.D. dissertation).

Bar-Zohar, Michael and Eitan Haber The Quest for the Red Prince (Ali Hassan Salameh) (New York: William Morrow, and London: Weidenfeld and Nicolson, 1983), 232 pp.
The Israelis search for Fatah's terrorist mastermind. Reviewed by James M. Markham "Life and Death of a Terrorist" New York Times Book Review (July 10, 1983), pp. 3, 31.

Barth, Karl Gunther, Jutta Kohut, Jochen Schildt and Christoph Bertram "Gaddafi's World" 33 World Press Review (March 1986), pp. 25-27.

Becker, Jillian "The Centrality of the PLO" in Benjamin Netanyahu, ed. Terrorism: How the West Can Win (New York: Farrar, Straus, Giroux, 1986), pp. 98-102.

Becker, Jillian, et al. The PLO: The Rise and Fall of the Palestine Liberation Organisation (London: Weidenfeld and Nicholson, 1984), 303 pp.
Reviewed by Bruce Hoffman in 6, 1 TVI: Terrorism Violence Insurgency Journal (Summer 1985), pp. 57-58, and David Pryce-Jones "How to Mislead a People and Ruin a Cause" 63, 1 Encounter (UK) (1984), pp. 61-64.

Belack, C. N. Transnational Terrorism and World Politics: A Case Study of the Palestine Arab Resistance Movement (Columbia University, Ph.D. dissertation, 1984).

Bennett, Ralph Kinney "Iran's Government by Extermination" 120 Reader's Digest (March 1982), pp. 23-26.

Boggio, Philippe "Abu Nidal: Mystery Man of International Terrorism" The Guardian (October 31, 1982), p. 12.

Bourret, J. C. Wie ein Franzoesisches Sonderkommando die in Nov. 1979 Besetzte Moskee in Mekka Befreite (Paris: editions France Empire, 1981); a shorter version appeared in 22, 6 Der Spiegel (1981), pp. 144ff.
The article discusses methods used to extract the holders of the holy shrine in Mecca.

Brugman, J. "Zondaar of Gelovige: De Theologische Achtergrond van het Islamitische Terrorism (Sinner or Believer: The Theological Background of Islamic Terrorism" 23, 412 Hollands Maandblad (March 1982), pp. 19-24.

Butenschon, Nils A. "PLO som Arabisk Aktor: Skisse til en Analysemodell (The PLO as an Arab Actor: A Tentative Outline for an Analytical Model)" 2 Internasjonal Politikk (Norway) (1981), pp. 201-217.

Carlson, Sevinc "Where the Oil Is and How it Moves" paper presented at the Conference on Political Terrorism and Energy: The Threat and Response, Washington, D.C., Georgetown University Center for Strategic and International Studies, May 1, 1980

Chomsky, Noam "International Terrorism: Diplomacy by Other Means" 20 Canadian Dimension (February 1987), pp. 37-40. A discussion of recent bombings in Tunisia.

Christopher, Warren, et al. American Hostages in Iran: The Conduct of a Crisis (New Haven: Yale University Press, 1985), 443 pp.
Reviewed by Jim Hoagland in Washington Post Book World (May 19, 1985), p. 5.

"A Chronology of Significant Attacks on Israel and Israeli Reprisal Operations" 5, 4 TVI: Terrorism Violence Insurgency Journal (Spring 1985), pp. 26-30.

Clarke, Thurston By Blood and Fire: The Attack on the King David Hotel (New York: Putnam, 1981), 304 pp.

Cobban, Helena The PLO: People, Power and Politics (New York: Cambridge, 1984), 305 pp.
Reviewed by Daniel Pipes "The Past and Present of the PLO" Washington Post Book World (March 25, 1984), pp. 8, 13.

Cobban, Helena "The PLO in the Mid-1980s: Between the Gun and the Olive Branch" 38, 4 International Journal (Canada) (1983), pp. 635-651.

Cooley, John K. Libyan Sandstorm (New York: Holt, Rinehart and Winston, 1982).

Dam, Kenneth W. "Terrorism in the Middle East" 84 Department of State Bulletin (December 1984), pp. 73-74.

Department of Defense Commission on Beirut International Airport Terrorist Act, October 23, 1983 Report (Washington, D.C.: The Commission, 1983), 141 pp.

Dhaher, Ahmed The PLO (University of West Virginia, Ph.D. dissertation, 1975).

"A Discussion with Yasser Arafat" 11, 2 Journal of Palestine Studies (1982), pp. 3-15.

Diskin, Abraham "Trends in Intensity Variation of Palestinian Military Activity: 1967-1978" 16, 2 Canadian Journal of Political Science (1983), pp. 335-348.

Doumergu, Emil Saudi Arabia and the Explosion of Terrorism in the Middle East (Great Current of History Library Book, Institute on Economic Policy, 1983), 137 pp.

Dubberstein, W. H. "The Middle East: Political and Security Assessment - An Overview", in Robert A. Kilmarx and Yonah Alexander, eds. Business and the Middle East: Threats and Prospects (New York: Pergamon, 1982).

Dyad, A. My Home, My Land: A Narrative of the Palestinian Struggle (New York: Rouleau, 1981).

"Shafik El-Hout, PLO Representative; Senator Richard G. Lugar; Senator Alan M. Cranston; Judith Kipper, Middle East Expert: Interview" 85 Meet The Press (October 20, 1985), 10 pp.

Fadl Allah, Muhammed Hussein "Islam and Violence in Political Reality" 4, 4-5 Middle East Insight (1986), pp. 4-13.

Frangi, Abdallah The PLO and Palestine (London: Zed, 1983), 256 pp.

Frankel, Norman "Political Terrorism: Causes and Prognosis: The Cases of Israel and Northern Ireland" paper presented to the annual convention of the International Studies Association/Midwest, Loyola University of Chicago, October 16-18, 1980.

Garfincle, Adam M. "Sources of the Al-Fatah Mutiny" 27, 3 Orbis (1983), pp. 603-640.

Gazit, Shlomo "The Myth and Reality of the PLO" in Benjamin Netanyahu, ed. International Terrorism: Challenge and Response (London: Transaction, 1981).

Finiewski, Paul "La Charte Nationale Palestinienne: Ce Que Veut L'OLP (The Palestinian National Charter: What the PLO Wants)" 48, 1 Rivista di Studi Pol. Int. (Italy) (1981), pp. 33-56.

Glick, Edward B. "Arab Terrorism and Israeli Retaliation: Some Moral, Psychological, and Political Reflections" in David C. Rapoport and Yonah Alexander, eds. The Rationalization of Terrorism (Frederick, Maryland: University Publications of America, 1982).

Golan, Galia "Soviet-PLO Relations" 16 Jerusalem Quarterly (1980), pp. 121-136.

Goldberg, Giora "Haganah, Irgun and 'Stern': Who Did What?" 25 Jerusalem Quarterly (1982), pp. 116-120.

Gregory, Harry Khadafy (New York: Paper Jacks, 1986), 173 pp., photos.
An "instant book" published in May 1986, includes material on the US bombing of Libya in mid-April in reaction to Libyan sponsorship of terrorist attacks on US citizens.

Hassassian, Manuel Sarkis Armenians as a National Minority in the Middle East (University of Cincinnati, Department of Political Science, Ph.D. dissertation).

Hazelton, Lesley "Respectable Terrorism" 261 Harpers (October 1980), p. 28-30.

Hechiche, Abdelwahab "Self-Determination and the Palestinians" paper presented to the annual convention of the International Studies Association, Los Angeles, March 18-22, 1980.

Hellman, Peter "Smadar's Will to Live" 127 Reader's Digest (Canada) (September 1985), pp. 37-42.
The story of Smadar Haran, an Israeli woman harmed in a terrorist attack.

Hoffman, Bruce "Recent Trends in Palestinian Terrorism: II" (Santa Monica: The Rand Corporation, P-7076, 1985).

Hudson, Michael C. "The Palestinians: Retrospect and Prospects" 78, 453 Current History (1980), pp. 22-25, 31, 39-41, 48.

Hudson, Michael C. "The US Decline in the Middle East: How Can It Be Stopped?" 26, 1 Orbis (1982), pp. 19-26.

Hurni, Ferdinand "Terrorism and the Struggle for Palestine" 28 Swiss Review of World Affairs (February 1979), pp. 14-23.

"Iran: Consequences of the Abortive Attempt to Rescue the American Hostages" 3, 1 Conflict (1981), pp. 55-77.

Isaac, Rael Jean "Liberal Protestants Versus Israel" 27, 8 Midstream (1981), pp. 6-14.
The criticizes stands of the National Council of Churches.

Israeli, Raphael, ed. The PLO in Lebanon: Selected Documents (New York: St. Martin's, 1984), 316 pp.
Reviewed by Daniel Pipes "The Past and Present of the PLO" Washington Post Book World (March 25, 1984), pp. 8, 13.

Jansen, Michael The Battle of Beirut: Why Israel Invaded Lebanon (London: Zed, 1982), 142 pp.

Kedourie, Elie "Political Terrorism in the Muslim World" in Benjamin Netanyahu, ed. Terrorism: How the West Can Win (New York: Farrar, Straus, Giroux, 1986), pp. 70-76.

Kestin, Hesh "Terror's Bottom Line" 137 Forbes (June 2, 1986), pp. 38-40.
The author claims that the PLO is going broke.

Kilmarx, Robert A. and Yonah Alexander, eds. Business and the Middle East: Threats and Prospects (New York: Pergamon, 1982), 272 pp.

Kimche, Jon "Carrington's 'Caviare'" 27, 6 Midstream (1981).
Discusses the PLO's reaction to UK Foreign Secretary Lord Carrington's European initiative.

Koch, Peter and Kai Hermann Assault at Mogadishu (London: Corgi, 1977).

Koshelev, V. S. "Iz Istorii Tainykh Antibritanskikh Organizatsii v Egipte 1870-1934 GG (Excerpts from the History of the Secret Anti-British Organizations in Egypt, 1870-1924)" 1 Narody Azii i Afriki (USSR) (1980), pp. 111-119.

Kurtzer, D. C. Palestine Guerrilla and Israeli Counter-Guerrilla Warfare: The Radicalization of the Palestine Arab Community to Violence, 1949-1970 (Columbia University: Ph.D. dissertation, 1976).

Kurz, Anat and Areil Merari ASALA: Irrational Terror or Political Tool (Boulder, Colorado: Westview, 1985).

Laffin, John The PLO Connections (London: Corgi Books, 1982), 174 pp.

Lagerwist, Frank A. Israel and the Politics of Terrorism in the Middle East (Institute on Economic Policy, 1981), 143 pp.

Legrain, Jean-Francois "La 'Dissidence' Palestinienne (The Palestinian 'Dissidence')" 4 Esprit (France) (1984), pp. 17-31.

Lehman-Wilzig, Sam and Giora Goldberg "Religious Protest and Police Reaction in a Theo-Democracy: Israel, 1950-1979" 25, 3 Journal of Church and State (1983), pp. 491-505.

Leibel, Aaron "Terrorism, Settlements and Palestinians: How-and Why - They Voted in a Jerusalem Neighborhood" 12 Present Tense (Autumn 1984), pp. 6-10.

Leibstone, Marvin "Palestine Terror: Past, Present and Future: Some Observations" (Gaithersburg, Maryland: International Association of Chiefs of Police, 1979), 27 pp.

Lerman, Eran "The Palestinian Revolution and the Arab-Israeli Conflict: A New Phase?" 141 Conflict Studies (1982), 19 pp.

Lesch, Ann Mosley "The Palestine Problem" 34, 4 World Politics (1982), pp. 560-573.

Lever, Evelyne "L'OAS et les Pieds-Noirs" 43 Histoire (France) (1982), pp. 10-23.

Lewis, Bernard "Islamic Terrorism?" in Benjamin Netanyahu, ed. Terrorism: How the West Can Win (New York: Farrar, Straus, Giroux, 1986), pp. 65-69.

Lilienthal, Alfred M. "Middle East Terror: The Double Standard" 52 Vital Speeches (February 15, 1986), pp. 277-282.

Litani, Yehuda "Leadership in the West Bank and Gaza" 14 Jerusalem Quarterly (1980), pp. 99-109.

MacDonald, C. G. "Iran: Political and Security Assessment", in Robert A. Kilmarx and Yonah Alexander, eds. Business and the Middle East: Threats and Prospects (New York: Pergamon, 1982).

MacIntyre, Ron "Pussyfooting with the PLO" 5 New Zealand International Review (January-February 1980), pp. 19-21.

Marchese, Stelio "Alle Origini del Terrorismo Strategico (Origins of Strategic Terrorism)" 21, 1 Storia e Pol. (Italy) (1982), pp. 257-275.
A look at whether the Soviets or the Chinese are responsible for disseminating an ideology which led to the general acceptance of terrorism in the Near East.

Mead, James M. "Lebanon Revisited" 67, 9 Marine Corps Gazette (1983), pp. 64-73.
A view of the role of the US 22d Marine Amphibious Unit during February-May 1983, including a look at the terrorist bombing of the US Embassy.

Melman, Yossi The Master Terrorist: The True Story Behind Abu Nidal (New York: Adama, 1986), 215 pp.

Merari, Ariel PLO: Core of World Terror (Jerusalem: Carta, 1983), 31 pp.

Merari, Ariel "Political Terrorism and Middle Eastern Instability" in N. Novik and J. Starr, eds. Challenges in the Middle East (New York: Praeger, 1981), pp. 101-112.

Merari, Ariel and Yosefa Braunstein "Shi'ite Terrorism: Operational Capabilities and the Suicide Factor" 5, 2 TVI Journal (Fall 1984), pp. 7-9.

Miller, Aaron David The PLO and the Politics of Survival (New York: Praeger, 1983), 132 pp., also available in 99, 11 Washington Papers (Center for Strategic and International Studies, Georgetown University).

Milson, Menahem "How to Make Peace with the Palestinians" 71, 5 Commentary (1981), pp. 25-35.

Miner, William Allen The Legal Implications of a Palestinian Homeland (Monterey: Naval Postgraduate School, Master's thesis, June 1979), 110 pp.

Mishal, Shaul "Nationalism Through Localism: Some Observations on the West Bank Political Elite" 17, 4 Middle Eastern Studies (UK) (1981), pp. 477-491.

Mottahedeh, Roy Parviz "Iran's Foreign Devils" 38 Foreign Policy (Spring 1980).

Moughrabi, Fouad "The PLO--A High Risk Insurgency?" paper presented to the panel on the Role of Terrorism in Ethnic Nationalism at the annual convention of the International Studies Association/South, University of Florida, October 29-31, 1981.

Muslih, Muhammad Y. "Moderates and Rejectionists Within the Palestine Liberation Organization" 30 Middle East Journal (Spring 1976), pp. 127-140.

Nassar, Jamal R. Non State Actors in the Middle East: A Case Study of the Palestine Liberation Organization (University of Cincinnati, Ph.D. dissertation, 1978).

Nisan, Mordechai "PLO Messianism: Diagnosis of a Modern Gnostic Sect" 7, 3 Terrorism (1984), pp. 299-312.

Norton, Augustus R. Moscow and the Palestinians (University of Miami Center for Advanced International Studies, 1974).

Norton, Augustus R. "The Palestinian State Under PLO Leadership" paper presented at the annual meeting of the Midwest Political Science Association, Chicago, April 1976.

O'Ballance, Edgar Language of Violence: The Blood Politics of Terrorism (San Rafael, California: Presidio, 1979), 365 pp. O'Ballance concentrates on the futures of the Palestinian terrorists, and notes their allies in other terrorist groups.

Oney, Earnest R. "The Revolutionary in Iran, Religion and Politics in a Traditional Society" 6 Clandestine Tactics and Technology (Gaithersburg, Maryland: International Association of Chiefs of Police, 1980).

Peck, M. C. "The Arab States of the Gulf: A Political and Security Assessment", in Robert A. Kilmarx and Yonah Alexander, eds. Business and the Middle East: Threats and Prospects (New York: Pergamon, 1982).

Peck, M. C. "The Middle East and Energy: Sources of Threat", in Yonah Alexander and Charles K. Ebinger, eds. Political Terrorism and Energy: The Threat and Response (New York: Praeger, 1982).

Perlmutter, Amos, Michael Handel and Uri Bar-Joseph Two Minutes Over Baghdad (London: Vallentine, Mitchell, 1982), 191 pp.

Piotrowski, Jerzy "The Palestine Question: Evolution of the PLO Stance" 10 Studies on the Developing Countries (1979), pp. 37-56.

Pipes, Daniel In the Path of God: Islam and Political Power (New York: Basic, 1983).

Plascov, Avi "A Palestinian State? Examining the Alternatives" Adelphi Papers (London, 1981).

Prill, Norbert J. "Die Anerkennung der PLO durch die Vereinten Nationen" 59 Die Friedens-Warte (1976), pp. 208-225.

Randal, Jonathan C. Going All the Way: Christian Warlords, Israeli Adventurers, and the War in Lebanon (New York: Viking, 1983), 304 pp.

Rawls, Lucia Wren "Obstacles to a Peaceful Settlement: Mirror Images in P.L.O. and Zionist Political Doctrines", paper presented to the 24th annual convention of the International Studies Association, Mexico City, April 5-9, 1983.

Rayfield, Gordon The Righteous Executioners: A Comparative Analysis of Jewish Terrorists of the 1940s and Palestinian Terrorists of the 1970s (City University of New York, Political Science Department: Ph.D. dissertation, 1980).

Reed, Stanley, III "Dateline Syria: Fin De Regime?" 39 Foreign Policy (Summer 1980), pp. 176-190.

Rokach, Livia Israel's Sacred Terrorism: A Study Based on Moshe Sharett's Personal Diary and Other Documents (Belmont, Mass.: Association of Arab-American University Graduates, 1982), 73 pp.

Rokach, Livia "Israeli State Terrorism: An Analysis of the Sharett Diaries" 9, 3 Journal of Palestine Studies (Spring 1980) pp. 3-28.

Rolef, Susan Hattis, ed. Violence as Reality: Assassination and Massacre in the Arab World (Jerusalem: Carta, 1983), 35 pp.

Rondot, Pierre "Quelques Aspects du Probleme Palestinien (Some Aspects of the Palestinian Problem)" 356, 5 Etudes (France) (1982), pp. 581-594.

Rubenberg, Cheryl The PLO: Its Institutional Infrastructure (Belmont, Massachusetts: Institute of Arab Studies, 1983), 66 pp.

Rubinstein, C. L. "The Lebanon War: Objectives and Outcomes" 37, 1 Australian Outlook (1983), p. 10-17.

Sabel, Robbie "How Israel Copes with Terrorism" 17, 2 International Society of Barristers Quarterly (April 1982), pp. 274-282.

Savory, R.M. "The Religious Environment in the Middle East" in Robert A. Kilmarx and Yonah Alexander, eds. Business and the Middle East: Threats and Prospects (New York: Pergamon, 1982).

Scott, Charles W. Pieces of the Game: The Human Drama of Americans Held Hostage in Iran (Atlanta, Ga.: Peachtree, 1984), 407 pp.

Scott, Marvin "What is the PLO Worth: Through Smart Investments, It May Have Made Billions" Parade (September 21, 1986), pp. 17-18.
 The author looks at liquid assets in banks and stocks, as well as business ventures (real estate, farms, airlines, duty-free shops), contributions, and narcotics trafficking.

Selhami, Mohamed "J'ai Rencontre Les 'Hommes Suicide'" 1203 Jeune Afrique (January 25, 1984), pp. 40-50. (in French)
 A look at the Islamic fanatics who join Iranian terrorist squads, the article is replete with haunting photos of potential killers.

Shah, Mowahid Hussain "Wars of National Liberation: The Palestinian Progress Under International Law" 31, 1 Pakistan Horizon (1978), pp. 3-23; Part II in 31, 2-3 (1978), pp. 3-31.

Shapira, Anita "The Debate in Mapai on the Use of Violence: 1932-1935" 2, 1 Zionism (Israel) (1981), pp. 99-124.

Shepherd, Naomi "Violence and Counter-Violence" 12 Present Tense (Autumn 1984), pp. 10-15.
A discussion of Palestinian terrorism in Israel.

al-Shuaibi, Issa "The Development of Palestinian Entity-Consciousness" 9, 2 Journal of Palestine Studies (1980), pp. 50-70, 99-124.

Sick, Gary All Fall Down: America's Tragic Encounter with Iran (New York: Random House, 1985), 366 pp.
Reviewed by Jim Hoagland in Washington Post Book World (May 19, 1985), p. 5.

Silverberg, Sanford R. "From Violence to a Morning Coat: The Legitimation of the P.L.O.", paper presented to the 24th annual convention of the International Studies Association, Mexico City, April 5-9, 1983.

Sim, Richard "Kurdistan: The Search for Recognition" 124 Conflict Studies (1980).

Sisco, Joseph J. "Middle East: Progress or Lost Opportunity?" 61, 3 Foreign Affairs (1983), pp. 611-640.

Smiklo, Charmaine The US and the Palestine Problem: A Case for US Recognition of the PLO (Claremont Graduate School, Department of Political Science, Ph.D. dissertation, 1982).

Sobel, Lester A., ed. Palestinian Impasse: Arab Guerrillas and International Terror (New York: Facts on File, 1978).

Spiegel, Steven L. "The Middle East: A Consensus of Error" 73, 3 Commentary (1982), pp. 15-24.

Stone, Julius "Liberation Movements: Arab and Jewish" 18 Quadrant (September-October 1974), pp. 56-63.

Tabbara, Lina Mikdadi Surviving the Siege of Beirut: A Personal Account (London: Onyx Press, 1983), 152 pp.

Tadayon, K. M. "The Changing Image of Iran in the United States: Open-Ended-Format Surveys Before and After the Hostage Crisis" 30, 2 Gazette: International Journal for Mass Communication Studies (Netherlands) (1982), pp. 89-95.

Tavin, Eli and Yonah Alexander, eds. Psychological Warfare and Propaganda: Irgun Documentation (Wilmington: Scholarly Resources, Inc. 1982), 300 pp.
The compilers offer Irgun communiques, speeches, letters, and other writings from 1937 to 1948.

Taylor, Alan R. "The PLO in Inter-Arab Politics" 11, 2 Journal of Palestine Studies (1982), pp. 70-81.

Thackrah, John Richard "The Palestine Liberation Organisation Until 1970" 63 War in Peace (March 1984).

Thauby Garcia, Gernando "Conflicto del sur del Libano (The Conflict in Southern Lebanon)" 97, 5 Rev. de Marina (Chile) (1980), pp. 420-426.

Tophoven, Rolf "PLO-Swischen Terror und Diplomatie" Aus Politik und Zeitgeschichte (December 1979), pp. 17-34.

Toubi, Jamal "Social Dynamics in War-Torn Lebanon" 17 Jerusalem Quarterly (1980), pp. 83-109.

Turki, Fawaz "The Passions of Exile: The Palestine Congress of North America" 9, 4 Journal of Palestine Studies (1980), pp. 17-43.

"TVI Interview: Rafi Eitan, March 27, 1985" 5, 4 TVI: Terrorism Violence Insurgency Journal (Spring 1985), pp. 22-25.

Tzur, Daniel "La Guerra del Libano: Buscando las Raices del Conflicto Arabe-Israeli (The War in Lebanon: Searching for Roots of the Arab-Israeli Conflict)" 37, 407-408 Estudios Centroamericanos (El Salvador) (1982), pp. 879-896.

"A US Offensive at the UN: Statements by the US Delegation Before the General Assembly" 144, 3 World Affairs (1981-1982), pp. 196-295.
Includes a statement before the UN on the extradition of Ziad Abu Eain to Israel in 1979 for a terrorist bombing.

Vashitz, Joseph "Towards Changes in the Middle East" 19, 1-2 International Problems (Israel) (1980), pp. 18-20.

Vatikiotis, P. J. "The Spread of Islamic Terrorism" in Benjamin Netanyahu, ed. Terrorism: How the West Can Win (New York: Farrar, Straus, Giroux, 1986), pp. 77-84.

Walters, Ronald W. "The Black Initiatives in the Middle East" 10, 2 Journal of Palestine Studies (1981), pp. 3-13.

Wasserstein, Bernard "New Light on the Moyne Murder" 26, 3 Midstream (1980), pp. 30-38.

Wessner, Charles Wakefield Bureaucratic Response to Urban Terrorism, or the Security Bureaucracy's Responses to the F.L.N.'s Urban Terrorism Campaign to Algiers, October, 1956 to October, 1957 (Fletcher School of Law and Diplomacy, Tufts University, Ph.D. dissertation, 1980).

Wilkinson, Paul "After Tehran" Conflict Quarterly (1981), pp. 5-14. also available in 238, 1385 Contemporary Review (UK) (1981), pp. 281-290.

Wilson, R. D. Cordon and Search (Aldershot: Gale and Polden, 1949).
How the British handled terrorism in Palestine.

Wise, Charles Dean The Impact of Palestinian Terror on the Arab/Israeli Conflict (University of Oklahoma at Norman, Political Science Department, Ph.D. dissertation, 1980), 256 pp.

Wolf, John B. "Middle Eastern Death Squads" 6, 4 Update Report (Gaithersburg, Maryland: International Association of Chiefs of Police, 1980).

Wright, Robin B. Sacred Rage: The Crusade of Modern Islam (New York: Linden Press/Simon and Schuster, 1985).

Yaniv, Avner "Phoenix or Phantom? The PLO After Beirut" 7, 3 Terrorism (1984), pp. 313-322.

Yodfat, Aryeh Y. and Yuval Arnon-Ohanna PLO Strategy and Tactics (New York: St. Martin's and London: Croom Helm, 1981), 225 pp.

Yonay, Ehud "Who's Watching the PLO?" 24 New West (September 24, 1979), pp. 80-83.

Zabih, Sepehr "Aspects of Terrorism in Iran" 463 Annals of the American Academy of Political and Social Science (September 1982), pp. 84-94.

Zamir, Meir "Politics and Violence in Lebanon" 25 Jerusalem Quarterly (1982), pp. 3-26.

LATIN AMERICA

La Accion Terrorista en Uruguay (Montevideo: Direccion Nacional de Relaciones Publicas, 1979-1981), 32 pp.

Aguilera Peralta, Gabriel "Quantitative Effects of State Political Terror in Guatemala in Relation to the Popular Movement" 9, 27 Estudios Sociales Centroamericanos (Costa Rica) (1980), pp. 217-249.

Aguilera Peralta, Gabriel "Terror and Violence as Weapons of Counter-Insurgency in Guatemala" 7, 2-3 Latin American Perspectives (Spring-Summer 1980), pp. 91-113.

Aguilera Peralta, Gabriel Edgardo, et al. Dialectica del Terror en Guatemala (San Jose, Costa Rica: Ediciones Universitaria Centroamericana, 1981), 281 pp.

Alonso Pineiro, Armando Cronica de la Subversion en la Argentina: con un Estudio Preliminar (Depalma, 1980), 173 pp.

Anderson, Thomas P. "The Ambiguities of Political Terrorism in Central America" 4, 1-4 Terrorism (1980), pp. 267-276.

"The Argentine Military Junta's Final Report on the War Against Subversion and Terrorism, April 1983" 7, 3 Terrorism (1984), pp. 323-340.

Arostegui, Martin "Revolutionary Violence in Central America" 4 International Security Review (Spring 1979).

Asencio, Diego C. and Susan Morrisey Livingstone, interviewer "Terrorism: 'The Original Cheap Shot'" 146, 1 World Affairs (1983), pp. 42-53.
An interview with a US Ambassador who was one of several hostages taken at a Dominican Embassy party in Bogota on February 27, 1980.

Barkey, D. W. and D.S. Eitzen "Toward an Assessment of Multi-National Corporate Social Expenditures in Relation to Political Stability and Terrorist Activity: The Argentine Case" 34, 4 Inter-American Economic Affairs (1981), pp. 77-90.

Black, George Triumph of the People: The Sandinista Revolution in Nicaragua (London, 1981).

Booth, John A. "A Guatemalan Nightmare: Levels of Political Violence: 1966-1972" 22, 2 Journal of Interamerican Studies and World Affairs (1980), pp. 195-225.

Bouchey, L. Francis and Alberto M. Piedra Guatemala: A Promise in Peril (Washington, D.C.: Council for Inter-American Security, 1980), 91 pp.

Bowen, Gordon L. "Guatemala: A New Form of Totalitarianism? State Terrorism and Cycles of 'Disappearances'" 111 Commonweal (February 10, 1984), pp. 76-78.

Branch, Taylor and Eugene Propper Labyrinth: The Pursuit of the Letelier Assassins (New York: Viking, 1982), 555 pp.

Casas, Ulises Origen Desarrollo del Movimiento Revolucionario Colombiano (Bogota, 1980).

Castaneda, Jorge Nicaragua: Contradicciones en la Revolucion (Mexico City, 1980).

Castro Caycedo, German Del ELN al M-19 Once Anos de Lucha Guerrillera (Bogota, 1980).
Includes interviews with Jaime Arenas and Jaime Bateman.

Castro, Rojas Gaspar Como Secuestramos a Niehous (Caracas: Editorial Fuentes, Ediciones Tres Continentes, 1979), 249 pp.

"Christians Fall Victim to Terrorist Violence in Peru" 28 Christianity Today (October 5, 1984), pp. 90-91.

Devine, Frank J. El Salvador: Embassy Under Attack (New York: Vantage, 1981).

Di Giovanni, Jr. "US Policy and the Marxist Threat to Central America" 128 Backgrounder (Washington, D.C.: The Heritage Foundation, October 15, 1980), 16 pp.

Diaz Silva, Ezequiel Los Secretos de Neihous (Caracas: Publicaciones Seleven, distribuye Merca Libros, 1979), 277 pp.

Dunkerley, James The Long War: Dictatorship and Revolution in El Salvador (London: Junction Books, 1982).

Ellner, Steve "Political Party Dynamics in Venezuela and the Outbreak of Guerrilla Warfare" 34, 2 Inter-American Economic Affairs (1980), pp. 3-24.

Endozain, Placido Archbishop Romero: Martyr of Salvador (Guildford: Lutterworth Press, 1981).

Fonseca, Carlos Sandino: Guerrillero Proletario (Managua, 1980).

Foster, Douglas "Guatemala: On the Green Path" 10 Mother Jones (November-December, 1985), pp. 12-14.

Fragoso, Heleno Claudio Terrorismo e Criminalidade Politica (Rio de Janeiro: Forense, 1981), 136 pp.

Garcia Marquez, Gabriel Los Sandinistas (Bogota, 1979).

Gerlach, Allen "El Salvador: Background to the Violence" 239, 1386 Contemporary Review (UK) (1981), pp. 1-7.

Gillespie, Richard Soldiers of Peron: Argentina's Montoneros (New York: Oxford University Press, and Oxford: Clarendon, 1982), 310 pp.

Gonzalez LaPeyre, Edison Violencia y Terrorismo (Santo Domingo, Dominican Republic: Omega, 1980), 399 pp.

Gorney, Cynthia "Voices from a Bogota Jail: Why Did Folk Say 'What a Shame' When the Terrorists Were Nabbed?" Washington Post (June 7, 1981), pp. D-1, D-5.
A look at the activities of the M-19.

Gravely, Edmund K. "Bitterman Slaying Isolates Guerrillas, Bolsters Summer Institute of Linguistics, Bogota" 25 Christianity Today (April 10, 1981), pp. 70-72.

"Guatemala: Nowhere to Run" 233 Nation (September 5, 1981), p. 167.

Guy, John James "El Salvador: Another Domino?" The World Today (August 1980).

Halperin, Ernst "From Peron to Somoza: The New Terrorism" 1, 4 Washington Quarterly (Autumn 1978), pp. 110-114.

Hoeffel, Paul Heath "The Sheraton Murder Case" 130 New York Times Magazine (September 6, 1981), p. 28.
A discussion of the deaths of Michael P. Hammer, Mark D. Pearlman, and Jose Rodolfo Viera in El Salvador.

Holland, Max and Kai Bird "Colombia: The Carlos Connection" 240 Nation (June 22, 1985), p. 759.

Jenkins, Brian Michael "Colombia's Bold Gamble for Peace" 5, 2 TVI Journal (Fall 1984), pp. 10-19.

Keagh, Dermot Romero, El Salvador's Martyr (Dublin, 1981).

Kemp, Peter "Russia Against the Tupamaros" Spectator (April 16, 1977), pp. 8-9.

Kruger, Alexander "El Salvador's Marxist Revolution" 137 Backgrounder (Washington, D.C.: The Heritage Foundation, April 10, 1981), 18 pp.

Landazabal Reyes, Fernando La Subversion y el Conflicto Social (Bogota: Ediciones Tercer Mundo, 1980), 157 pp.

Lanz Rodriguez, Carlos El Caso Neihous y la Corrupcion Administrativa (Caracas: Editorial Fuentes, Ediciones Tres Continents, 1979), 188 pp.

Lara, Patricia Siembra Vientos y Recogeras Tempestades (Bogota, 1982).
Lara offers biographies of M-19 leaders, a chronology, and documents.

Litt, John and James Kohl "The Guerrillas of Montevideo" 214 The Nation (February 28, 1972), pp. 269-272.

Livingstone, Susan Morrisey "Terrorism: 'The Original Cheap Shot': An Interview with Ambassador Diego Asencio" 146, 1 World Affairs (Summer 1983), pp. 42-53.

Livingstone, Susan Morrisey "Terrorist Wrongs Versus Human Rights: An Interview with Assistant Secretary of State Elliott Abrams" 146, 1 World Affairs (Summer 1983), pp. 69-78.

McClintock, Cynthia "Why Peasants Rebel: The Case of Peru's Sendero Luminoso" World Politics (October 1984), pp. 48-84.

McClory, Robert J. "Church Money Aids Terrorists" 19 National Catholic Reporter (August 123, 1983), p. 3.
A note on the misuse of Church money in Puerto Rico.

McLellan, Andrew C. "Right-wing Terror Paralyzes Guatemalan Labor" 35 AFL-CIO Free Trade Union News (September 1980), pp. 3-9.

Mercado, Roger El Partido Comunista del Peru: Sendero Luminoso (Lima: Ediciones de Cultura Popular, 1982).

Millet, Richard "The Politics of Violence: Guatemala and El Salvador" 80, 463 Current History (1981), pp 70-74, 88.

Montgomery, Tommie Sue The Salvadoran Revolution: Origins and Evolution (Boulder, Colorado, 1982).

Mulgannon, Terry "Traveling in El Salvador: Personal Glimpses of a Torn Country" 5, 2 TVI Journal (Fall 1984), pp. 20-22.

"Peru's Ancient Incas are Reborn in a Terrorist Movement"
Business Week (August 30, 1982), p. 45
A discussion of the aims and objectives of the Sendero
Luminoso terrorists.

Pinto Flores, Aquiles Yo fui Rehen del M-19 (Bogota: Canal
Ramirez-Antares, 1980), 225 pp.

Premo, Daniel L. "Political Assassination in Guatemala: A Case
of Institutionalized Terror" 23, 4 Journal of Inter-American
Studies and World Affairs (November 1981), pp. 429-456.

Radu, Michael S. "Terror, Terrorism, and Insurgency in Latin
America" 28, 1 Orbis (Spring 1984), pp. 27-40.

Ranly, Ernest W. "Under the Peruvian Volcano: The Church,
Terrorism, and Democracy" 113 Commonweal (February 14, 1986),
pp. 78-82.

Raushenbush, Richard The Terrorist War in Guatemala
(Washington, D.C.: Council for Inter-American Security,
Educational Institute, 1982).

Revolutionary Strategy in El Salvador, second edition (London:
Tricontinental Society, 1983), 56 pp.

Robinson, Steve "Argentina's Disappeared" 4 Life (September
1981), pp. 38-44.

Romero Carranza, Ambrosio El Terrorismo en la Historia
Universal y en la Argentina (Buenos Aires: Ediciones DePalma,
1980), 294 pp.

Rovira, Alejandro Subversion, Terrorismo, Guerra
Revolucionaria (Montevideo, 1981), 29 pp.

Russell, Charles A. "Latin America: Regional Review" 4, 1-4
Terrorism (1980), pp. 277-292.

Silva, Geraldo Eulalio do Nascimento e "Ocupacao da Embaixada
Americana em Bogota (Occupation of the American Embassy in
Bogota)" 330 Rev. do Inst. Hist. e Geor. Brasileiro (1981),
pp. 187-198.

Sloan, John "Political Terrorism in Latin America" paper
presented to the annual meeting of the Southwest Social
Science Association, San Antonio, Texas, March 17-19, 1982.

Smith, Peter H. "Argentina: The Uncertain Warriors" 79, 454
Current History (February 1980), pp. 62-65, 85-86.

Soto, Pedro Juan "Fiction or Reality: Testimony of an Author
in Crisis" 9, 3 Caribbean Review (Summer 1980), pp. 15, 45.
The father of one of the terrorists who participated in the
Cerror Maravilla incident claims that his son was set-up by a
Puerto Rican policeman. A related story is Tomas Stella
"Cerror Maravilla: Injustice in Puerto Rico" 9, 3 Carribean
Review (Summer 1980), pp. 12-15, 44-45.

Taylor, Robert W. and Harry E. Vanden "Defining Terrorism in El Salvador: 'La Matanza'" 463 Annals of the American Academy of Political and Social Science (September 1982), pp. 106-118.

Terrorism in Argentina: Evolution of Terrorist Delinquency in Argentina (Buenos Aires: Republica Argentina, Poder Ejecutivo Nacional, 1980), 442 pp.
Lists the major terrorist actions and includes newspaper reports of terrorist assassinations.

"Terrorism: The New Global War" 2 Latin American Times (May 1980), pp. 10-15.
The article concentrates on the M-19's seizure of the Dominican Republic's Embassy in Bogota in February, 1980.

Rehen: Testimonios de Tito Livio: Rehen del M-19 (Publicaciones America, 1980), 111 pp.

Torrens, James "An Education in Terror at El Salvador's Universities" 149 America (December 24, 1983), pp. 411-413.

"U.S. Condemns Salvadoran Death Squads" 7, 3 Terrorism (1984), pp. 347ff.

de Villemarest, Pierre F. Strategists of Fear: Twenty Years of Revolutionary War in Argentina (Geneva, 1981).

Watson, John C. Social Mobilization, Socio-Economic Development, Political Institutionalization and Political Violence in South America (University of New Orleans, Department of Political Science, Ph.D. dissertation).

Weber, Henri Nicaragua: The Sandinist Revolution (London, 1981).

ASIA

Baker, Edward J. "Politics in South Korea" 81, 474 Current History (1982), pp. 173-178.
Discusses the assassination of President Park Chung-hee in 1979.

Basu, P. K. "Terror in Bhangore" 17, 12 Economic and Political Weekly (1982), pp. 424-425.

"'Born' in the U.S.: Terrorist Training in the South" 32 World Press Review (September 1985), pp. 39-40.
A summary of Sikh terrorism.

Chakravarty, S. R. "Bengal Revolutionaries in Burma" 19, 1-2 Quarterly Review of Historical Studies (India) (1979-80), pp. 42-49.

Chapman, William "A Philippine Laboratory of Revolution: In Davao, the Poor are with the Enemies of Marcos" Washington Post (May 19, 1985), pp. D1-D2.
A discussion of the roots of support of the New Peoples Army.

Clague, Peter Iron Spearhead: The True Story of a Communist Killer Squad in Singapore (Singapore: Heinemann Educational Books, 1980), 153 pp.

Cloughley, B. W. "The Troubles in Nagaland (India)" 6, 1 TVI: Terrorism Violence Insurgency Journal (Summer 1985), pp. 35-38.

Fedorov, V. "Left Extremism in the Political Life of the Eastern Countries" 5 Aziia i Afrika Segodnia (USSR) (1983), pp. 13-16.

Gonick, Cy "The Delhi Riots" 19 Canadian Dimension (September-October, 1985), pp. 23-25.

Gregor, A. James and Maria Hsia Chang "Terrorism: The View from Taiwan" 5, 3 Terrorism (1981), pp. 233-264.

Guiart, Jean "New Caledonia: Behind the Revolt" 6, 1 TVI: Terrorism Violence Insurgency Journal (Summer 1985), pp. 23-25.

International Renegades: North Korean Diplomacy Through Terror (Seoul: Korean Overseas Information Service, 1983), 106 pp.

An International Terrorist Clique: North Korea (Seoul: Korean Overseas Information Service, 1983), 51 pp.

Jiwa, Salim The Death of Air India Flight 182 (Canada, 1986). A look at the bombing of an aircraft in Canada.

Kodikara, S. V. "The Separatist Eelam Movement in Sri Lanka: An Overview" 37, 2 India Quarterly (April-June 1981), pp. 194-212.

Lopez, Eugenio and Steve Psinakis Two Terrorists Meet (San Francisco: Alchemy Books, 1981), 346 pp. Memoirs of a leader in the Philippino resistance to Marcos.

"Materials on Massacre of Korean Officials in Rangoon" 7, 4 Korea and World Affairs (South Korea) (1983), pp. 735-764.

Milman, Joel and Mark Dowie "A Brazen Act of Terrorism: The Killing of Henry Liu" 10 Mother Jones (May 1985), pp. 17-26. A discussion of the killing of a Taiwanese journalist in the US.

Mitchell, Jared "A Nation Losing Control: Sri Lanka's Almost Civil War" 98 Macleans (February 18, 1985), pp. 30ff.

Munro, Ross H. "The New Khmer Rouge" 80 Commentary (December 1985), pp. 19-38. A look at terrorism in the Philippines.

Muramatsu, Takeshi "Japan's Terror Groups" in Benjamin Netanyahu, ed. Terrorism: How the West Can Win (New York: Farrar, Straus, Giroux, 1986), pp. 106-108.

Murphy, Denis "Violence in the Philippines" 153 America (November 2, 1985), pp. 278-281.

Nath, Shaileshwar Terrorism in India (New Delhi: National Publishing House, 1980), 350 pp.

Richardson, Leon D. "Crime and Punishment in the People's Republic of China" 5, 4 TVI: Terrorism Violence Insurgency Journal (Spring 1985), pp. 52-53.

Richardson, Leon D. "The Tamil Separatist Problem" 6, 1 TVI: Terrorism Violence Insurgency Journal (Summer 1985), pp. 31-34.

Sanders, Sol W. "'The Sword' That is Pointing at Pakistan's Zia" 9 Business Week (1981), p. 60.
A look at a Kabul-based terrorist organization that seeks to overthrow the Pakistani government.

Siriweera, W. I. "Recent Developments in Sinhala-Tamil Relations" 20, 9 Asian Survey (September 19809), pp. 903-913.

US House of Representatives, Committee on Foreign Affairs The Consequences of the Aquino Assassination, Hearings and Mark Up (Washington, D.C.: September 13, October 6, 18, 1983).

Weatherbee, Donald E. "Communist Revolutionary Violence in the ASEAN States" 10, 3 Asian Affairs: An Am. Review (1983), pp. 1-17.

Wheen, Francis "The Burning of Paradise: Sri Lanka's Drift to Violence" 102 New Statesman (July 17, 1981), p. 13.

Wilson, A. "Sri-Lanka: State Terrorism" 16, 27 Economic and Political Weekly (1981), p. 1144.

Young, P. Lewis "New Caledonia: In Conflict" 6, 1 TVI: Terrorism Violence Insurgency Journal (Summer 1985), pp. 26-30.

AFRICA

Akinsanya, Adeoye "The Entebbe Rescue Mission: A Case of Aggression?" 34, 3 Pakistan Horizon (1981), pp. 12-35, reprinted in 9, 2 Journal of African Studies (1982), pp. 46-57.
Although the Arab hijackers and Idi Amin's regime violated international law, so did the Israeli rescuers.

Breytenbach, Breyten The True Confessions of an Albino Terrorist (New York: Farrar Straus Giroux, 1985).
Breytenbach is a noted poet who was imprisoned for his alleged ties with the African National Congress.

Campbell, Keith "Prospects for Terrorism in South Africa" 14, 2 South Africa International Quarterly (October 1983), pp. 397-417.

Carmichael, D.J.C. "Of Beasts, Gods, and Civilized Men" 6, 1 Terrorism (1985), pp. 3-18.

du Plessis, J. "The 'Just Struggle' and War of Words in Southern Africa" 6 South Africa Forum Position Paper No. 7 (April 1983).

Foot, M.R.D. Resistance (London, 1978).

Friedland, Elaine A. Comparative Study of the Development of Revolutionary Nationalist Movements in Southern Africa-- FRELIMO (Mozambique) and the African National Congress of South Africa (City University of New York, Political Science Department, Ph.D. dissertation, 1980).

Friedland, Elaine A. "South Africa and Instability in Southern Africa" 463 Annals of the American Academy of Political and Social Science (September 1982), pp. 95-105.

Hough, M. South Africa, Counter-Insurgency, Terrorism, and Publicity: Factual Review (Pretoria, South Africa: Institute for Strategic Studies, University of Pretoria, 1981), 19 pp.

Jakonya, T.J.B. "The Effects of the War on the Rural Population of Zimbabwe" 5 Journal of South African Affairs (April 1980), pp. 133-147.

Kentridge, S. "Pathology of a Legal System: Criminal Justice in South Africa" 128, 3 University of Pennsylvania Law Review (January 1980), pp. 603-621.

Khapoya, Vincent B. "The Politics of Decision: A Comparative Study of African Policy Toward the Liberation Movements" 12 (University of Denver Monograph Series in World Affairs, 1974- 75), 88pp.
  Khapoya develops a 9-point scale of support for liberation groups, and uses national aggregate data to test theories about the determinants of support.

Magstadt, T.M. "Ethiopia Great Terror" 25, 4 Worldview (1982), pp. 5-6.

Marais, N. "Effective Action Against the African National Congress" 6 South Africa Forum Position Paper No. 5 (March 1983).

"More Terrorism to Come, Say South African Guerrillas After Bloody Bank Takeover" 57 Jet (February 21, 1980), p. 15.

Morris, Michael Spence Lowdell South African Political Violence and Sabotage, 1 July-31 December 1982 (Cape Town, South Africa: Terrorism Research Center, 1982), 49 pp.
  Includes vignettes, incidents, a graph, and a table. Other time frames are also available.

Rich, Paul "Insurgency, Terrorism and the Apartheid System in South Africa" 32, 1 Political Studies (UK) (March 1984), pp. 68-85.

Searle, Chris "Struggling Against the 'Bandastan': An Interview with Attati Mpakati" 21, 1 Race and Class (Spring 1980), pp. 389-401.
Socialist political exile Mpakati has suffered many attempts to kill him--his hands were blown off by a letter bomb.

Sherman, Richard F. Eritrea in Revolution (Brandeis University, Political Science Department, Ph.D. dissertation, 1980).

Sundiata, Ibrahim K. "The Structure of Terror in a Small State: Equatorial Guinea" in Robin Cohen, ed. African Islands and Enclaves (Beverly Hills: Sage, 1983), pp.81-100.

Theodoropoulos, Christos "Support for SWAPO's War of Liberation in International Law" 26, 2 Africa Today (1979), pp. 39-48.

von Lowis, H. "SWAPO's Design for South West Africa/Namibia" 6 South Africa Forum Position Paper No. 6 (March 1983).

Wagoner, Fred E. Dragon Rouge: The Rescue of Hostages in the Congo (Washington, D.C.: National Defense University, 1980).

Willers, David "The Politics of Violence in South Africa" 11, 1 South Africa International (July 1980), pp. 29-41.

UNITED STATES

"Abortion Terrorism: The Toll Rises" 13 Ms, (March 1985), p. 19.

Alexander, Shana Anyone's Daughter: The Times and Trials of Patty Hearst (New York: Viking, 1979), 562 pp.

Al-Khashaf "Arab Terrorism American Style" 1 Clandestine Tactics and Technology (Gaithersburg, Maryland: International Association of Chiefs of Police, 1974), 14 pp.

Allen, Bob "Terrorism: Death on America's Doorstep" Genesis (1980), pp. 23-25, 98-99.
A sensationalistic treatment rife with factual errors.

Alpert, Jane Growing Up Underground (New York: William Morrow).
A look at how a well-educated young women's views moved from those of a radical terrorist to a feminist.

Alpert, Jane "I Bombed the Federal Building" 348 Rolling Stone (July 23, 1981), pp. 20-23, 62-63.
A former new leftist notes how she assisted two Quebec terrorists who hijacked a plane to Cuba in 1969 and helped her lover Sam Melville bomb 8 government and corporate buildings.

Audsley, David "Posse Comitatus: An Extremist Tax Protest Group" 6, 1 TVI: Terrorism Violence Insurgency Journal (Summer 1985), pp. 13-16.

Avrich, Paul The Haymarket Tragedy (Princeton University Press, 1984), 535 pp.
Reviewed by Nick Kotz "The Bomb That Shook America" Washington Post Book World (September 2, 1984), p. 5.

Avrich, Paul The Modern School Movement: Anarchism and Education in the United States (Princeton, New Jersey: Princeton University Press, 1980).
A discussion of attempts by Alexander Berkman and his colleagues to assassinate John D. Rockefeller in 1913-1914.

Blumberg, Janice Rothschild "The Bomb that Healed: A Personal Memoir of the Bombing of the Temple in Atlanta, 1958" 73, 1 American Jewish Historian (1983), pp. 20-38.

Bocklet, Richard "FBI Efforts to Make the US a 'Hard Target'; Despite its Open Borders, so far the US has Stayed Largely Free of Major Terrorist Attacks" 118 Scholastic Update (May 16, 1986), pp. 21-22.

Buckelew, Alvin H. Terrorism and the American Response (San Rafael, California: Mira Academic Press, 1984), 161 pp.

Bush, George "Prelude to Retaliation: Building a Governmental Consensus on Terrorism" 7, 1 SAIS Review (Winter-Spring 1987), pp. 1-9.

Casolaro, Dan "Are Mobsters, Terrorists Behind High Computer Crime Losses?" 13, 1 Security Systems Digest (January 13, 1982), pp. 1-3.

Charters, David A. "Terrorism and the 1984 Olympics" Conflict Quarterly (Summer 1983), pp. 37-47.

Collier, Peter and David Horowitz "Doing It: The Inside Story of the Rise and Fall of the Weather Underground" 379 Rolling Stone (September 30, 1982), pp. 19, 21-24, 26, 29-30, 35-36, 95-96, 98, 100.
Their lives were focused on violence, drugs, and sexual politics.

Cordes, Bonnie "Armenian Terrorism in America" 5, 1 TVI Journal (Summer 1984), pp. 22-27.

Crossen, Cynthia "Can Patty Hearst Blame it on F. Lee Bailey?" 3 American Lawyer (June 1981), pp. 16-21.
A look at Patty Hearst's suit to overturn her conviction on grounds that her attorney's judgment was compromised by his book contract about the case.

Davis, James R. The Terrorists: Youth, Bikes and Prison Violence (San Diego: Grossmont, 1978).

Decter, Midge "Notes from the American Underground" 73, 1 Commentary (1982), pp. 27-33.

DiLaura, Arnold E. "Preventing Terrorism: An Analysis of National Strategy" 7, 1 SAIS Review (Winter-Spring, 1987), pp. 11-26.

Diliberto, Gioia "The Radical Odyssey of Terrorist Kathy Boudin Ends with a Bang, Then a Whimper" 16 People (November 9, 1981), pp. 46-47.

Dixon, Senator Alan J. "The Terror Next Time" 33, 10 Playboy (October 1986), pp. 96-98, 122, 156-157.
A U.S. Senator warns that the US is poorly prepared for a major domestic terrorist attack.

Domestic Terrorism (Washington, D.C.: National Governors' Association, May 1979), 120 pp.

Downes, Richard "The Future Consequences of Illegal Immigration" 11, 2 The Futurist (April 1977), pp. 125-127.
Downes suggests that a possible outcome of continued Mexican immigration into the US is nuclear terrorism.

Dudley, J. Wayne "Hate Organizations of the 1940s: The Columbians, Inc." 42, 3 Phylon (1981), pp. 262-274.

Duncan, Evan "Terrorist Attacks on U.S. Official Personnel Abroad" 81 Department of State Bulletin (April 1981), pp. 34-37.

"Economic Sanctions to Combat International Terrorism" 149 Current Policy Special Report (Washington, D.C.: US Department of State, July 1986), 5 pp.
Adapted from a report prepared by the Department of State in response to a request from Senators Richard G. Lugar and Frank H. Murkowski for an analysis of the advisability of economic sanctions as a diplomatic tool to combat international terrorism.

Englade, Kenneth F. "Terrorism: in the Name of God and Country" 76 Liberty (January-February 1981), pp. 2-6.
The author warns that terrorism might be expected from Nazis, the KKK, the Christian Patriots Defense League.

Faber, Nancy "Long Since Returned to an Ordinary Life as a Young Mother, Patty Hearst Still Thinks About her Safety" 17 People (February 1, 1982), pp. 67-69.

Farrell, William Regis The United States Government Response to Terrorism, 1972-1980: An Organizational Perspective (Ann Arbor: University of Michigan, Ph.D. dissertation, 1981), 312 pp.

"FBI Analysis of Terrorist Incidents in the United States, 1982, Report prepared by Terrorist Research and Analytical Center, Terrorism Section, Criminal Investigation Division" in FBI Oversight and Authorization, Hearing before the Subcommittee on Security and Terrorism of the Committee on the Judiciary, US Senate (Washington, D.C.: 98th Congress, First session, February 2, 1983), pp. 43-65.

"FBI Reports Terrorism Spared in 1981" 7, 1 Law Enforcement News (January 11, 1981), p. 11.

"Feds Investigating Links Between Weather Underground, BLA, Foreign Terrorist Groups" 2, 10 Organized Crime (October 1981), pp. 1, 6, also available in 12, 22 Security Systems Digest (October 28, 1981), pp. 1,9.

Francis, Samuel T. "The Jackal Reborn: The Brinks Robbery and Terrorism in the United States" 7, 1 International Security Review (Spring 1982), pp. 99-124.

Francis, Samuel T. The Terrorist Underground in the United States (Washington, D.C.: The Nathan Hale Institute, 1984).

Franks, Lucinda "The Seeds of Terror" 131 New York Times Magazine (November 22, 1981), pp. 34-76.
A look at the Weather Underground, centering on Katherine Boudin and Diana Oughton.

Freed, Donald and Fred Landis Death in Washington: The Murder of Orlando Letelier (London: Zed, 1980).

Gitlin, Todd "White Heat Underground" 233 Nation (December 19, 1981), pp. 657, 669-674.
A history of the Weather Underground.

Gleason, John "A Poisson Model of Incidents of International Terrorism in the United States" 4, 1-4 Terrorism (1980), pp. 259-276.

Gonzales, Lawrence "The Targeting of America: A Special Report on Terrorism" 30 Playboy (May 1983), pp. 80-186.

Hearst, Patricia Campbell with Alvin Moscow Every Secret Thing (New York: Doubleday, 1981), 466 pp.
Reviewed by Jonathan Yardley "Patricia Hearst: Living to Tell the Tale" Washington Post Book World (December 20, 1981), p. 3.

Hearst, Patricia Campbell and Alvin Moscow "Patty Hearst: The California Heiress Relives the Terror of Kidnapping and Brainwashing by the SLA" 17 People (February 1, 1982), pp. 44-52.
Excerpts from Hearst's Every Secret Thing. A similar excerpt appeared in 29 Playboy (March 1982), pp. 77-81.

Hoffman, Bruce "The Cuban Anti-Castro Terrorist Movement" 5, 1 TVI Journal (Summer 1984), pp. 15-21.

Hoffman, Bruce "The Jewish Defense League" 5, 1 TVI Journal (Summer 1984), pp. 10-14.

Hofman, Steven "National Forces of Armed Liberation (i.e., FALN): A Puerto Rican Terrorist Group" (Washington, D. C.: Library of Congress, CRS, July 25, 1978), 7 pp.

Hurt, Henry "Search for a Terrorist Gang" 127 Reader's Digest (December 1985), pp. 166-174.
The hunt for members of the Sam Melville-Jonathan Jackson Unit.

"Incidents of Terrorism and Hijackings in the US 1980-1983" 5, 1 <u>TVI Journal</u> (Summer 1984), pp. 30-39.

"International Terrorism" <u>Gist</u> (Washington, D.C.: US Department of State, Bureau of Public Affairs, May 1987), 2 pp.
A review of the extent of the problem, including statistical summaries, and US efforts to combat terrorism.

Jenkins, Brian Michael "American Terrorism: More Bombast or Bomb Blasts?" 1, 4 <u>TVI Journal</u> (1980), pp. 2-8.

Jenkins, Brian Michael "The Spread of Violence: Will Terrorism Rise in the U.S.?" <u>Current</u> (November 1981), pp. 11-16.

Jenkins, Brian Michael "Terrorism in the United States" 5, 1 <u>TVI Journal</u> (Summer 1984), pp. 1-3, also available as (Santa Monica: The Rand Corporation, P-6474, May 1980), P6474), 20 pp.

Jenkins, Brian Michael "The Terrorist Threat to the Olympics" 5,1 <u>TVI Journal</u> (Summer 1984), pp. 51ff.

Jenkins, Brian Michael "The U.S. Response to Terrorism: A Policy Dilemma" 5, 4 <u>TVI: Terrorism Violence Insurgency Journal</u> (Spring 1985), pp. 31-35, also available in <u>Armed Forces Journal International</u> (April 1985), pp. 39-45.

Jenkins, Brian Michael, Sorrel Wildhorn and Marvin M. Lavin "Intelligence Constraints of the 1970s and Domestic Terrorism, prepared for the US Department of Justice" (Santa Monica: The Rand Corporation, 1982), 22 pp.

Judis, John "When the 'Visible Saints' Come Marching In" 46 <u>Progressive</u> (January 1982), pp. 21-23.
A look at the origins and values of the Weather Underground, comparing them to Protestant evangelicals.

Kavey, Fred "Animal Liberation: The New Trend in Terrorism" 29 <u>Guns & Ammo</u> (June 1985), pp. 28-32.

Kinney, Jean <u>An American Journey: The Short Life of Willy Wolfe</u> (New York: Simon and Schuster, 1979), 319 pp.
Wolfe was one of the members of the Symbionese Liberation Army.

"Law Makers and Law Enforcers Discuss Domestic Terrorism with Neil C. Livingstone, Philip C. Cox, George Bradford, Samuel T. Francis, Dario Marquez, and Michael K. Pilgrim" 7 <u>International Security Review</u> (Spring 1982).

Lerner, Steve "Terror Against Arabs in America: No More Looking the Other Way" 195 <u>New Republic</u> (July 28, 1986), pp. 20-23.

Lowry, Heath W. "The United States Congress and Adolf Hitler on the Armenians" 3,2 <u>Political Communication and Persuasion</u> (1985).

Mallowe, Mike "The City as a Sitting Duck: Philadelphia and Terrorists" 72 Philadelphia Magazine (July 1981), pp. 112-121. Argues that Philadelphia's tradition of giving material aid to diverse groups makes it particularly vulnerable. Notes the 1976 threatened poisoning of the water supply and the success of IRA fugitive Michael O'Rourke in hiding for 2 years in the city.

Marcotte, Paul "Terrorism Fears Hiked; Will Violence Spread to US?" 72 American Bar Association Journal (October 1, 1986), p. 42.

Meese, Edwin, III "The Five Tiers of Domestic Action" in Benjamin Netanyahu, ed. Terrorism: How the West Can Win (New York: Farrar, Straus, Giroux, 1986), pp. 165-167.

Melnichak, Joseph M. "Domestic Terrorism in America" 6, 1 TVI: Terrorism Violence Insurgency Journal (Summer 1985), pp. 17-19.

Meltzer, Milton The Truth About the Ku Klux Klan (New York: F. Watts, 1982), 120 pp.

"Miami: Melting Pot for the Hemisphere" 15, 28 Crime Control Digest (July 13, 1981), pp. 2-3.

Monroe, Charles P. "Addressing Terrorism in the United States" 463 Annals of the American Academy of Political and Social Science (September 1982), pp. 141-148. Looks at FBI successes in balancing civil rights and national security.

Motley, James Berry "Target America: The Undeclared War" in Neil C. Livingstone and Terrell E. Arnold, eds. Fighting Back: Winning the War Against Terrorism (Lexington: Lexington Books, 1986), pp. 59-84.

National Governors' Association Domestic Terrorism (Washington, D.C.: Center for Policy Research, 1979), 313 pp.

"Organized Crime in California: Part 2: Terrorism" (Bureau of Organized Crime and Criminal Intelligence, Office of the Attorney General of California, 1980).

"O-T-C Capsule Terrorism Escalates; Is Product Security Realistic?" 57 Advertising Age (March 24, 1986), pp. 1ff. Notes product recalls by Smith Kline Beckman in the wake of contamination of nonprescription drugs in the US.

Pinsky, Mark I. "The 'Quiet' Death of Alex Odeh: Terrorism Comes to Orange County" 13 Present Tense (Winter 1986), pp. 6-12. A discussion of the assassination in California of an Arab American political activist.

"Playboy Interview: Patricia Hearst" 29 Playboy (March 1982), pp. 69ff (14 pp).

Public Report of the Vice President's Task Force on Combatting Terrorism (Washington, D.C.: US Government Printing Office, February 1986).

Purnell, Susanna and Eleanor Wainstein "The Problems of US Businesses Operating Abroad in Terrorist Environments" (Santa Monica: The Rand Corporation, 1981).

Quainton, Anthony C. E. "US Prepares for Terrorism" 42, 5 The Shingle, Philadelphia Bar Association Quarterly Magazine (September-November 1979).

Rabinowitz, D. "Testing Haig Resolve Against Terrorists: The Case of Eain, Abu" 185, 24 New Republic (1981), pp. 12-14.

"Radicals Revisited: Weather Underground" 145 America (November 7, 1981), pp. 271.

Rankin, Ken "Safety Measures May Avert Tragedy of Food Tampering" 20 Nation's Restaurant News (March 10, 1986), p. F38.

Romeo, Peter "Fearful of Terrorism, Vacationers Stay in U.S." 20 Nation's Restaurant News (February 17, 1986), pp. 1-2.

Rose, Gregory E. "The Terrorists are Coming" 5 Politics Today (July-August 1978), pp. 22-26, 52, 54.
Argues that restrictions on the FBI will limit our ability to respond to domestic terrorism.

Sansing, John "No Man is Told by God What is the Right Way" 16 Washingtonian (March 1981), pp. 69-77.
Another look at the Hanafi Muslims.

Sater, William F. "Violence and the Puerto Rican Separatist Movement" 5, 1 TVI Journal (Summer 1984), pp. 4-9.

Shaw, Peter "The End of the Seventies" 185 New Republic (December 23, 1981), pp. 21-23.
A look at the October 1981 killings by the Weather Underground.

Sick, Gary "Terrorism: Its Political Uses and Abuses" 7, 1 SAIS Review (Winter-Spring, 1987), pp. 27-38.

Simpson, Peggy "A Strange Definition of Terrorism: Abortion Clinic Violence" 10 Working Woman (April 1985), p. 44.

Smith, Brent L. "Antiterrorism Legislation in the United States: Problems and Implications" 7, 2 Terrorism (1984), pp. 213-232.

Stein, Jeff "An Army in Exile" 12 New York (September 10, 1979), pp. 42-49.
Stein notes that the Cuban Nationalist Movement has extended operations out of Miami, and is now active in New York and New Jersey.

Steinberg, Jeffrey, et al. The Terrorist Threat to the 1984
Los Angeles Olympics: An EIR Multi-Client Special Report (New
York: Executive Intelligence Review, 1984), 145 pp.

Stocking, Kathleen "Ann Arbor's Famous Radicals, Then and Now:
A Personal Remembrance" 5 Monthly Detroit (February 1982), pp.
73-82.
A former student radical remembers the actions of the
University of Michigan members of the Weathermen and Pun
Plamondon, cofounder of the White Panther Party who was
charged with bombing the Ann Arbor CIA office.

Sturken, Barbara "Customer Refund Bill Faces Key Opposition in
N. Y. Legislature: Repayment of Cancellations Over Terrorism"
45 Travel Weekly (March 6, 1986), p. 3.

"Surrogate Warfare: The Threat Within" in Uri Ra'anan, Robert
L. Pfaltzgraff, Jr., Richard H. Shultz, Ernst Halperin, and
Igor Lukes Hydra of Carnage: International Linkages of
Terrorism: The Witnesses Speak (Lexington, Mass.: Lexington
Books, 1986), pp. 609-620.

"Terrorism in the United States" (Alexandria, Va.: Risks
International, 1982).

"Terrorism: 'The Plague of Modern Society'" 7 Washington
Spectator (September 1, 1981), reprinted in 73 Texas Observer
(September 25, 1981), pp. 16-18.
Argues that terrorism in the US is minor and largely racial.

Turner, Harry L. "Two Women: Lolita Lebron and Marie Haydee
Torres" 4 Nuestro (October 1980), pp. 39-40.
A discussion of women and the Armed Forces for the National
Liberation of Puerto Rico.

"Uncle Sam's Antiterrorism Plan" 24, 2 Security Management
(February 1980), pp. 39-50.

"US Can't Cope with World Terrorism, 4 Experts Argue" 13, 1
Security Systems Digest (January 13, 1982), pp. 8-9.

US House of Representatives, Committee on the Judiciary,
Subcommittee on Civil and Constitutional Rights "Domestic
Security Measures Relating to Terrorism: Hearings" (Ninety-
Eighth Congress, Second Session, February 8 and 9, 1984), 138
pp.

US Senate, Committee on the Judiciary, Subcommittee on
Security and Terrorism "Domestic Security (Levi) Guidelines):
Hearings" (Washington, D.C.: 97th Congress, Second Session,
June 24, 25, August 11 and 12, 1982), 587 pp.

"US Terrorism Cases Double in 1981, FBI's Webster Says" 16, 2
Crime Control Digest (January 11, 1982), p. 6; also available
in 13, 1 Security Systems Digest (January 13, 1982), p. 7.

Vestermark, Seymour D., Jr. "Extremist Groups in the US" 1
Clandestine Tactics and Technology (Gaithersburg, Maryland:
International Association of Chiefs of Police, 1974).

Wallop, Malcolm "The Role of Congress" in Uri Ra'anan, Robert L. Pfaltzgraff, Jr., Richard H. Shultz, Ernst Halperin, and Igor Lukes <u>Hydra of Carnage: International Linkages of Terrorism: The Witnesses Speak</u> (Lexington, Mass.: Lexington Books, 1986), pp. 251-258.

Webster, William H. "Fighting Terrorism in the United States" in Benjamin Netanyahu, ed. <u>Terrorism: How the West Can Win</u> (New York: Farrar, Straus, Giroux, 1986), pp. 168-170.

Webster, William H. "Terrorism in the United States" 6, 1 <u>Ohio Northern University Law Review</u> (1979), pp. 1-3.
The Director of the Federal Bureau of Investigation discusses the extent of terrorism in the US, and how his organization combats it.

Webster, William H. "The View of the Federal Bureau of Investigation" 17, 2 <u>International Society of Barristers Quarterly</u> (April 1982), pp. 283-295.
The Director of the FBI contributes to a symposium on terrorism and the law.

Weed, Steven <u>My Search for Patty Hearst</u> (New York: Crown, 1976).
Hearst's boyfriend describes his experiences during her kidnapping by the SLA.

Weiss, Ellen R. "Islamic Terrorist Threat in U.S. " 5, 1 <u>TVI Journal</u> (Summer 1984), pp. 28-29.

Wohl, James P. "A Terrorist's Guide to the 1984 Olympics" <u>Playboy</u> (May 1983).

Wolf, John B. "Terrorist Death Squad Activity in the United States" 6, 5 <u>Update Report</u> (Gaithersburg, Maryland: International Association of Chiefs of Police, 1980).

Wolf, John B. and G. R. Zoffer "The Menace of Terrorism in the United States" 41, 3 <u>Human Events: The National Conservative Weekly</u> (January 3, 1981), pp. 10-15.

Woods, Randall B. "The Miss Stone Affair" 32, 6 <u>American Heritage</u> (1981), pp. 26-29.
A look at the kidnapping of missionary Ellen M. Stone in September 1901 by Macedonian revolutionaries.

Woods, Randall B. "Terrorism in the Age of Roosevelt: The Miss Stone Affair, 1901-1902" 31, 4 <u>American Quarterly</u> (1979), pp. 478-495.

Wurth, Don E. "The Heinekin Kidnapping: A Case Study" 5, 1 <u>TVI Journal</u> (Summer 1984), pp. 40-42.

Responses

GENERAL

Amos, John W., II and Russell H. S. Stolfi "Controlling International Terrorism: Alternatives Palatable and Unpalatable" 463 Annals of the American Academy of Political and Social Science (September 1982), pp. 69-83.

Bass, Gail, Brian Michael Jenkins, Konrad Kellen and David Ronfeldt "Options for US Policy on Terrorism" (Santa Monica: The Rand Corporation, R-2764-RC, July 1981).

Beyl, R. A. "International Terrorism" 49, 1 Police Chief (1982), pp. 112-114.

Bienen, Henry and R. Gilpin "Economic Sanctions as a Response to Terrorism" 3, 1 Journal of Strategic Studies (May 1980), pp. 89-98.
The authors find that with very few exceptions, sanctions have not worked.

Blair, Robert A. "Fighting Terrorism: A Dissenting View" 146, 1 World Affairs (Summer 1983), pp. 114ff.

Branco, Frederico "A Worldwide Trend: The Need for Global Action" 32 World Press Review (September 1985), p. 35.

Cavanagh, Suzanne "US Government Agencies Dealing with Terrorism" (Washington, D.C.: Library of Congress, CRS, February 3, 1978), 11 pp.

Celmer, Marc A. Terrorism, U.S. Strategy, and Reagan Policies (Westport, Connecticut: Greenwood, 1987), 132 pp.

Civiletti, Benjamin R. "Terrorism: The Government's Response Policy" FBI Law Enforcement Bulletin (January 1979), pp. 19-22.

Clark, Robert S. "Guidelines in Scientific Research: Terrorism" Police Chief (May 1978), p. 87.

Colby, William E. "Taking Steps to Contain Terrorism" <u>New York Times</u> (July 8, 1984), p. 21E.

Collins, Whit "Counter-Terrorist Technology for Everyday Use" <u>Security World</u> (October 1978), pp. 18-20.

Daly, John Charles, moderator <u>Terrorism: What Should be our Response?</u> (Washington, D.C.: American Enterprise Institute, 1982), 25 pp.

"Data for Anti-Terrorism Trainers" 6, 11 <u>Training Aids Digest</u> (November 1981), pp. 7-8.

Delmas, Claude "Terrorism and the Open Society" 30, 5 <u>NATO Review</u> (December 1982), pp. 12-17.
A look at how the Atlantic Alliance is concerned.

Dobson, Christopher and Ronald Payne <u>Counterattack: The West's Battle Against the Terrorists</u> (New York: Facts on File, 1982), 198 pp.
Chapters cover actions taken by the UK, US, Israel, FRG, the Netherlands, France, Italy, Spain, and private corporations.

Drake, W. "Terrorism Preparedness for Local Elected Officials" (Washington, D.C.: Aimret, Inc., c/o National League of Cities, 1979-1980).
A $98,000 contract designed to provide a working conference and related activities for the mayors of the nation's 60 largest cities.

Dreher, Edward T. and James W. Manger "Investigation of Terrorist Activities" 4 <u>Clandestine Tactics and Technology</u> (Gaithersburg, Maryland: International Association of Chiefs of Police, 1983).

Evans, Ernest "Toward a More Effective U.S. Policy on Terrorism", in Yonah Alexander and Charles K. Ebinger, eds. <u>Political Terrorism and Energy: The Threat and Response</u> (New York: Praeger, 1982).

Farrell, William Regis "Organized to Combat Terrorism" in Neil C. Livingstone and Terrell E. Arnold, eds. <u>Fighting Back: Winning the War Against Terrorism</u> (Lexington: Lexington Books, 1986), pp. 49-58.

Farrell, William Regis <u>The U.S. Government Response to Terrorism: In Search of an Effective Strategy</u> (Boulder: Westview, 1982), 142 pp.
In his Ph.D. disseration at the University of Michigan, Farrell looks at definitions, organizational perspectives and priorities, and aspects of military involvement.

Ferrarotti, Franco "Even Terrorists are Human Beings" 43 <u>La Critica Sociologica</u> (Autumn 1977), in Italian.
Although we condemn their actions, we should nonetheless consider sparing the lives of terrorists.

<u>Figgie Report, Part 2: The Corporate Response to Fear of Crime</u>
(New York: Research and Forecasts, Inc., 1080), 91 pp.
A survey of Fortune 1000 senior executives on personal and
corporate responses and attitudes toward crime and personal
protection.

Flores, David A. "Export Controls and the U.S. Effort to
Combat International Terrorism" 13, 2 <u>Law and Policy in
International Business</u> (1981), pp. 521-590.

Fontain, Roger "Latin America" paper presented at the
Conference on Political Terrorism and Energy: The Threat and
Response, Washington, D.C., Georgetown University Center for
Strategic and International Studies, May 1, 1980

Frostmann, H. M. <u>International Political Terrorism and the
Approaching Emergence of the Authoritarian State</u> (1981), 146
pp.

Gallagher, Richard J. "Crisis Management--The Need--The
Response" 6 <u>Clandestine Tactics and Technology</u> (Gaithersburg,
Maryland: International Association of Chiefs of Police,
1979).

Gal-Or, Naomi <u>International Cooperation to Suppress Terrorism</u>
(New York: St. Martin's and London: Croom Helm, 1985), 390 pp.

Gellman, Barton "Though Terrorism May be Hard to Define, This
Administration Takes it Seriously" 13 <u>National Journal</u>
(September 12, 1981), pp. 1631-1635.

Georges-Abeyie, Daniel E. "Terrorism and the Liberal State: A
Reasonable Response" 4, 3 <u>Police Studies</u> (Fall 1981), pp. 34-
53.

Green, Leslie C. "Terrorism and Its Responses" 8, 1 <u>Terrorism</u>
(1985), pp. 33-78.

Hartman, Geoffrey "The Response to Terror: Introductory Notes"
5, 2 <u>Human Rights Quarterly</u> (May 1983), pp. 113-115.
An introduction to a symposium on Terror in the Modern Age:
The Vision of Literature, The Response of Law.

Hasbrook, Edward D. "United States Foreign Policy Through
Cloak and Dagger War Operations: Terrorism or Mandate of
National Security?" 11 <u>Oklahoma City University Law Review</u>
(Spring 1986), pp. 159-205.

Herold, H. "Perspektiven der Internationalen Fahnung Nach
Terroristen" 4 <u>Kriminalistik</u> (April 1980), pp. 165-171.

Hewitt, Christopher <u>The Effectiveness of Anti-Terrorist
Policies</u> (Lanham: University Press of America, 1984).

Hewitt, Christopher "Effectiveness of Counter-Terrorist
Policies" (contract research with the US Department of State,
Bureau of Intelligence and Research, Office of Long Range
Assessments and Research, 1981).

The study examines 5 major terrorist campaigns and government countermeasures.

Information Spectrum, Inc. Risk Assessment Techniques: A Handbook for Program Management Personnel (Washington, D.C.: US Government Printing Office, July 1983).

"Interpol's Resolutions on Terrorism" 6, 1 TVI: Terrorism Violence Insurgency Journal (Summer 1985), pp. 6-7.

"Interpol's Response to Terrorism" 6, 1 TVI: Terrorism Violence Insurgency Journal (Summer 1985), pp. 3-5.

Jenkins, Brian Michael "Combatting Terrorism: Some Policy Implications" (Santa Monica: The Rand Corporation, P-6666, August 1981), 11 pp., presented to the US Department of State Conference on Terrorism in the 1980s, May 21-22, 1981.

Jenkins, Brian Michael "Fighting Terrorism: An Enduring Task" (Santa Monica: The Rand Corporation, P-6585, February 1981), 8 pp.

Jenkins, Brian Michael "International Terrorism: Choosing the Right Target" (Santa Monica: The Rand Corporation, P-6597, March 1981), 8 pp.

Jenkins, Brian Michael "A Strategy for Combatting Terrorism" (Santa Monica: The Rand Corporation, P-6624, May 1981), 8 pp.

Jenkins, Brian Michael "Testimony Before the Senate Governmental Affairs Committee Regarding Senate Bill Against Terrorism, January 27, 1981" (Santa Monica: The Rand Corporation, P-6586, February 1981), 16 pp.

Jenkins, Brian Michael "A US Strategy for Combatting Terrorism" 3, 2-3 Conflict (1981), pp. 167-176.

Jones, Peter M. "The U.S. Stand Against International Terrorism; What are the U.S. Government's Policies Against Terrorism Abroad?" 118 Scholastic Update (May 16, 1986), pp. 19-20.

Kaiser, Frederick "Federal Anti-Terrorism Policy, Procedures, and Structure" (Washington, D.C.: Library of Congress, CRS, May 26, 1978), 9 pp.

Kerr, Donald M. "Coping With Terrorism" 8, 2 Terrorism (1985), pp. 113-126.

Kerstetter, Wayne R. "Terrorism and Intelligence" 3, 1-2 Terrorism (1979), pp. 109-115.
Kerstetter explains the process of analyzing intelligence data, and suggests that this process would be enhanced if the US government had a centrally-located data base on terrorism. He also suggests that a clearinghouse of information on terrorism be set up among nation-states.

Ketcham, Christine C. and Harvey J. McGeorge, II "Terrorist Violence: Its Mechanics and Countermeasures" in Neil C. Livingstone and Terrell E. Arnold, eds. Fighting Back: Winning the War Against Terrorism (Lexington: Lexington Books, 1986), pp. 25-34.

Kobetz, Richard W. "Anti-Terrorism Training Program Must Consider Basic Approaches to All Types of Threats" 6, 9 Training Aids Digest (September 1981), pp. 1, 6.

Kobetz, Richard W. "Ex-Hostage Laingen Warns Police: Train Now for Domestic Terrorism Incidents" 7, 3 Training Aids Digest (March 1982), pp. 1, 5.

Kupperman, Robert H. and Robert A. Friedlander "Terrorism and Social Control: Challenge and Response" 6, 1 Ohio Northern University Law Review (1979), pp. 52-59.
  After arguing that the terrorist threat is likely to increase in the next decade, particularly in the US, the authors suggest that intelligence, "high-pass" security barriers, and effective crisis management systems are needed.

Kupperman, Robert H. with Debra Van Opstal and David Williamson, Jr. "Terror, The Strategic Tool: Response and Control" 463 Annals of the American Academy of Political and Social Science (September 1982), pp. 24-38.

Labich, Kenneth "Coping with the Fear of Terror" 113 Fortune (May 26, 1986), pp. 57-59.

Laxalt, Paul "The Agenda for International Action" in Benjamin Netanyahu, ed. Terrorism: How the West Can Win (New York: Farrar, Straus, Giroux, 1986), pp. 186-189.

Lefever, Ernest W. Revolution, Terrorism, and US Policy (Washington, D.C.: Ethics and Public Policy Center, 1983), 13 pp.

Leventhal, Paul "Congressional Response" paper presented at the Conference on Political Terrorism and Energy: The Threat and Response, Washington, D.C., Georgetown University Center for Strategic and International Studies, May 1, 1980

Levy, Rudolf Intelligence in Terrorism Counter-action

Livingstone, Neil C. "Fighting Terrorism: The Private Sector" 3, 2-3 Conflict (1981), pp. 177-222.

Livingstone, Neil C. "Taming Terrorism: In Search of a New US Policy" 7 International Security Review (Spring 1982).

Livingstone, Neil C. The War Against Terrorism (Lexington: D.C. Heath, 1982), 219 pp.
  Reviewed by Danile E. Georges-Abeyie 75, 1 Journal of Criminal Law and Criminology (Spring 1984), p. 316.

Livingstone, Neil C. and Terrell E. Arnold "Fighting Back" in Neil C. Livingstone and Terrell E. Arnold, eds. Fighting Back: Winning the War Against Terrorism (Lexington: Lexington Books, 1986), pp. 229-248.

Livingstone, Neil C. and Terrell E. Arnold, eds. Fighting Back: Winning the War Against Terrorism (Lexington: Lexington Books, 1986), 288 pp.

Marvil, David "The Role of the Federal Energy Management Agency" paper presented at the Conference on Political Terrorism and Energy: The Threat and Response, Washington, D.C., Georgetown University Center for Strategic and International Studies, May 1, 1980

McEwen, Michael T. and Stephen Sloan "Terrorism Preparedness on the State and Local Level: An Oklahoma Perspective" Clandestine Tactics and Technology (Gaithersburg, Maryland: International Association of Chiefs of Police, 1980).

McGregor, Miriam "Terrorism Insurance for Travelers" National Underwriter--Life and Health Edition (May 17, 1986), p. 3.

Merari, Ariel, ed. On Terrorism and Combatting Terrorism: Proceedings of an International Seminar, Tel Aviv, 1979 (Tel Aviv: Jaffee Center for Strategic Studies, Tel Aviv University, and Frederick, Maryland: University Publications of America, 1984).

Mickolus, Edward F. Combatting International Terrorism: A Quantitative Analysis (New Haven, Conn.: Yale University, Department of Political Science, Ph.D. dissertation, 1981), 600 pp.
The author shows how quantitative methods can be used to study terrorism in general, specific terrorist campaigns, negotiating in hostage incidents, international legal approaches, etc. The rationale for the variables used in the ITERATE II dataset is also offered.

Miller, Abraham H. "Responding to the Victims of Terrorism: Psychological and Policy Implications" in Richard H. Shultz, Jr. and Stephen Sloan, eds. Responding to the Terrorist Threat: Security and Crisis Management (New York: Pergamon, 1980), pp. 93-104.

Miller, Rueben "Governments' Responses to International Terrorism" paper presented to the annual convention of the International Studies Association, Atlanta, March 27-31, 1984 (updated for the Graduate School of International Studies, University of Denver, 1985).

Motley, James B. US Strategy to Counter Domestic Political Terrorism (Washington, D.C.: National Defense University Press, 1983), 136 pp.

Netanyahu, Benjamin, ed. International Terrorism: Challenge and Response: Proceedings of the Jerusalem Conference on International Terrorism (New Brunswick: Transaction Books, and Jerusalem: Jonathan Institute, 1981), 383 pp.

Blurb reads: "In 1979, several world renowned politicians, ambassadors, academicians and journalists met at the Jerusalem Conference on Terrorism to discuss the origins, nature, and future of terrorism and to propose measures for combatting and defeating the international terror movements. This conference marked a turning point in the world's understanding of the problem of terrorism and what has to be done about it."

Netanyahu, Benjamin "Terrorism: How the West Can Win" in Benjamin Netanyahu, ed. Terrorism: How the West Can Win (New York: Farrar, Straus, Giroux, 1986), pp. 199-226, same title in 129 Reader's Digest (July 1986), pp. 110-115.

Netanyahu, Benjamin, ed. Terrorism: How the West Can Win (New York: Farrar, Straus, Giroux, 1986), 254 pp.
   Reviewed by John Gross 135 New York Times (April 25, 1986), pp. 23, C30; 127 Time (April 14, 1986), pp. 48-54; and Robert McFarlane "What Should Be Done About Terrorism" 16, 20 Washington Post Book World (May 18, 1986), pp. 1, 10.

Oakley, Robert B. "International Terrorism: Current Trends and the US Response" 706 Current Policy (Washington, D.C.: US Department of State, Bureau of Public Affairs, May 15, 1985), 7 pp.
   A reprint of a statement given by the Director of the Office for Counter-Terrorism and Emergency Planning, US Department of State, before the Senate Committees on Foreign Relations and on the Judiciary. Oakley discusses statistical trends, US policy, US actions, and the reason for increasing international cooperation.

Ofri, Arie "Intelligence and Counter-terrorism" 28, 1 Orbis (Spring 1984), pp. 41-52.

O'Neill, Bard E. and James Motley "Global Terrorism: What Should the US Do? Summary" in The 1980s: Decade of Confrontation? Proceedings of the Eighth Annual National Security Affairs Conference 13-15 July 1981, cosponsored by the National Defense University and the Under Secretary of Defense for Policy (Washington, D.C.: National Defense University Press, Fort Lesley J. McNair, 1981), pp. 237-241.

Patko, Imre "Az Egyesult Allamok Ket Taktikaja az 'Emberi Jogoktol' a 'Nemzetkozi Terrorizmusig' (The Two Tactics of the United States: From 'Human Rights' to 'International Terrorism')" 36, 3 Tarsadalmi Szemle (Hungary) (1981), pp. 61-72.
   Patko claims that the US shifted from concern for human rights under the Carter administration to combatting terrorism in the Reagan administration.

Peck, Malcolm C. "The Middle East" paper presented at the Conference on Political Terrorism and Energy: The Threat and Response, Washington, D.C., Georgetown University Center for Strategic and International Studies, May 1, 1980

Perez, Francis H. "Combatting Terrorism in the 1980s" 49, 1 Police Chief (1982), pp. 129-130.

Petrakis, Gregory "Counter-Terrorism: Measures for Meeting this Transnational Phenomenon" paper presented to the spring conference of the National Capital Area Political Science Association and the Internatioanl Studies Association-D.C. Chapter, Mount Vernon College, Washington, D.C., February 28, 1981.

Pfaltzgraff, Robert L., Jr. "Implications for American Policy" in Uri Ra'anan, Robert L. Pfaltzgraff, Jr., Richard H. Shultz, Ernst Halperin, and Igor Lukes Hydra of Carnage: International Linkages of Terrorism: The Witnesses Speak (Lexington, Mass.: Lexington Books, 1986), pp. 289-300.

Public Report of the Vice President's Task Force on Combatting Terrorism (Washington, D.C.: US Government Printing Office, 1986), 36 pp.
The report reviews and evaluates US policy and programs, describes the role of Congress, discusses the viewpoint of the American people, and examines the effect of the media. The group recommends improving international cooperation, enhancing intelligence capabilities, eliminating loopholes and ensuring coordination throughout the executive branch.

Quainton, Anthony C. E. "Combatting Terrorism: A Strategy of Partnership" 5 Police Chief (May 1980), pp. 22-24.

Quainton, Anthony C. E. "US Antiterrorism Program" 80, 2040 Department of State Bulletin (July 1980), pp. 75-77.
Using CIA statistics, Ambassador Quainton gives an overview of the terrorist problem and how the US deals with it.

Rabin, Yitzhak "An International Agency Against Terrorism" in Benjamin Netanyahu, ed. Terrorism: How the West Can Win (New York: Farrar, Straus, Giroux, 1986), pp. 182-185.

"Retailers, Manufacturers Aren't Letting Terrorism Scare Them" 200 Housewares (May 21, 1986), pp. 1-2.

Revel, Jean-Francois "Democracy Versus Terrorism" in Benjamin Netanyahu, ed. Terrorism: How the West Can Win (New York: Farrar, Straus, Giroux, 1986), pp. 196-198.

Rivers, Gayle The Specialist: Revelations of a Counterterrorist (New York: Stein and Day, 1985).

Rosenbaum, David M. "The United States" paper presented at the Conference on Political Terrorism and Energy: The Threat and Response, Washington, D.C., Georgetown University Center for Strategic and International Studies, May 1, 1980

Ryans, John K., Jr. and William L. Shanklin "How Managers Cope with Terrorism" 23, 2 California Management Review (Winter 1980), pp. 66-72.

Saddy, Fehmy "International Terrorism, Human Rights, and World Order" 5, 4 Terrorism (1982), pp. 325-352.

Sarkesian, Sam C. "Defensive Responses" in Uri Ra'anan, Robert L. Pfaltzgraff, Jr., Richard H. Shultz, Ernst Halperin, and Igor Lukes <u>Hydra of Carnage: International Linkages of Terrorism: The Witnesses Speak</u> (Lexington, Mass.: Lexington Books, 1986), pp. 201-220.

Sherizen, Sanford "US Policies and Practices Concerned with the Export of Crime Control Technology" paper presented at the convention of the International Studies Association, Toronto, March 24, 1979, 25 pp.
Sherizen looks at regulations of such exports, including police training, security equipment, and other forms of assistance.

Shultz, George "U.S. Government and Business: Our Common Defense Against Terrorism" 654 <u>Current Policy</u> (Washington, D.C.: US Department of State, Bureau of Public Affairs, February 4, 1985), 3 pp.
A reprint of an address by the US Secretary of State before the American Society for Industrial Security, Arlington, Virginia.

Shultz, Richard H., Jr. "Policy Responses to Terrorist Tactics: A Critical Review" paper presented to the annual convention of the International Studies Association, Los Angeles, March 18-22, 1980, published as "The State of the Operational Art: A Critical Review of Anti-Terrorist Programs" in Richard H. Shultz, Jr. and Stephen Sloan, eds. <u>Responding to the Terrorist Threat: Security and Crisis Management</u> (New York: Pergamon, 1980), pp. 18-58.

Shultz, Richard H., Jr. and Stephen Sloan, eds. <u>Responding to the Terrorist Threat: Security and Crisis Management</u> (New York: Pergamon, 1980), 261 pp.

Sloan, Stephen "Simulating Terrorism: An Analysis of Findings Related to Tactical, Behavioral and Administrative Responses of Participating Police and Military Forces" paper presented at the annual convention of the International Studies Association, Los Angeles, March 18-22, 1980, published in Richard H. Shultz, Jr., and Stephen Sloan, eds. <u>Responding to the Terrorist Threat: Security and Crisis Management</u> (New York: Pergamon, 1980), pp. 115-133.

St. John, Peter "Analysis and Response of a Decade of Terrorism" <u>International Perspectives (Canada)</u> (September-October 1981), pp. 2-5.
In the 1980s, we are likely to see more resorts to assassinations and high-tech terrorism, along with more resort to terrorism in the North-South conflict. Intelligence networks, police, and the press must cooperate against this threat.

Stinson, James and Edward Samuel Heyman "Analytic Approaches for Investigating Terrorist Crimes" 6 <u>Clandestine Tactics and Technology</u> (Gaithersburg, Maryland: International Association of Chiefs of Police, 1980).

Stohl, Michael "The Failure of the Reagan Administration's Counter-terrorism Policy" 12 World (Fall 1985), pp. 39-43.

Stohl, Michael "Responding to the Terrorist Threat: Fashions and Fundamentals" in Michael Stohl, ed. The Politics of Terrorism; Third Edition: Revised and Expanded (New York: Marcel Dekker, 1987).

Stohl, Michael "Terrorism, States and State Terrorism: The Reagan Administration in the Middle East" Arab Studies Quarterly (Spring 1987).

Sweet, William "Anti-Terrorism: New Priority in Foreign Policy" Editorial Research Reports (March 27, 1981), pp. 231-248.

Tanham, George "Southeast Asia" paper presented at the Conference on Political Terrorism and Energy: The Threat and Response, Washington, D.C., Georgetown University Center for Strategic and International Studies, May 1, 1980

Taylor, Robert W. "Managing Terrorist Incidents" 12, 4 The Bureaucrat (Winter 1983-84), pp. 53-58.
The author borrows liberally from CIA and US State Department statistics to look at the scope of the problem and difficulties the US bureaucratic system poses in combatting it.

"Ten Responses: Proposals for Terrorist Crises" 32 World Press Review (September 1985), p. 40.

"Terrorism Alters Many European Travel Plans" 42 Footwear News (May 12, 1986), pp. 1-2.

Trent, Darrell M. "A National Policy to Combat Terrorism" 9 Policy Review (Summer 1979), pp. 41-54.

"TVI Interview: Commander Ray Kendall, Secretary General of Interpol" 6, 1 TVI: Terrorism Violence Insurgency Journal (Summer 1985), pp. 8-11.

"TVI Interview: John Simpson, President of Interpol's General Assembly" 6, 1 TVI Journal (Summer 1985), p. 12.

The US Government Anti-Terrorism Program, prepared by the Executive Committee on Terrorism for the Special Coordination Committee of the National Security Council (US Department of Justice, June 1979).

US Senate "Act for Rewards for Information Concerning Terrorist Acts: S. 2625" (Washington, D.C.: 98th Congress, 2nd Session, May 2, 1984), 7 pp.
Sponsored by Senators Thurmond and Denton.

US Senate, Committee on the Judiciary, Subcommittee on Security and Terrorism Government Files: Retention or Destruction? Hearing (Washington, D.C.: US Government Printing Office, October 5, 1981), 564 pp.

Vedovato, Giuseppe "L'Apporto Internationale alla Lotta Contro il Terrorismo e la Criminalita Organizzata" 50, 3 <u>Rivista di Studi Politici Internazionali</u> (July-September 1983), pp. 451-458.

Wardlaw, Grant <u>Political Terrorism: Theory, Tactics, and Counter-Measures</u> (Cambridge: Cambridge University Press, 1982).

Wardlaw, Grant "State Response to International Terrorism: Some Cautionary Comments" in Robert O. Slater and Michael Stohl, eds. <u>Current Perspectives on International Terrorism</u> (London: Macmillan, 1987).

Waugh, William Lee, Jr. <u>International Terrorism: How Nations Respond to Terrorists--A Comparative Policy Analysis</u> (Salisbury, North Carolina: Documentary Publications, 1982), 326 pp.

Waugh, William Lee, Jr. <u>International Terrorism: Theories of Response and National Policies</u> (University of Mississippi, Ph.D. dissertation, 1980), 350 pp.

Wilkinson, Paul "Double Standards: Barriers to International Cooperation" 32 <u>World Press Review</u> (September 1985), pp. 36-37.

Wilkinson, Paul "Proposals for a Liberal-Democratic Government Response to Terrorism and Low-Intensity Violence at Domestic and International Levels" in Brian Michael Jenkins, conference director <u>Terrorism and Beyond: An International Conference on Terrorism and Low-Level Conflict</u> (Santa Monica: The Rand Corporation, R-2714-DOE/DOJ/DOS/RC, December 1982), pp. 203-232.

Wilkinson, Paul "Proposals for Government and International Responses to Terrorism" in Paul Wilkinson, Guest Editor "British Perspectives on Terrorism 5, 1-2 <u>Terrorism</u> (1981), pp. 161-193.

Wilkinson, Paul "Terrorism, International Dimensions: Answering the Challenge" 113 <u>Conflict Studies</u> (1979), 22 pp.

Williams, Sharon G. <u>Insurgency Terrorism: Attitudes, Behavior and Response</u> (City University of New York, Political Science Department, Ph.D. dissertation, 1980).

Wolf, John B. "Antiterrorism: Objectives and Operations" 4 <u>Clandestine Tactics and Technology</u> (Gaithersburg, Maryland: International Association of Chiefs of Police, 1978).

Wolf, John B. "Anti-Terrorism: Technological, Corporate and Personal Considerations" 6, 2 <u>Update Report</u> (Gaithersburg, Maryland: International Association of Chiefs of Police, 1980).

Wolf, John B. "Assessing the Performance of a Terrorist and an Anti-Terrorist Organization" in Donald E. J. MacNamara and

Philip John Stead, eds. New Dimensions in Transnational Crime (New York: John Jay, 1982).

Wolf, John B. "Enforcement Terrorism" 3, 4 Police Studies: The International Review of Police Development (1981), pp. 45-54.

Wolf, John B. Fear of Fear: A Survey of Terrorist Operations and Controls in Open Societies (New York: Plenum, 1981), 256 pp.

Wolf, John B. "Target Analysis, Parts I and II" 4 Clandestine Tactics and Technology (Gaithersburg, Maryland: IACP, 1978).

Zerb, Milton R. "Defending Against Terrorism: Practical Lessons for the Diplomat" Georgetown Magazine (March-April, 1983), pp. 13-14, 21.

PHYSICAL SECURITY AND EXECUTIVE PROTECTION

"Adequacy of U.S. Marine Corps Security in Beirut" 7, 3 Terrorism (1984), pp. 341-346.

"An Interview with Ed Best, Director of Security at the Los Angeles Olympics" 5, 2 Terrorism, Violence, Insurgency Journal (Fall 1984), pp. 1-6.

Andriole, Stephen J. and Judith Ayres Daly "Potential Application of Computer-Based Crisis Management Aids to Problems of Physical Security" in Joel J. Kramer, ed. The Role of Behavioral Science in Physical Security: Proceedings of the Third Annual Symposium, May 2-4, 1978 (Washington, D.C.: National Bureau of Standards Special Publication 480-38, 1979), pp. 47-74.

Applebome, Peter "Jack Sparks, Secret Agent" 13 Texas Monthly (February 1985), pp. 88ff.
A profile of the head of the International Association of Research, a private anti-terrorist group.

"Assessment of Terrorism as It Impacts on the Business Community" (Harvard Business School and Yale School of Business and Management, joint student research project, August 1980).

Ashley, Steven "Can Technology Stop Terror in the Air?" 227 Popular Science (November 1985), pp. 68-73.

"Atkins to Keep Buyers out of Europe 90 Days; Other Retail Firms React to Terrorism" 16 Daily New Record (April 18, 1986), pp. 2-3.
Frederick Atkins, Inc., an import-export firm, fears terrorist attacks in Europe.

Australian Parliament Protective Security Review: Report; Unclassified Version (Canberra: Australian Government Publishing Service, 15 May 1979), 360 pp.

Bell, J. Bowyer "The Terrorist Threat to US Businesses Abroad" 5 Enterprise (August 1981), pp. 2-4.

Bevan, Thomas E. "Biosensor for Assessment of Defence Performance Capability" in Joel J. Kramer, ed. The Role of Behavioral Science in Physical Security: Proceedings of the Third Annual Symposium, May 2-4, 1978 (Washington, D.C.: National Bureau of Standards Special Publication 480-38, 1979), pp. 1-6.

Blum, J. "The Protection of Persons and Installations at Risk: The German Way" Police Studies (December 1978), pp. 53-61.

Chase, Dennis "Coping With Terrorism: Wary Execs 'Looking Over Shoulder'" 57 Advertising Age (April 21, 1986), pp. 3-4.
  Corporate executives are wary of flying to Europe. Includes related article on executive trips.

Chester, C.V., G. A. Cristy, and E.P. Wigner "Emergency Technology" (Oak Ridge, Tennessee: US Department of Energy, Oak Ridge National Laboratory, 1980).
  The research analyzes potential large scale threats to public health and safety from program areas of DOE responsibility, and develops countermeasures to eliminate them or reduce the hazard to the public. Terrorist attacks are included in the scope of inquiry.

Cole, Richard B. Executive Security: A Corporate Guide to Effective Response to Abduction and Terrorism (New York: Wiley, 1980), 323 pp.

Cooper, H. H. A. "Evaluating the Terrorist Threat: Principles of Applied Risk Assessment" 6 Clandestine Tactics and Technology (Gaithersburg, Maryland: International Association of Chiefs of Police, 1979).

Cooper, H. H. A. and Richard W. Kobetz "Advanced Counterterrorism Training" 5, 6 Assets Protection (November/December 1980), pp. 21-24.

Cooper, Vi Bashian "Waging War on Corporate Terrorism" 8 Colorado Business (August 1981), pp. 148-151.

Denton, R. W., C. Dorman, LCDR, USN, and R. J. Fyfe Program for the Protection of Offshore Energy Assets (Panama City, Florida: Naval Coastal Systems Laboratory, March 1974, NSCL Report 203-74).

Dunkin, T. "Terrorists Beware!--Werbell's Cobray School" 5, 1 Soldier of Fortune (January 1980), pp. 46-50.

Ebersole, John F., LCDR, USCG "International Terrorism and the Defense of Offshore Facilities" 105, 9 U.S. Naval Institute Proceedings (September 1979), pp. 919ff.

"Executive Protection Program (EPP)" 59 Personnel Journal (November 1980), pp. 915-917.

A guideline for dealing with and responding to terrorist activities involving corporate employees and their families both in the US and overseas.

Feiler, Stuart I. "Terrorism: Is Tourism Really the Target?" 20 Hotels and Restaurants International (October 1986), pp. 85-88.
Includes a list of 55 active terrorist groups.

FitzPatrick, T.K. "The Prudent Traveler: A Basic Primer" 5, 6 Assets Protection (November-December 1980), pp. 25-29.

Flanagan, J. C. "Terrorism and US Industry" (Washington, D.C.: US Department of Commerce, Bureau of Domestic Commerce, for the US Department of Justice Law Enforcement Assistance Administration, 1980).
A study of terrorist objectives in attacking US corporate interests.

Gallery, Sherry M. "Guarding Against Terrorism" Dun's Business Month (September 1986), p. 72.

Gillan, Linda "Oil Field Terrorism: Nobody Wants the Bomb" 193 World Oil (October 1981), pp. 140-142.
Gillan warns that Federal agencies are not equipped to handle a terrorist attack on US oil fields.

Godwin, Nadine "Insurance Firm Adds Terrorism Coverage" 45 Travel Weekly (April 21, 1986), p. 4.
An interview with Edward S. Shulman, President of Access America, Inc.'s on anti-terrorism services.

Graham, Ellen "Seeking Security: Terrorism Bolsters Use of More Bodyguards by More Corporations; Muscle and Street Savvy are Tools of the Practitioner; Attending the Best Parties; How to Spot Would-be Killer" Wall Street Journal (May 1, 1986), p. 1.

"Halt: Boon from Barrier Boom" 109 Fortune (February 6, 1984), p. 13
A discussion of hydraulic steel barricades manufactured by Delta Scientific Corporation.

Harris, Douglas H. "Link Analysis of Threats and Physical Safeguards" in Joel J. Kramer, ed. The Role of Behavioral Science in Physical Security: Proceedings of the Third Annual Symposium, May 2-4, 1978 (Washington, D.C.: National Bureau of Standards Special Publication 480-38, 1979), pp. 17-22.

Harvey, Michael "A New Corporate Weapon Against Terrorism" 28 Business Horizons (January-February 1985), pp. 42-47.

Heard, Alex "Bugging the Bomb Detectors" Washington Post Magazine (November 16, 1986), pp. 11-12.
A satiric look at the charlatans working in the field of executive protection.

Henze, Paul B. "Coping With Terrorism" 9 Fletcher Forum (Summer 1985), pp. 307-323.

A look at Soviet support for terrorism, and how management should handle terrorism.

International Symposium on Maritime Security and Terrorism (Arlington, Va.: ISIS Associates, 1981), 78 pp.

Jacobson, Kenneth H. "The Corporation and International Terrorism" (Menlo Park, California: Business Intelligence Program, SRI International, 1981), 20 pp.

Jenkins, Brian Michael, ed. Terrorism and Personal Protection (Stoneham, Massachusetts: Butterworth, 1985), 480 pp.
 Contents include How Terrorists Look at Kidnappings; Kidnapping as a Terrorist Tactic; Kidnapping in the US; An Economic Analysis of Security, Recovery, and Compensation in Terrorist Kidnapping; The Payment of Ransom; Managing the Episode; Negotiations with Kidnappers; The Hostage Recovery; Talking to Terrorists; The Function and Use of Bodyguards; Protecting the Office; Transportation Security; Avoiding Capture and Surviving Captivity; Reentry.

Kapstein, Jonathan "How US Executives Dodge Terrorism Abroad" Business Week (May 12, 1986), p. 40.

Karen, R. "Corporations and Governments: Delicate Balance in Security Matters" 24, 3 Security Management (March 1980), pp. 10-17.

Karpel, Craig S. "The Victims of Terrorism Strike Back" 10 Penthouse (August 1979), pp. 71-72, 174-180.
 A look at how the International Security Group provides executive protection courses.

Killam, E. W. "Terrorism: An Introduction for Rural Law Enforcement Officers" 28, 4 Law and Order (April 1980), pp. 38-44.

Kilmarx, Robert A. "Terrorism and Business: Future Prospects" paper presented at the Conference on Political Terrorism and Energy: The Threat and Response, Washington, D.C., Georgetown University Center for Strategic and International Studies, May 1, 1980

Kobrin, Stephen "Political Risk: A Review and Reconsideration" Journal of International Business Studies (Spring 1979).

Kobrin, Stephen "When Does Political Instability Result in Increased Investment Risk?" 12 Columbia Journal of World Business (Fall 1978).

Kocher, Charles Horace Terrorism: Threat to Industrial Security (California State University at Long Beach, M.S. thesis, 1978), 121 pp.

Kraar, Louis "The Multinationals Get Smarter about Political Risks" Fortune (March 24, 1980), p. 92.

Kuhne, Robert J. and Robert F. Schmitt "The Terrorist Threat to Corporate Executives: Many Multinational Corporations are Forming Crisis Management Teams which Deal with the Eventuality of a Terrorist Threat Using the Same Techniques They Apply to Other Management Problems" 22 Business Horizons (December 1979), pp. 77-82.

Lamb, John and James Etheridge "DP: The Terror Target" 32 Datamation (February 1, 1986), pp. 44-46.
European computer facilities have recently come under attack.

Leibstone, Marvin "Corporation Terror: Violence and the Business Community" (Gaithersburg, Maryland: International Association of Chiefs of Police, 1980), 21 pp.

Leibstone, Marvin "Terrorism and the International Business Community" 6 Clandestine Tactics and Technology (Gaithersburg, Maryland: International Association of Chiefs of Police, n.d.).

Levinson, Eric "Site Hardening" 5, 6 Assets Protection (November/December 1980), pp. 29-35.

Lewis, G. W. "Biotechnology Predictors of Physical Security Personnel Performance" (San Diego, California: US Department of Defense, US Navy, Personnel Research and Development Center, 1981).
The research determines the feasibility of using biotechnology procedures such as event related brain potentials, muscle activity, and other psychophysiological measures to improve predictions of personnel reliability and performance effectiveness. Reactions to terrorist attacks and improving security guard vigilance are key areas of inquiry.

Livingstone, Neil C. "Fighting Terrorism: The Private Sector" 3, 2-3 Conflict (1981), pp. 177-219.

Lofting, Christopher "On Terrorism: Advice to the Wary" 368 Journal of Commerce and Commercial (April 18, 1986), pp. 1Aff.
An interview with Ed De Santis and Anthony Scotti, including discussions of Pinkerton's protection of executives.

MacBain, M. "Will Terrorism Go to Sea?" 24, 8 Security Management (August 1980), pp. 76-94, reprinted from Sea Power (January 1980).

Mack, Toni "Looking Out for Number One" 134 Forbes (December 31, 1984), pp. 126-127.
A discussion of the increasing use of bodyguards for executive protection.

"Major Points to Consider for Better Executive Protection" 12, 2 Security Letter (January 18, 1982), pp. 1-4.

Malley, Joseph A. "Preparing and Protecting Personnel and Property Prior to a Terrorist Attack" in Patrick J. Montana and George S. Roukis, eds. Managing Terrorism: Strategies for the Corporate Executive (Westport, Conn.: Quorum Books, 1983), pp. 73-90.

Marks, Jim "Terrorism: An International Threat" 41 <u>Journal of Insurance</u> (September-October 1980), pp. 13-18.

Marvil, David L. "The Role of the Federal Emergency Management Agency in Response to the Consequences of Terrorism" in Brian Michael Jenkins, conference director <u>Terrorism and Beyond: An International Conference on Terrorism and Low-Level Conflict</u> (Santa Monica: The Rand Corporation, R-2714-DOE/DOJ/DOS/RC, December 1982), pp. 266-272.

McClure, Brooks "Corporate Vulnerability---And How to Assess It", paper presented at the Conference on Political Terrorism and Energy: The Threat and Response, Washington, D.C., Georgetown University Center for Strategic and International Studies, May 1, 1980, published in Yonah Alexander and Charles K. Ebinger, eds. <u>Political Terrorism and Energy: The Threat and Response</u> (New York: Praeger, 1982).

McClure, Brooks "Operational Aspects of Terrorism" 17 <u>Williamette Law Review</u> (Winter 1980), pp. 165-184.

McDowell, Charles and John P. Harlan "Police Response to Political Crimes and Acts of Terrorism: Some Dimensions for Consideration" paper presented to the annual convention of the American Society of Criminology, Toronto, October 30-November 2, 1975.

McGeorge, Harvey J., II and Christine Ketcham "Protection of Senior Executives" 146, 3 <u>World Affairs</u> (Winter 1983-84), pp. 277ff.

McGeorge, Harvey J., II and Charles F. Vance "Executive Protection: Living Long in a Dangerous World" in Neil C. Livingstone and Terrell E. Arnold, eds. <u>Fighting Back: Winning the War Against Terrorism</u> (Lexington: Lexington Books, 1986), pp. 95-108.

McGuire, E. Patrick "International Terrorism and Business Security" 65 <u>Conference Board Information Bulletin</u> (October 1979), 22 pp.
 Although offering a creditable study of measures which corporations can and have taken to prevent terrorist acts, McGuire frequently uses incommensurable statistics to illustrate points.

Melanson, Philip H. <u>The Politics of Protection: The US Secret Service in the Terrorist Age</u> (New York: Praeger, 1984), 215 pp.

Metz, George F. "Teaching Officers How to Deal with Terrorist Vehicle Ambushes" 6, 7 <u>Training Aids Digest</u> (July 9181), pp. 1-2.

Michal, Ed "Diplomatic Protection" <u>Foreign Service Journal</u> (June 1981), pp. 23-25, 40.

Moin, David and J. D. Kidd "Retailers' Trips in Jeopardy" 151 <u>Womens Wear Daily</u> (April 28, 1986), pp. 1-2.
 Purchasing agents fear terrorist attacks in Europe.

Montana, Patrick J. and Stacey M. Krinsky "Organizations Serving the Executive Protection Field" in Patrick J. Montana and George S. Roukis, eds. Managing Terrorism: Strategies for the Corporate Executive (Westport, Conn.: Quorum Books, 1983), pp. 135-160.

Montgomery, John M. "The Effective Use of Intrusion Alarms" 5 Clandestine Tactics and Technology (Gaithersburg, Maryland: International Association of Chiefs of Police, n.d.).

Moore, Arthur C. "The Bunkerization of Washington" 21 Washingtonian (July 1986), pp. 96-97.
A look at security measures at the White House and elsewhere in Washington.

Moore, R. T. "Computerized Site Security Monitor and Response System" 3, 1 Journal of Security Administration (June 1980), pp. 29-41.

"Multinational Firms Act to Protect Overseas Workers from Terrorism" Wall Street Journal (April 29, 1986), pp. 31-33.

Newcomer, H. A. and J. W. Adkins "Terrorism and the Business Executive" 59, 11 Personnel Journal (1980), pp. 913-915.

NiCastro, James R., B. Woolson and J. Blancy "An Overview of the Machine Analysis of the Internal Threat (MAIT) Analysis System" in Joel J. Kramer, ed. The Role of Behavioral Science in Physical Security: Proceedings of the Third Annual Symposium, May 2-4, 1978 (Washington, D.C.: National Bureau of Standards Special Publication 480-38, 1979), pp. 23-28.

Nudell, Mayer and Norman Antokol "Contingency Planning for Terrorism: Part 1" 33 Risk Management (July 1986), pp. 20-23.
A former State Department terrorism expert discusses security measures business executives and corporations can take, and the utility of risk insurance policies.

Nudell, Mayer and Norman Antokol "Contingency Planning for Terrorism: Part 2" 33 Risk Management (August 1986), pp. 30-35.
Article includes a chart on a possible crisis management center configuration, emergency notification and initial activities, and the planning process.

Nydele, Ann "Designing for Terrorism and Other Aggressions" 174 Architectural Record (January 1986), pp. 37-40.

Oakley, Robert B. "Combating International Terrorism" 667 Current Policy (Washington, D.C.: US Department of State, Bureau of Public Affairs, March 5, 1985), 7 pp.
A reprint of a statement by the Director of the Office for Counter-Terrorism and Emergency Planning of the US Department of State, before the Subcommittees on Arms Control, International Security, and Science and on International Operations of the House Foreign Affairs Committee. Oakley gives statistics on terrorism in 1984, then explains the goals of US counterterrorism policy, citing the need for effective

coordinated action, protection of US presence abroad, international cooperation, and effective intelligence efforts. New initiatives are also discussed.

Olin, W. Ronald "An Evaluation of the United States Counter Terrorism Response Capability" <u>Police Chief</u> (June 1979), pp. 34, 36.

O'Reilly, Brian "Business Copes With Terrorism" 113 <u>Fortune</u> (January 6, 1986), pp. 47-52.
Includes a related article on terrorism against business.

Perez, Marta Brito "Clandestine Tactics and Technology" 48 <u>Police Chief</u> (May 1981), pp. 50-51.
A discussion of a service provided on the International Association of Chiefs of Police, which gives information on terrorism to subscribers.

"Personal and Family Security: Security Against Terrorism" 25 minute 16 mm. color film (Motorola Teleprograms, Inc., 1975).

Pizer, Harry "Executive Protection: The View From the Private Security Sector" in Richard H. Shultz, Jr. and Stephen Sloan, eds. <u>Responding to the Terrorist Threat: Security and Crisis Management</u> (New York: Pergamon, 1980), pp. 105-114.

Purnell, Susanna W. and Eleanor S. Wainstein "The Problems of US Businesses Operating Abroad in Terrorist Environments" (Washington, D.C.: The Rand Corporation, R-2842-DOC, November 1981), 103 pp.

Reber, J. R. "Threat Analysis Methodology" 2 <u>Clandestine Tactics and Technology</u> (Gaithersburg, Maryland: International Association of Chiefs of Police, 1976).

"Release of General Dozier is a Blow Against Terrorism and a Reminder to Improve DP Efforts" 12, 3 <u>Security Letter</u> (February 1, 1982), p. 3.
A discussion of computers in police work against terrorism.

Rescorla, R. "Adapting and Adopting: Tailoring the Company Security Plan to Meet the Terrorist Challenge" 1, 7 <u>TVI Journal</u> (1980), pp. 7-12.

Robb, Maureen "US Strives to Combat Terrorism at Sea Through The International Maritime Organization" 368 <u>Journal of Commerce and Commercial</u> (May 19, 1986), p. 12A.

Russell, A. Lewis <u>Corporate and Industrial Security</u> (Houston: Gulf, 1980), 275 pp.

Russell, Charles A. "Businesses Becoming Increasing Targets" in Patrick J. Montana and George S. Roukis, eds. <u>Managing Terrorism: Strategies for the Corporate Executive</u> (Westport, Conn.: Quorum Books, 1983), pp. 55-72.

Ryans, John K., Jr., and William L. Shanklin "How Managers Cope with Terrorism" 23 <u>California Management Review</u> (Winter 1980), pp. 66-72.

Ryans, John K., Jr., and William L. Shanklin "Terrorism and the Multinational Company" 30, 2 Business (March-April 1980), pp. 2-7.

"Safety Tips for Safe Travel" (Washington, D.C.: US Department of Defense, 1986, available from the DOD Public Affairs Office).
Advice on how to avoid of minimize trouble with terrorists. Although originally intended for DOD employees and families, the guide was made available to the public. There is no indication on the pamphlet of where it is printed.

Schnabolk, Charles Physical Security: Practices and Technology (Boston: Butterworths, 1983), 388 pp.

Scotti, A. "How to Purchase an Armored Vehicle" 6 Assets Protection (January/February 1981).

Scotti, A. "Transportation Security: Ambush Countermeasures and Tactics" 5 Clandestine Tactics and Technology (Gaithersburg, Maryland: International Association of Chiefs of Police, n.d.).

Shapiro, Stacy "Airlines' War Risk Rates Likely to Rise in Light of Losses Linked to Terrorism" 19 Business Insurance (July 1, 1985), pp. 2-3.

Shaw, Paul D. "Planning for Executive Protection" 3 Clandestine Tactics and Technology (Gaithersburg, Maryland: International Association of Chiefs of Police, 1976).

Shultz, George "Enhancing Diplomatic Security" 788 Current Policy (Washington, D.C.: US Department of State, Bureau of Public Affairs, February 14, 1986), 4 pp.
A reprint of a statement by the US Secretary of State before the Senate Committee on Foreign Relations, in which he outlines the changes the administration proposes for protecting US embassies and other overseas facilities.

Shultz, Richard H. "International Terrorism: Operational and R&D Countermeasures" 5 Clandestine Tactics and Technology (Gaithersburg, Maryland: International Association of Chiefs of Police, 1979).

Siljander, Raymond P. Terrorist Attacks: A Protective Service Guide for Executives, Body Guards and Policemen (Springfield: Thomas, 1980), 342 pp.

"Study Discusses Steering Clear on Terror Attacks on Vehicles" 7, 22 Law Enforcement News (December 21, 1981), p. 2.

"Survival Tactics" 22 minute 16 mm. color film (Woroner Films, Inc., Motorola Teleprograms, Inc., 1973).

"Terrorism: Safety Tips" Business Week (July 8, 1985), pp. 109-110.

Tophoven, Rolf GSG9: German Response to Terrorism (Koblenz: Bernard and Graefe Verlag, 1984), 124 pp.

"Traveling Incognito: Terrorism Threatens US Athletes" 8 _Women's Sports and Fitness_ (September 1986), p. 20.

Tuthill, Mary "Cloak-and-Dagger Men Aid Executives" 70 _Nation's Business_ (August 1982), p. 67.

"US Trains Elite Task Force to Deal With Terrorists" 13, 3 _Security Systems Digest_ (February 10, 1982), pp. 1, 7.

Unsworth, Edwin "Dealing with Fears of Terrorism: UK Report" 368 _Journal of Commerce and Commercial_ (April 30, 1986), p. 19A.

Van Aartrijk, Peter, Jr. "Terrorism Rises, Cover Demand Grows" _National Underwriter Property and Casualty--Employee Benefits Edition_ (April 6, 1987), pp. 13-15.

"Vehicle Ambush Counter-attacks" 18 minute 16 mm. color film (Charles S. MacCrone Productions).

"Vehicle Under Attack: Officer Survival of Incendiary Ambush" 15 minute 16 mm. color film (William Brose Productions, 1973).

Viggiano, John F. "Protecting the Traveling Executive" 5 _Clandestine Tactics and Technology_ (Gaithersburg, Maryland: International Association of Chiefs of Police, 1979).

Virtanen, Michael "House Moves Antiterrorism Bills, Seeks Stricter Seaport Security" 45 _Travel Weekly_ (March 20, 1986), pp. 1-2.

"Vulnerability of Chemical Plants to Terrorism: An Examination (Interview with Neil C. Livingstone)" 63 _Chemical and Engineering News_ (October 21, 1985), pp. 7-13.

"Wackenhut to Form Anti-Terrorism Unit to Assist Companies" _Wall Street Journal_ (April 28, 1986), pp. 18-34.

Wainstein, Eleanor S. and Susanna W. Purnell "Effects of Terrorism on Business Operations" in Patrick J. Montana and George S. Roukis, eds. _Managing Terrorism: Strategies for the Corporate Executive_ (Westport, Conn.: Quorum Books, 1983), pp. 123-134.

Weinstein, Sidney, Curt Weinstein and Raymond Nolan "Neurophysiological Operant and Classical Conditioning Methods in Rats in the Detection of Explosives" in Joel J. Kramer, ed. _The Role of Behavioral Science in Physical Security: Proceedings of the Third Annual Symposium, May 2-4, 1978_ (Washington, D.C.: National Bureau of Standards Special Publication 480-38, 1979), pp. 7-16.

Winkler, H. B. "Study of the Need for Ocean Industry Protection" 4, 1 _Journal of Security Administration_ (1981), pp. 11-25.

Wright, Steve "New Police Technologies: An Exploration of the Social Implications and Unforeseen Impacts of Some Recent Developments" 15, 4 Journal of Peace Research (1978), pp. 305-322.

Yallop, J.H. Protection Against Terrorism (Chichester: B. Rose, 1980), 92 pp.

MILITARY RESPONSES

Albrecht, Lelia "Iran Raid Commander Charlie Beckwith Quits the Army, but not the Fight" 16 People (August 31, 1981), p. 25.

Alexander, Joseph "Countering Tomorrow's Terrorism" 107 US Naval Institute Proceedings (July 1981), pp. 45-50.
Looks at several armed rescue operations.

Alon, Hanan, Lt. Col. "Terrorism and Countermeasures: Analysis Versus a Participant's Observations" in Brian Michael Jenkins, conference director Terrorism and Beyond: An International Conference on Terrorism and Low-Level Conflict (Santa Monica: The Rand Corporation, R-2714-DOE/DOJ/DOS/RC, December 1982), pp. 233-242.

Barnett, R. W. "The US Navy's Role in Countering Maritime Terrorism" 6, 3 Terrorism (1983), pp. 469-480.

Beckwith, Col. Charlie A. and Donald Knox Delta Force:: The U.S. Counter-Terrorist Unit and the Iran Hostage Rescue Mission (New York: Harcourt Brace Jovanovich, 1983), 310 pp.
The Iran rescue mission as viewed by the leader of the Delta Force. Reviewed by Richard Harwood in "Eagle Claw: Debacle in the Desert" Washington Post Book World (November 6, 1983), pp. 3-14.

Bishara, Ghassan "The Political Repercussions of the Israel Raid on the Iraqi Nuclear Reactor" 11, 3 Journal of Palestine Studies (1982), pp. 58-76.

Boyle, Francis A. "International Law in Time of Crisis: From the Entebbe Raid to the Hostages Convention" 75 Northwestern University Law Review (1980), pp. 769-856.

Charters, David "Swift and Bold: An Appraisal of Hostage Rescue Operations" 1 Conflict Quarterly (Summer 1980), pp. 26-33.

Earl, Robert L. "A Matter of Principle" 109, 2 US Naval Institute Proceedings (1983), pp. 29-36.
Argues that the mission to rescue the US hostages in Iran in April 1980 was inflexible because of its built-in constraints.

Fairley, H. Scott "State Actors, Humanitarian Intervention and International Law: Reopening Pandora's Box" 10 Georgia Journal of International and Comparative Law (1980), pp. 29-63.

Farrell, William R. "Military Involvement in Domestic Terror Incidents" 34 <u>Naval War College Review</u> (July/August 1981), pp. 53-66.
 Constitutional and statutory law severely limits military involvement.

Ferraro, Vincent and Elizabeth Doherty "The Doctrine of Military Necessity in a Guerrilla War" paper presented to the annual convention of the International Studies Association, Los Angeles, March 18-22, 1980.

Friedlander, Robert A. "Retaliation as an Anti-Terrorist Weapon: The Israeli Lebanon Incursion and International Law" 8 <u>Israel Yearbook on Human Rights</u> (1978), pp. 63-77.

Gazit, Shlomo "Risk, Glory, and the Rescue Operation" 6, 1 <u>International Security</u> (Summer 1981), pp. 111-135.
 Commanders planning a rescue should include territory, terrain, composition of the hostage group, and characteristics of the terrorists. Gazit looks at the failed US Iranian rescue operation.

Geraghty, T. <u>Who Dares Wins: The Story of the Special Air Services</u> (London: Arms and Armour Press, 1980).

Geyer, Georgie Anne "Living in a World of Irregulars: Are American Fighting Men Becoming Sitting Ducks in Today's Unconventional Wars?" 119 <u>American Legion</u> (November 1985), pp. 26-28.

Gordon, Don "Terrorism: Are We Losing the War? 4, 3 <u>Defense and Diplomacy</u> (March 1986), pp. 38-44.

Hayden, Thomas "Antiterrorist Contingency Readiness" 105 <u>US Naval Institute Proceedings</u> (March 1979), pp. 100-103.
 Argues for a Navy/Marines team to aid the FBI and police.

Hickman, William F. "Did it Really Matter?" 36, 2 <u>Naval War College Review</u> (1983), pp. 17-30.
 A discussion of the effects of a December 1979 US naval buildup in the Indian Ocean and the Arabian sea during the Tehran Embassy crisis.

Iverson, Wayne "No Way to San Jose for Third World Cops" 50 <u>Progressive</u> (April 1986), p. 18.
 An examination of problems in police anti-terrorism training.

Jenkins, Brian Michael "We Needn't Rule Out the Use of Force Against Terrorists" 104 <u>Los Angeles Times</u> (May 21, 1985), p. II-5.

Jonas, George <u>Vengeance</u> (New York: Simon and Schuster, 1984), 376 pp.
 A study of "Avner," the leader of the Mossad team who tracked down and killed Black Septembrists involved in the murder of the Israeli Olympics team in 1972. Reviewed, unfavorably, by Christian Williams "Adventures in the Terrorist Trade" <u>Washington Post Book World</u> (July 1, 1984), p. 8.

Klare, Michael T. "Low-Intensity Conflict: The New U.S. Strategic Doctrine" 241 Nation (December 28, 1985), pp. 698-705.

Livingstone, Neil C. "Proactive Responses to Terrorism: Reprisals, Preemption, and Retribution" in Neil C. Livingstone and Terrell E. Arnold, eds. Fighting Back: Winning the War Against Terrorism (Lexington: Lexington Books, 1986), pp. 109-133.

McGowan, Robert, et al. The Day of the S.A.S.: The Inside Story of How Britain Ended the Seige of Princess Gate (London: Express Newspapers, 1980), 64 pp.

McGuire, Frank "Arming Against Terrorism" 4,3 Defense and Diplomacy (March 1986), pp. 49-52.

Menarchik, E. Douglas "Strike Against Terror! The Entebbe Raid" 31, 5 Air University Review (1980), pp. 65-76.

Mirvahabi, Farin "Entebbe: Validity of Claims in International Law" 6 Philippines Year Book of International Law (1977), pp. 58-91, reprinted in 17 Revue de Droit Penale Militaire et de Droit de la Guerre (1978), pp. 627-676.

Moorer, Thomas H. "The Raid" paper presented at the Conference on Political Terrorism and Energy: The Threat and Response, Washington, D.C., Georgetown University Center for Strategic and International Studies, May 1, 1980

Motley, James Berry "The Case for a Multinational Strike Force" 4, 3 Defense and Diplomacy (March 1986), pp. 45-47.

Norman, Geoffrey "Black Berets to the Rescue" 89 Esquire (April 11, 1978), pp. 43-46.
Is the US Army prepared to combat terrorism?

"Retaliating Against Libya" 12, 25 Security Systems Digest (December 9, 1981), p. 8.

Rivers, Gayle The War Against the Terrorists: How to Win It (New York: Stein and Day, 1986).
A New Zealander who claims to have battled terrorists around the world suggests that a team of 1000 well trained men can defeat terrorists. He also offers 10 precautions to take before you board a plane and 9 recommendations to follow if you are on a hijacked plane.

Roberts, Guy B. "Covert Responses: The Moral Dilemma" paper presented at the Joint Services Committee on Professional Ethics Conference on Terrorism, National War College, Fort McNair, Washington, D.C., January 10-11, 1985, published in Neil C. Livingstone and Terrell E. Arnold, eds. Fighting Back: Winning the War Against Terrorism (Lexington: Lexington Books, 1986), pp. 133-144.

Ronhovde, Kent "The Use of Federal Military Forces for the Purpose of Combatting Domestic Terrorism: Limitations Imposed by the Posse Comitatus Act" (Washington, D.C.: Library of Congress, CRS, September 20, 1978), 39 pp.

Sarazin, James "Wonder Machines to the Rescue" 123, 17 Manchester Guardian (October 19, 1980), p. 12.
A discussion of the quick-strike forces commanded by the FRG's Colonel Wegener and France's Prouteau, plus some of the difficulties experienced by Italy's Carabinieri General Carlo Alberto della Chiesa in establishing a similar force.

Thackrah, John Richard "Army-Police Cooperation Against Terrorism" Police Journal (January-March, 1983).

Thackrah, John Richard "Police-Public Cooperation Against Terrorism" Police and Society Research Centre Papers (Summer 1983).

Thompkins, Thomas C. "Military Countermeasures to Terrorism in the 1980s" (Santa Monica: The Rand Corporation, N-2178-RC, August 1984).

Toensing, Victoria "The Legal Case for Using Force" in Neil C. Livingstone and Terrell E. Arnold, eds. Fighting Back: Winning the War Against Terrorism (Lexington: Lexington Books, 1986), pp. 145-156.

Tovar, B. Hugh "Active Responses" in Uri Ra'anan, Robert L. Pfaltzgraff, Jr., Richard H. Shultz, Ernst Halperin, and Igor Lukes Hydra of Carnage: International Linkages of Terrorism: The Witnesses Speak (Lexington, Mass.: Lexington Books, 1986), pp. 231-250.

Truby, J. David "Red Light for Blue Light" 1, 3 TVI Journal (1980), pp. 2-5.

Umozurike, U. O. "The Israelis in Entebbe: Rescue or Aggression?" 12 Verfassung und Recht in Ubersee (1979), pp. 383-392.

Wilkinson, Paul "Adaptation for the Struggle Against Terrorism of International Cooperation Between the Police and Security Services" paper presented at the Council of Europe Conference on the Defence of Democracy Against Terrorism in Europe, November 1980.

Wolf, John B. "Intelligence Operations and Terrorism" 7, 1 Update Report (Gaithersburg, Maryland: International Association of Chiefs of Police, 1981).

Wright, Jeffrey W. "Terrorism: A Mode of Warfare" 64, 10 Military Review (1984), pp. 35-45.
A summary of recommendations made in the Report of the Department of Defense Commission on Beirut International Airport Terrorist Act (October 23, 1983).

Zafren, Daniel "The Israeli Rescue Raid in Uganda: A Violation of International Law?" (Washington, D.C.: Library of Congress, CRS, July 26, 1976), 17 pp.

INTERNATIONAL LEGAL APPROACHES

ABA Standing Committee on World Order Under Law "Model American Convention on the Prevention and Punishment of Certain Serious Forms of Violence Jeopardizing Fundamental Rights and Freedoms, with Appendices" (Washington, C.C.: Division of Public Service Activities, American Bar Association, 1980), 15 pp.

"1984 Act to Combat International Terrorism" 84 Department of State Bulletin (December 1984), p. 86.

Adams, T. "Law and the Lawless - Terrorism - The International Legal Perspective" 1, 7 TVI Journal (1980), pp. 3-8.

"ADL Asks States to Adopt Legislation Outlawing Paramilitary Training Camps" 4 Pennsylvania Law Journal Report (February 23, 1981), p. 5.

Aldrich, George H. Alfred P. Rubin, Harry H. Almond, Jr., and Frits Kalshoven "Protocols Additional to the Geneva Convention of the Laws of War" Proceedings of the American Society of International Law (1980), pp. 191-212.

Almond, Harry H., Jr. "The Legal Regulation of International Terrorism" 3, 2-3 Conflict (1981), pp. 143-166.

Almond, Harry H., Jr. "Using the Law to Combat Terrorism" in Neil C. Livingstone and Terrell E. Arnold, eds. Fighting Back: Winning the War Against Terrorism (Lexington: Lexington Books, 1986), pp. 157-174.

"American Courts and Modern Terrorism: The Politics of Extradition" 13, 3 New York University Journal of International Law and Politics (Winter 1981), pp. 617-644.

Anawalt, Howard C. "The Peaceful Use of Presidential Power: The International Court of Justice, The Algerian Intervention and the US Supreme Court" paper presented to the panel on the Iran Hostage Crisis and International Law at the 23rd annual convention of the International Studies Association, Cincinnati, Ohio, March 24-27, 1982.

Arnold, Terrell E. "Rewriting the Rules of Engagement" in Neil C. Livingstone and Terrell E. Arnold, eds. Fighting Back: Winning the War Against Terrorism (Lexington: Lexington Books, 1986), pp. 175-190.

"Arrest on Suspicion (Great Britain)" 49 Journal of Criminal Law (May 1985), pp. 147-149. A discussion of McKee v. Chief Constable of Northern Ireland (1985), 1 All E.R. 1 (H.L.).

Aston, Clive C. International Law and Political Terrorism (Westport: Greenwood, 1982).

Aston, Clive C. "International Legislation Against Political Terrorism" in A. Martin, ed. Political Terrorism: A United Nations Association Special Report (New York: UNAUSA, March, 1980).

Aymond, M. "Procedural Problems of Extradition" 60, 1-2 Revue de Droit Penal et de Criminologie (January-February, 1980), pp. 7-14.

Baker, Mark B. "The South American Legal Response to Terrorism" 3 Boston University International Law Journal (Winter 1985), pp. 67-97.

Banoff, Barbara Ann and Christopher H. Pyle "'To Surrender Political Offenders': The Political Offense Exception to Extradition in United States Law" 16, 2 New York University Journal of International Law and Politics (Winter 1984), pp. 169-210.

Barkey, David W. and D. Stanley Eitzen "Toward an Assessment of Multi-National Corporate Social Expenditures in Relation to Political Stability and Terrorist Activity: The Argentine Case" 34, 4 Inter-American Economic Affairs (Spring, 1981), pp. 77-90.

Bazler, Michael J. "Capturing Terrorists in the 'Wild Blue Yonder': International Law and the Achille Lauro and Libyan Aircraft Incidents: Symposium on International Terrorism '86" 8 Whittier Law Review (Summer 1986), pp. 685-709.

Bazler, Michael J. and Terry Porvin "International Terrorism: A Selected Bibliography" 8 Whittier Law Review (Summer 1986), pp. 793-800.

Becker, W. "Survey of Laws Against Terrorism" 33, 3 Neue Polizei (February 1979), pp. 23-27.

Beichman, Arnold "A War Without End" 11 American Spectator (April 1978), pp. 20-23.
Beichman believes that we should give terrorists certain capital punishment, treating them as enemy agents.

Bernhardt, J. Peter "The Provisional Measures Procedure of the International Court of Justice Through US Staff in Tehran: Fiat Iustitia, pereat curia?" 20 Virginia Journal of International Law (Spring 1980), pp. 557-613.

Berns, Walter "Constitutional Power and the Defense of Free Government" in Benjamin Netanyahu, ed. Terrorism: How the West Can Win (New York: Farrar, Straus, Giroux, 1986), pp. 149-154.

Bialos, Jeffrey P. and Kenneth I. Juster "The Libyan Sanctions: A Rational Response to State-Sponsored Terrorism?" 26 Virginia Journal of International Law (Summer 1986), pp. 799-855.

Bigay, J. "Extradite or Punish" 60, 1-2 Revue de Droit Penal et de Criminologie (January-February 1980), pp. 113-125.

Bishop, Joseph W., Jr., "Law in the Control of Terrorism and Insurrection: The British Laboratory Experience" 42, 2 Law and Contemporary Problems (Spring 1978), pp. 141ff.

Blishchenko, Igor Pavlovich and N. Zhdanov Terrorism and International Law (Moscow: Progress Publishers, 1984), 286 pp.

Blum, Yehuda Z. "The Legality of State Response to Acts of Terrorism" in Benjamin Netanyahu, ed. Terrorism: How the West Can Win (New York: Farrar, Straus, Giroux, 1986), pp. 133-138.

de Boubee, G. R. "European Convention for the Repression of Terrorism and the Law of Extradition" 60, 1-2 Revue de Droit Penal et de Criminologie (January-February 1980), pp. 63-78.

Boire, Martin C. "Terrorism Reconsidered as Punishment: Toward an Evaluation of the Acceptability of Terrorism as a Method of Societal Change or Maintenance" 20 Stanford Journal of International Law (Spring 1984), pp. 45-134.

Boyle, Francis A. "International Law in Time of Crisis: From the Entebbe Raid to the Hostages Convention" 75 Northwestern University Law Review (December 1980), pp. 769-856.

Boyle, Francis A. "Preserving the Rule of Law in the War Against International Terrorism" 8 Whittier Law Review (Summer 1986), pp. 735-745.

Brady, Julio A. "The Threat of Terrorism to Democracy: A Criminal Justice Response" 8, 3 Terrorism (1986), pp. 205-212.

Bremer, L. Paul "Practical Measures for Dealing with Terrorism" 913 Current Policy (Washington, D.C.: US Department of State, Bureau of Public Affairs, January 22, 1987), 4 pp.

Bremer, L. Paul "Terrorism and the Rule of Law" 947 Current Policy (Washington, D.C.: US Department of State, Bureau of Public Affairs, April 23, 1987), 4 pp.

Browne, Marjorie "Comparison of Legislation on International Terrorism" (Washington, D.C.: Library of Congress, CRS, October 18, 1979), 13 pp.

Busuttil, James J. "The Bonn Declaration on International Terrorism: A Non-Binding International Agreement on Aircraft Hijacking" 31, 3 International and Comparative Law Quarterly (July 1982), pp. 474-487.

Carbonneau, Thomas E. "Terrorist Acts--Crimes or Political Infractions? An Appraisal of Recent French Extradition Cases" 3, 2 Hastings International and Comparative Law Review (Winter 1980), pp. 265-298.

Carlton, Charles "Judging Without Consensus: The Diplock Courts in Northern Ireland" 3 Law and Policy Quarterly (April 1981), pp. 225-242.

A look at the nonjury trials in which a single judge uses modified rules of evidence and lowered standards for the admission of confessions.

"Case Concerning United States Diplomatic and Consular Staff in Tehran (United States v. Iran)" 45 _International Court of Justice_ (Order of May 12, 1981).

Cavanagh, Suzanne "Analysis of Terrorism Jurisdiction in the Proposed FBI Charter, and Alternative Definitions of Terrorism" (Washington, D.C.: Library of Congress, CRS, September 18, 1979), 11 pp.

Cavanagh, Suzanne "The Complexities of Developing a Federal Response to Domestic Terrorism: An Overview" (Washington, D.C.: Library of Congress, Congressional Research Service, December 3, 1982), 30 pp.

Celada, Raymond "Protocol II of Geneva Conventions and Domestic Terrorists" (Washington, D.C.: Library of Congress, Congressional Research Service, December 3, 1981), 5 pp.

Chamberlain, Kevin "Collective Suspension of Air Services with States Which Harbour Hijackers" 32, 3 _International and Comparative Law Quarterly_ (July 1983), pp. 616-632.

Chinkin, Christine "The Foreign Affairs Powers of the US President and the Iranian Hostages Agreement: _Dames and Moore v. Reagan_" 32, 3 _International and Comparative Law Quarterly_ (July 1983), pp. 600-615.

Clarizio, Jeanne B. "Striking at the Heart of Liberty" 72 _American Bar Association Journal_ (January 1986), pp. 38-39.

Constance, George Wesley _Obstacles That Block UN Efforts to Control International Terrorism_ (New School for Social Research, Ph.D. dissertation, 1981), 282 pp.

Constantinople, George R. "Towards a New Definition of Piracy: The Achille Lauro Incident" 26 _Virginia Journal of International Law_ (Spring 1986), pp. 723-753.

"Convention on the Physical Protection of Nuclear Materials, Done at Vienna, October 26, 1979, opened for Signature, March 3, 1980" 18 _International Legal Materials_ (1979), pp. 1419, 1422-31.

Council of Europe _International Co-Operation in the Prosecution and Punishment of Acts of Terrorism_ (Strasbourg: The Council, 1983), 19 pp.

"Council of Europe: Recommendation Concerning International Cooperation in the Prosecution and Punishment of Acts of Terrorism" 21, 1 _International Legal Materials_ (January 1982), pp. 199-201.

"Criminal Injury to Persons: Compensation of Victims in Northern Ireland" 44 _Journal of Criminal Law_ (February 1980), pp. 53-54.

D'Amato, Anthony and Alfred P. Rubin "What Does Tel-Oren Tell
Lawyers? Judge Bork's Concept of the Law of Nations is
Seriously Mistaken" 79 American Journal of International Law
(January 1985), pp. 92-113.
A discussion of the decision in Tel-Oren v. Libyan Arab
Republic 726 f. 2d   774 (D.C. Cir. 1894), and comments and
criticisms by Rubin.

"Defense Lawyers in Terrorist Trials" 5 Kriminalistik (1980),
p. 203.

"Defining Terrorism" 9 National Law Journal (September 15,
1986), p. 12.

DeGostin, Robert "Terrorism and Title 18 of the US Code"
(Washington, D.C.: Library of Congress, CRS, July 11, 1977),
23 pp.

Delaney, Robert F. "World Terrorism Today" 9 California
Western International Law Journal (Summer 1979), pp. 450-460.

Dinstein, Yoram "Comments on the Fourth Interim Report of the
International Law Association Committee on International
Terrorism (1982)" 7, 2 Terrorism (1984), pp. 163-168.

Dugard, John "International Terrorism and the Just War" 12
Stanford Journal of International Studies (1977), pp. 21ff.

Eig, Larry "Proposed Act to Combat International Terrorism
(S.333): Expansion of Restriction of Existing Presidential
Statutory Authority?" (Washington, D.C.: Library of Congress,
CRS, August 14, 1980), 8 pp.

"European Communities: Agreement Concerning the Application of
the European Convention on the Suppression of Terrorism Among
the Member States" 19, 2 International Legal Materials (March
1980), pp. 325-326.

Evans, Alona E. "Perspectives on International Terrorism" 17
Willamette Law Review (Winter 1980), pp. 151-164.
A paper presented to a symposium on International Law and
Foreign Policy in the 1980s.

Falsgraf, William W. "The Bar Responds to Terrorism:
President's Page" 71 American Bar Association Journal
(September 1985), p. 8.

Falvey, Anne "Legislative Responses to International
Terrorism: International and National Efforts to Deter and
Punish Terrorists" 9 Boston College International and
Comparative Law Journal (Summer 1986), pp. 323-359.

Feith, Douglas J. "International Responses" in Uri Ra'anan,
Robert L. Pfaltzgraff, Jr., Richard H. Shultz, Ernst Halperin,
and Igor Lukes Hydra of Carnage: International Linkages of
Terrorism: The Witnesses Speak (Lexington, Mass.: Lexington
Books, 1986), pp. 265-286.

Ferencz, Benjamin B. "When One Person's Terrorism is Another Person's Heroism" 9 Human Rights (Summer 1981), pp. 38-42. A short history of legal efforts to prevent terrorism and crimes against humanity.

Fields, Louis G., Jr. "Terrorism: A Summary of Applicable US and International Law" in E. Nobles Lowe and Harry D. Shargel, eds. Legal and Other Aspects of Terrorism (New York: Practicing Law Institute, Course Handbook Series Number 310, 1979), also available in Brian Michael Jenkins, conference director Terrorism and Beyond: An International Conference on Terrorism and Low-Level Conflict (Santa Monica: The Rand Corporation, R-2714-DOE/DOJ/DOS/RC, December 1982), pp. 247-265.

Fields, Louis G., Jr. "Terrorism and the Rule of Law: Society at the Crossroads" 6, 1 Ohio Northern University Law Review (1979), pp. 4-12.
The Assistant Legal Advisor of the Department of State examines global and regional measures taken to combat terrorism.

Flores, David A. "Export Controls and the U.S. Effort to Combat International Terrorism" 13, 2 Law and Policy in International Business (1981), pp. 521-590.

Flynn, Edith "Political Prisoners and Terrorists in American Correctional Institutions" in Ronald D. Crelinsten, Danielle Laberge-Altmejd and Denis Szabo, eds. Terrorism and Criminal Justice: An International Perspective (Toronto: Lexington, 1978).

Freestone, David "Legal Responses to Terrorism: Towards European Cooperation?" in Juliet Lodge, ed. Terrorism: A Challenge to the State (Oxford: Martin Robertson, 1981).

Friedlander, Robert A. "Comment: Unmuzzling the Dogs of War" 7, 2 Terrorism (1984), pp. 169-174.

Friedlander, Robert A. "Looking at the World Idealistically" 13, 2 Case Western Reserve Journal of International Law (Spring 1981), pp. 307-310.

Friendlander, Robert A. "On the Prevention of Violence" 25, 2 Catholic Lawyer (Spring 1980), pp. 95-105.

Friedlander, Robert A. "The PLO and the Rule of Law: A Reply to Dr. Anis F. Kassim" 10, 2 Denver Journal of International Law and Policy (Winter 1981), pp. 221-235.

Friedlander, Robert A. "Seeking Legal Remedies--Domestic and International" 17, 2 International Society of Barristers Quarterly (April 1982), pp. 296-306.

Friedlander, Robert A. "Terrorism and International Law: Recent Developments" 13, 3 Rutgers Law Journal (1982).

Friedlander, Robert A. "Terrorism and National Liberation Movements: Can Rights Derive from Wrongs?" 13,2 Case Western Journal of International Law (1981), pp. 281-289.

Friedlander, Robert A. "Terrorism and Self-Determination: The Fatal Nexus" 7 Syracuse Journal of International Law and Commerce (Winter 1979-1980), pp. 263-268.

Friedlander, Robert A. "Terrorism and the Law: What Price Safety?" (Gaithersburg, Maryland: International Association of Chiefs of Police, 1979), 27 pp.

Friedlander, Robert A. Terrorism: Documents of International and Local Control (Dobbs Ferry: Oceana, 1979).

Friedlander, Robert A. Terrorism: Documents of International and Local Control--From the Terror Decade of the 1970's to the Dangerous Decade of the 1980's, vol. III (Dobbs Ferry, New York: Oceana Publications, 1981).

Garvey, Jack I. "Repression of the Political Emigre--The Underground to International Law: A Proposal for Remedy" 90 Yale Law Review (November 1980), pp. 78-120.
A look at emigres who are attacked in the US by agents from their nation of citizenship.

Gemmer, K. H. "Search for Wanted Persons and Everyday Police Activities: Writs, Search Criteria and Pursuit of Terrorists" Kriminalistik (1980), pp. 2-7.

Gilbert, Geoffrey S. "Terrorism and the Political Offence Exemption Reappraised" 34, 4 International and Comparative Law Quarterly (October 1985), pp. 695-723.

Ginossar, Shalev "Outlawing Terrorism" 13, 2 Israel Law Review (April 1978), pp. 150-159.
The author argues for dropping amnesty laws in such cases, expediting trial procedures (with no evidence or arguments in mitigation of sentence allowable), mandatory life imprisonment or death sentences, and creation of a "supracriminal" law.

Glaser, David M. "Murder in the Casbah or the Effect of Morocco's Reservation to the Vienna Convention on Diplomatic Relations" 11, 2 New York University Journal of International Law and Politics (Fall 1978), pp. 299-322.

Glassman, David L. "Keeping 'The Wild' Out of 'The Wild Blue Yonder': Preventing Terrorist Attacks Against International Flights in Civil Aviation" 4 Dickinson Journal of International Law (Spring 1986), pp. 251-274.

Goldberg, Arthur "Diplomatic Immunity and Terrorism: The Vienna Convention" 151 New Zealand Law Journal (May 1985).

Goldie, L.F.E. "Combatting International Terrorism: The UN Developments" 31 Naval War College Review (Winter 1979), pp. 49-60.

Gordon, Edward "Freeze, Thaw May Squeeze Law: What's Happening
to Those Iranian Assets?" International Practitioner's
Notebook (November 19, 1980), pp. 1-7.

Gordon, Edward "Trends: The Blocking of Iranian Assets" 14, 4
International Lawyer (Fall 1980), pp. 659-688.

Greaves, Douglas "The Definition and Motivation of Terrorism"
13 Australian Journal of Forensic Science (June 1981), pp.
160-166.

Green, Leslie C. "Canada's Role in the Development of the Law
of Armed Conflict" 18 Canadian Year Book of International Law
(1980), pp. 91ff.

Green, Leslie C. "Niceties and Necessities--The Case for
Diplomatic Immunity" 19 International Perspectives (March-
April, 1980), pp. 19-23.
Includes a discussion of how the Canadians saved 6 US
diplomats in Iran.

Green, Leslie C. "The Tehran Embassy Incident--Legal Aspects"
19 Archiv des Volkerrechts (1980).

Green, Leslie C. "The Tehran Embassy Incident and
International Law" 38, 1 Behind the Headlines (1980) also
available in (Toronto: Canadian Institute of International
Affairs, 1980), 24 pp..

Green, Leslie C. and J. Lador-Lederer "Fourth Interim Report
of the Committee on International Terrorism" Report of the
Sixtieth Conference (International Law Association, 1982),
Annex 1, pp. 354-357.

Greer, D. S. "The Admissibility of Confessions Under the
Northern Ireland (Emergency Provisions) Act" 31 Northern
Ireland Legal Quarterly (Autumn 1980), pp. 205-238.

Greer, Steven C. "Supergrasses and the Legal System in Britain
and Northern Ireland" 102 Law Quarterly Review (April 1986),
pp. 198-249.
A discussion of informers that appear as principal witness
for the prosecution.

Hacker, Donald E. "The Application of Prisoner-of-War Status
to Guerrillas under the First Protocol Additional to the
Geneva Conventions of 1949" 2, 1 Boston College International
and Comparative Law Journal (1978), pp. 131-162.

Hall, J. W., Jr. "A Possible Legal Solution to International
Terrorism" 85, 2 Case and Comment (March-April, 1980), pp. 30-
36.
Argues that an international criminal court, although
desirable, is not feasible at present.

Handelman, Stephen "Countering the Terrorists" 31 World Press
Review (September 1984), p. 58.

Hannay, William M. "International Terrorism and the Political Offense Exception to Extradition" 18, 3 Columbia Journal of Transnational Law (1980), pp. 381-412.

Hannay, William M. "Legislative Reform of U.S. Extradition Statutes: Plugging the Terrorist's Loophole" 13 Journal of International Law (Fall, 1983).

Helms, Andrea R. C. "Procedural Democracy and the Terrorist Threat" 4 Police Studies (Winter 1982), pp. 23-32.

Horbatiuk, Kevin G. "Anti-Terrorism: The West German Approach" 3 Fordham International Law Forum (Spring 1980), pp. 167-191.

Horowitz, Irving Louis "Civil Liberties Dangers in Anti-Terrorist Policies" Civil Liberties Review (March 1977), pp. 25-32.

"International Cooperation to Suppress Terrorism" 9 Houston Journal of International Law (Autumn 1986), p. 154.

"International Law Association Paris Conference (1984)" 7, 2 Terrorism (1984), pp. 199-212.

"International Terrorism: Extradition--Decision of Paris Chambre d'Accusation, January 11, 1977" 18 Harvard International Law Review (1977), pp. 467ff.

"International Terrorism: Fourth Interim Report of the Committee" 7, 2 Terrorism (1984), pp. 123-146.

Intoccia, Gregory F. "International Legal and Policy Implications of an American Counter-Terrorist Strategy" 14 Denver Journal of International Law and Policy (Spring-Summer 1985), pp. 121-146.

du Jardin, J. "Particulars of the European Convention for the Repression of Terrorism Compared to Classical Extradition Law" 60, 1-2 Revue de Droit Penal et de Criminologie (January-February 1980), pp. 15-42.

Jetter, Sherry L. "International Terrorism: Beyond the Scope of International Law" 12 Brooklyn Journal of International Law (March 1986), pp. 505-552.

Jones, Nancy "US Law Applying to Terrorist Attacks Against Offshore Structures: Present Statutes and Jurisdictional Problems Associated with the Expansion of These Statutes" (Washington, D.C.: Library of Congress, CRS, August 24, 1977), 11 pp.

Kaiser, Frederick "Committees, Subcommittees, and Staff Members with Responsibility for US Anti-Terrorism Programs" (Washington, D.C.: Library of Congress, CRS, January 22, 1981), 3 pp.

Kassim, Anis "A Response to Professor Robert A. Friedlander: The PLO and the Rule of Law" 10 Denver Journal of International Law and Policy (Winter 1981), pp. 237-241.

Kittrie, Nicholas "Looking at the World Realistically" 13 <u>Case Western Reserve Journal of International Law</u> (1981), pp. 311-313.

Kittrie, Nicholas "Patriots and Terrorists: Reconciling Human Rights with World Order" 13,2 <u>Case Western Reserve Journal of International Law</u> (1981), pp. 291-305.
The author argues that the recent trend to limit the political offense exception should be reevaluated to avoid overcompensating for past abuses of the exception.

Kornblum, Allan N. and Lubomyr M. Jachnycky "America's Secret Court: Listening in on Espionage and Terrorism" 24 <u>Judges Journal</u> (Summer 1985), pp. 14-20.

Kuhn, Thomas Moddie <u>Terrorism in International Law</u> (University of South Africa: L.L.D. dissertation, 1980).

Kutner, Luis "Constructive Notice: A Proposal to End International Terrorism" 10 <u>Common Law Lawyer</u> (May-June 1985), pp. 1-16.

Larschan, Bradley "Extradition, The Political Offense Exception and Terrorism: An Overview of the Three Principal Theories of Law" 4, 2 <u>Boston University International Law Journal</u> (Summer 1986), pp.231-284.

"Legislative Proposals Regarding Diplomatic Security" 86 <u>Department of State Bulletin</u> (January 1986), pp. 47-48.
A transcript of Ambassador Ronald I. Spiers' testimony before Congress.

Leiser, Burton M. "Enemies of Mankind" in Benjamin Netanyahu, ed. <u>Terrorism: How the West Can Win</u> (New York: Farrar, Straus, Giroux, 1986), pp. 155-156.

Levinfeld, Barry "Israel's Counter-Fedayeen Tactics in Lebanon: Self-Defense and Reprisal Under Modern International Law" 21, 1 <u>Columbia Journal of Transnational Law</u> (1982).

Levine, Evyatar "A Landmark on the Road to Legal Chaos: Recognition of the PLO as a Menace to World Public Order" 10, 2 <u>Denver Journal of International Law and Policy</u> (Winter 1981), pp. 243-258.

Levine, Herbert M. "Does International Law Serve as a Constraint on Terrorism?", Chapter 18 in <u>World Politics Debated: A Reader in Contemporary Issues</u> (New York: McGraw-Hill, 1983).

Levitt, Geoffrey M. "International Law and the U.S. Government's Response to Terrorism" 8 <u>Whittier Law Review</u> (Summer 1986), pp. 755-762.

Levy, Harold J. "In Camera: An Interview with Serge Menarde" 4 <u>Canadian Lawyer</u> (September 1980), pp. 16-20.

Lillich, Richard B., ed. Transnational Terrorism, Conventions and Commentary: A Compilation of Treaties, Agreements, and Declarations of Especial Interest to the United States (Charlottesvile, Va.: Michie, 1982), 281 pp.

Liput, Andrew L. "An Analysis of the Achille Lauro Affair: Towards an Effective and Legal Method of Bringing International Terrorists to Justice" 9 Fordham International Law Journal (Spring 1986), pp. 328-372.

Liskofsky "The Abu Daoud Case: Law or Politics?" 7 Israel Year Book of Human Rights (1977), pp. 66ff.

Lockwood, Bert B. "Model American Convention on the Prevention and Punishment of Serious Forms of Violence, with Appendices" (Washington, D.C.: Division of Public Services, American Bar Association, Standing Committee on World Order Under Law, 1983), 17 pp.

"Lotta Contro Il Terrorismo" 46, 1 Rivista di Studi Politici Internazionali (January-March 1979), pp. 119-123.
Texts of resolutions passed at the interparliamentary conference, the North Atlantic Assembly, and the Council of Europe.

Lowe, E. Nobles and Harry D. Shargel, eds. Legal and Other Aspects of Terrorism (New York: Practising Law Institute, Course Handbook Series, Number 310, 1979), 864 pp.
Includes sections on legal aspects, government policy and response, international terrorism and security planning, with techniques for executive protection, and the CIA bibliography on terrorism.

Lowenfeld, Andreas F. and Robert B. Flynn "Analyzing the Applicable Laws in the Achille Lauro Aftermath" 194 New York Law Journal (November 1, 1985), p. 1.
A discussion of extradition laws.

Lubet, Steen and Morris Czaches "The Role of the American Judiciary in the Extradition of Political Terrorists" 71, 3 Journal of Criminal Law and Criminology (Fall 1980), pp. 193-210.

MacKay, Lorri L. "Some Problems with the Extradition of Transnational Terrorists" (London School of Economics and Political Science, Faculty of Economics, Department of International Relations, MSc Long Essay, 1986), 43 pp.

Magdelenat, Jean-Louis Les Droits et Obligations des Etats d'Assurer la Securite de l'Aviation Internationale Contre le Terrorisme (McGill University, D.C.L. dissertation, 1981).

McClure, Brooks "Operational Aspects of Terrorism" 17 Williamette Law Journal (Winter 1980), pp. 165-184.
A paper presented to a symposium on International Law and Foreign Policy in the 1980s.

McCredie, Jeffrey Allan "Contemporary Uses of Force Against Terrorism: The United States Response to Achille Lauro: Questions of Jurisdiction and its Exercise" 16 <u>Georgia Journal of International and Comparative Law</u> (Fall 1986), pp. 435-467.

McHugh, Lois "International Terrorism: International Legal Documentation" (Washington, D.C.: Library of Congress, CRS, January 20, 1978), 104 pp.

McNamara, Francis <u>Legal Aspects of the Fight Against Terrorism</u> (Houston: Investigative Research Foundation, 1983).

McWhinney, Edward "International Terrorism: United Nations Projects for Legal Controls" 7, 2 <u>Terrorism</u> (1984), pp. 175-184.

Melvin, Virginia A. "Redefining the Alien Tort Claims Act" 70 <u>Minnesota Law Review</u> (October 1985), pp. 211-240. A discussion of Tel-Oren v. Libyan Arab Republic 517 <u>F. Supp.</u> 542 (D.D.C. 1981) and Filartiga v. Pena-Irala 630 f.2d 876 (2d Cir. 1980) and how they affect the Palestine Liberation Organization.

Moore, J.B. "A Theoretical Overview of the Laws of War in a Post-Charter World, with Emphasis on the Challenge of Civil Wars, Wars of National Liberation, Mixed Civil-International Wars, and Terrorism" 31 <u>American University Law Review</u> (1982), pp. 841ff.

Munson, Valerie J. "The Case Concerning United States Diplomatic and Consular Staff in Tehran" 2 <u>California Western International Law Journal</u> (Summer 1981). pp. 543-568.

Murphy, John Francis "Comments on the Fourth Interim Report of the ILA Committee on International Terrorism (1982)" 7, 2 <u>Terrorism</u> (1984), pp. 193-198.

Murphy, John Francis <u>Legal Aspects of International Terrorism: Summary Report of an International Conference, December 13-15, 1978, Department of State, Washington, D.C.</u> (St. Paul, Minnesota: West, 1980), 74 pp.

Murphy, John Francis "Legal Controls and the Deterrence of Terrorism: Performance and Prospects" 13 <u>Rutgers Law Journal</u> (1982).

Murphy, John Francis <u>Punishing International Terrorism: The Legal Framework for Policy Initiatives</u> (Totowa, New Jersey: Rowman and Allanheld, 1985), 142 pp. Reviewed in <u>Foreign Affairs</u> (Fall 1986), p. 180.

Murphy, John Francis "Report on Conference on International Terrorism: Protection of Diplomatic Premises and Personnel, Bellagio, Italy, March 8-12, 1982" 6, 3 <u>Terrorism</u> (1983), pp. 481-496.

Murphy, John Francis <u>The United Nations and the Control of International Violence: A Legal and Political Analysis</u> (Totowa, New Jersey: Allanheld, Osmun Publishers, 1982), 212 pp.

Nagel, W. H. "A Social-Legal View on the Suppression of Terrorists" 8, 3 <u>International Journal of the Sociology of Law</u> (August 1980), pp. 213-226.

Nanes, Allan S. "Congressional Developments" 6, 1 <u>Terrorism</u> (1982), pp. 101-104.

Natter, Raymond "Survey of Federal and State Laws Concerning Terrorism" (Washington, D.C.: Library of Congress, CRS, December 14, 1977), 13 pp.

O'Brien, William V. "The Jus in Bello in Revolutionary War and Counterinsurgency" 18, 2 <u>Virginia Journal of International Law</u> (Winter 1978), pp. 193-244.

"Omnibus Antiterrorism Act of 1979" 6, 1 <u>Ohio Northern University Law Review</u> (1979), pp. 120-143.
A reprint of S.333, a bill submitted by Senator Abraham Ribicoff and others to establish, inter alia, sanctions against states aiding terrorists.

Oppermann, T. "The Part Played by International Law in Combatting International Terrorism" 25 <u>Law and State</u> (1982), pp. 116-135.

Ownby, Gordon T. "Law Schools Cancel Sessions Abroad in Terrorism's Wake" 132 <u>Chicago Daily Law Bulletin</u> (May 12, 1986), p. 1.

Palmer, E. <u>The Austrian Law on Extradition and Mutual Assistance in Criminal Matters</u> (1983).

Panzera, Antonio Filippo <u>Attivita Terroristiche e Diritto Internazionale</u> (Napoli: Jovene, 1978), 196 pp.

Passow, Sam "Terrorism and Corporate Liability" 5, 2 <u>TVI Journal</u> (Fall 1984), pp. 32-33.

Paust, Jordan J. "Entebbe and Self-Help: The Israeli Response to Terrorism" 2 <u>Fletcher Forum</u> (January 1978), pp. 86-92.

Paust, Jordan J. "Federal Jurisdiction Over Extraterritorial Acts of Terrorism and Nonimmunity for Foreign Violators of International Law Under the FSIA and the Act of State Doctrine" 23 <u>Virginia Journal of International Law</u> (Winter 1983), pp. 191-251.

Paust, Jordan J. "Responding Lawfully to International Terrorism: The Use of Force Abroad" 8 <u>Whittier Law Review</u> (Summer 1986), pp. 711-733.

Paust, Jordan J. "Terrorism and 'Terrorism-Specific' Statutes" 7, 2 <u>Terrorism</u> (1984), pp. 233-239.

Piper, Don C. "Documents Concerning the Achille Lauro Affairs and Cooperation in Combatting International Terrorism" 24 <u>International Legal Materials</u> (November 1985), pp. 1509-1565. Includes press briefings by US officials, Italian-US treaties, US legislation, and a statement in the UN by the President of the Security Council.

"The Political Offense Exception and Terrorism" 85 <u>Department of State Bulletin</u> (December 1985), pp 58-62.

Przetacznik, Franciszek <u>Protection of Officials of Foreign States According to International Law</u> (The Hague: Martinus Nijhoff, 1983), 390 pp.

Purdy, Chip "Foreign Intelligence Surveillance Act: Unconstitutional Warrant Criteria Permit Wiretapping if a Possibility of International Terrorism is Found" 17 <u>San Diego Law Review</u> (July 1980), pp. 963-977.

Rafat, Amir "The Iran Hostage Crisis and International Court of Justice: Aspects of the Case Concerning United States Diplomatic and Consular Staff in Tehran" 10 <u>Denver Journal of International Law and Policy</u> (1981).

Ravaschiere, V. P. "Terrorist Extradition and the Political Offense Exception: An Administrative Solution" 21, 1 <u>Virginia Journal of International Law</u> (Fall 1980), pp. 163-183.

"Report on Legislative Responses to International Terrorism" 8, 2 <u>Terrorism</u> (1985), pp. 147-164. A summary of a forum sponsored by the Center for Law and National Security, University of Virginia, in cooperation with the Institute for Studies in International Terrorism, State University of New York, held on October 3, 1984, at the US Capitol.

Reshetov, Yuri "International Terrorism: Legal Aspects" 15 <u>New Times (Moscow)</u> (April 1981), pp. 20-22.

Richard, Ghislaine "Air Transport Safety: Prevention and Sanctions" 10 <u>Annals of Air and Space Law</u> (1985), pp. 209-216.

Ripp, Rudolph K. "The United Nations Commission on Human Rights" 6, 4 <u>Terrorism</u> (1983), pp. 577-587.

Root, Anthony "Settlement of the Iranian Hostage Crisis: An Exercise of Constitutional and Statutory Executive Prerogative in Foreign Affairs" 13, 4 <u>New York University Journal of International Law and Politics</u> (1981), pp. 993-1048.

Rosenn, K. S. "Strengthening Juridical Responses to Terrorism: Practical Measures for Latin America" (Coral Gables, Florida, University of Miami School of Law, under contract to the US Department of State, Bureau of Intelligence and Research, Office of Long Range Assessments and Research, 1981).

Rosenstock, Robert "International Convention Against the Taking of Hostages: Another International Community Step Against Terrorism" 9 Denver Journal of International Law and Policy (Summer 1980), pp. 169-195.

Rosenthal, Betsy R. "Countering International Terrorism: Building a Consensus" 8 Whittier Law Review (Summer 1986), pp. 747-762.

Rostow, Eugene "Overcoming Denial" in Benjamin Netanyahu, ed. Terrorism: How the West Can Win (New York: Farrar, Straus, Giroux, 1986), pp. 146-148.

Rovine, Arthur "A Prudent Response" 72 American Bar Association Journal (January 1986), pp. 38-39.

Rubin, Alfred P. "Current Legal Approaches to International Terrorism" 7, 2 Terrorism (1984), pp. 147-162, also available in H. H. Han, ed., Terrorism, Political Violence and World Order (1984), pp. 433ff.

Rubin, Alfred P. "Terrorism and Piracy: A Legal View" 3, 1-2 Terrorism (1979), pp. 117-130.
 Rubin finds that the classical concept of piracy is closer to terrorism than is commonly believed. He suggests several ways of coordinating this body of law with laws of jurisdiction and armed conflict to clarify the international legal situation.

Rubin, Alfred P. "Terrorism and Social Control: An International Law Perspective" 6, 1 Ohio Northern University Law Review (1979), pp. 60-69.
 Domestically, "terrorism" is already covered by criminal law, and Rubin wonders if it is wise to treat such offenses as distinct juridically. Internationally, the terrorist problem is based upon the difference between jurisdiction to prescribe and to enforce, and calls for states to cooperate. Legal problems which arise from lack of international cooperation in general, and in specific cases, are addressed.

Rubin, Alfred P. "Terrorism and the Laws of War" 12 Denver Journal of International Law and Policy (Spring 1983), pp. 219-235.

Rubin, Alfred P. "Terrorism: 'Grave Breaches' and the 1977 Geneva Protocols" 192 Proceedings of the American Society of International Law (1980).

Samuels, Alec "Terrorism and English Law" 10 Kingston Law Review (April 1980), pp. 3-23.

Sayre, Robert M. "The War of Words: Can Diplomacy Be Effective?" in Neil C. Livingstone and Terrell E. Arnold, eds. Fighting Back: Winning the War Against Terrorism (Lexington: Lexington Books, 1986), pp. 85-94.

Schachter, Oscar "Self-Help in International Law: US Action in the Iranian Hostages Crisis" 37, 2 Journal of International Affairs (1984), pp. 231-246.

Schlaefer, Cindy Verne "American Courts and Modern Terrorism: The Politics of Extradition" 13, 3 New York University Journal of International Law and Politics (Winter 1981), pp. 617-643.

Shamgar, Meir "An International Convention Against Terrorism" in Benjamin Netanyahu, ed. Terrorism: How the West Can Win (New York: Farrar, Straus, Giroux, 1986), pp. 157-162.

Shamwell, Horace F., Jr. "Implementing the Convention on the Prevention and Punishment of Crimes Against Internationally Protected Persons, Including Diplomatic Agents" 6, 4 Terrorism (1983), pp. 529-544.

Silverberg, Sanford R. "Sanctuary and Irregular Warfare: Contortive International Law" Houston Journal of International Law (Spring 1980).

Singer, Eric H. "Terrorism, Extradition, and FSIA Relief: The Letelier Case" 19 Vanderbilt Journal of Transnational Law (Winter 1986), pp. 57-82.

Smith, Jeffrey H. "A Symposium on Terrorism and the Law: The Scope of the Problem" 17, 2 International Society of Barristers Quarterly (April 1982), pp. 267-273.

Sofaer, Abraham D. "The Political Offense Exception and Terrorism" 15 Denver Journal of International Law and Policy (Summer 1986), pp. 125-133.

Sofaer, Abraham D. "Terrorism and the Law" 64 Foreign Affairs (Summer, 1986), pp. 901-922.
A reprint of the Sulzbacher Lecture delivered at the Columbia University School of Law, April 5, 1986, by the Legal Adviser to the U.S. Department of State, a former federal district judge in New York.

Stanbrook, Ivor and Clive Stanbrook The Law and Practice of Extradition (Chichester: Barry Rose, 1980).

Stein, Ted L. "Contempt, Crisis and the Court: The World Court and the Hostage Rescue Attempt" 76, 3 American Journal of International Law (1982), pp. 499-531.

Sundberg, Jacob W. F. "Comments on the Fourth Interim Report of the Committee on International Terrorism" 7, 2 Terrorism (1984), pp. 185-192.

Suter, Keith An International Law of Guerrilla Warfare: The Global Politics of Lawmaking (London: F. Pinter, 1984), 192 pp.

"Terrorism Cutting Law School Sessions Abroad" 117 New Jersey Law Journal (May 22, 1986), p. 30.

Tomasevski, K. "Some Thoughts on Constraints Upon the Approach of International Law to International Terrorism" 27, 1 Yugoslav Review of International Law (1980), pp. 100-109.

Tomasevski, K. "The United Nations Activities Concerning the Problem of Terrorism" 66: 1-2 Archives of Legal and Social Sciences (1980), pp. 67-76. In Croatian with English summary.

Touret, Denis G. "Terrorism and Freedom in International Law" 2 Houston Journal of International Law (Spring 1980), pp. 363-373.

Tulkens, F., ed. "Extradition and Terrorism" 60, 1-2 Revue de Droit Penal et de Criminologie (January-February, 1980), 159 pp.
Proceedings of the 16th Franco-Belgo-Luxembourgian Meeting on Criminal Science, May 18-19, 1979.

Tulkens, F. "Political Offenses in Belgian Law and the Fate Reserved for It in the European Convention for the Repression of Terrorism" 60, 1-2 Revue de Droit Penal et de Criminologie (January-February 1980), pp. 79-94.

Tybor, Joseph R. "Accused Terrorist's Extradition Ok'd. Court: Don't let U.S. Become 'Social Jungle'" 3 National Law Journal (March 9, 1981), p. 8.
A discussion of the Abu Eain case.

"UK-US: Extradition Treaty Supplement Limiting Scope of Political Offenses to Exclude Acts of Terrorism (Done at Washington, June 25, 1985); Letters of Transmittal to the US Senate" 24 International Legal Materials (July 1985), pp. 1104-1109.

"US: Court of Appeals for the Seventh Circuit Decision in Eain v. Wilkes" 21, 2 International Legal Materials (March 1982), pp. 342-356.

"US: Hanoch Tel-Oren v. Libyan Arab Republic et al. 726 f.2d 774 (D.C. Cir. 1984) (Court of Appeals Decision and US brief submitted to the Supreme Court) 24 International Legal Materials (March 1985), pp. 370-434.

"US: 1984 Act to Combat International Terrorism (From US Public Law 98-533 of October 19, 1984)" 24 International Legal Materials (July 1985), pp. 1015-1018.

US Senate, Committee on the Judiciary, Subcommittee on Security and Terrorism "The Antiterrorism and Foreign Mercenary Act: Hearing on S. 2255" (Washington, D.C.: 97th Congress, 2nd session, September 23, 1982), 79 pp.

US Senate, Committee on the Judiciary, Subcommittee on Security and Terrorism "Bills to Authorize Prosecution of Terrorists and Others Who Attack US Government Employees and Citizens Abroad: Hearing" (Washington, D.C.: 99th Congress, First Session, July 30, 1985), 103 pp.
Session was conducted regarding S. 1373 Protection of US Government Personnel Act of 1985, S. 1429 Terrorist Prosecution Act of 1985, and S. 1508, Terrorist Death Penalty Act of 1985.

US Senate, Committee on the Judiciary, Subcommittee on Security and Terrorism "Legislative Initiatives to Curb Domestic and International Terrorism: Hearings" (Washington, D.C.: 98th Congress, 2nd session, June 5, 6, and 13, 1984), 194 pp. Sessions were conducted regarding S. 2470 Anti-Nuclear Terrorism Act of 1984, S. 2623 Aircraft Sabotage Act, S. 2624 Act for the Prevention and Punishment of the Crime of Hostage-Taking, S. 2625 Act for Rewards for Information Concerning Terrorist Acts, and S. 2626 Prohibition Against the Training or Support of Terrorist Organizations Act of 1984.

van den Wijngaert, C. "European Judicial Space in the Face of 'Euroterrorism' and the Safeguard of the Fundamental Human Rights of the Common Market" 33, 3 Revue Internationale de Criminologie et de Police Technique (July-September 1980), pp. 289-308.

van den Wijngaert, Christine The Political Offense Exception to Extradition (Antwerp: Kluwer-Deventer, 1980).

Vance, Cyrus R. "Terrorism: Scope of the Threat and Needs for Effective Legislation" Department of State Bulletin (March 1978), pp. 53-55.

"Violence Against Diplomats Condemned in Sixth Committee; Wide Variety of Legal Issues Also Considered" 21 UN Monthly Chronicle (October 1984), pp. 82-85.

Warbrick, Colin "The European Convention on Human Rights and the Prevention of Terrorism" 32, 1 International and Comparative Law Quarterly (January 1983), pp. 82-119.

Warbrick, Colin "The Prevention of Terrorism (Temporary Provisions) Act 1976 and the European Convention on Human Rights: The McVeigh Case" 32, 3 International and Comparative Law Quarterly (July 1983), pp. 757ff.

Watson, Alan "Law in a Reign of Terror" 3 Law and History Review (Spring 1985), pp. 163-168.

Wilkinson, Paul "Admissibility of Negotiations between Organs of the Democratic States and Terrorists", paper presented at the Council of Europe Conference on the Defence of Democracy Against Terrorism in Europe, November 1980, published in 48, 3 Rivista di Studi Politici Internazionali (July-September 1981), pp. 369-374.

Wilkinson, Paul "Problems of Establishing a European Judicial Area" paper presented at the Council of Europe Conference on the Defence of Democracy Against Terrorism in Europe, November, 1980.

Wilson, Clifton E. "Modern Challenges to Traditional Diplomatic Immunities" paper presented to the panel on the Iran Hostage Crisis and International Law at the 23rd annual convention of the International Studies Association, Cincinnati, Ohio, March 24-27, 1982.

Wright, Claudia "The Prohibition Against the Training or Support of Terrorist Organizations Act of 1984: Introduction" 13, 4 Journal of Palestine Studies (Summer 1984), pp. 134-144.

Yoder, Amos "The Effectiveness of UN Action Against International Terrorism: Conclusions and Comments" 6, 4 Terrorism (1983), pp. 587-592.
Some steps have been taken, but nuclear terrorism remains to be discussed.

Yoder, Amos "United Nations Resolutions Against International Terrorism" 6, 4 Terrorism (1983), pp. 503-517.
The 1981 UN resolution inspired several bilateral agreements.

Media and Terrorism

Alexander, Yonah "Terrorism, the Media and the Police" in Robert H. Kupperman and Darrell M. Trent, eds. Terrorism (Stanford University Press, 1980).

Altheide, David "Format Symbols and TV Coverage of Terrorism in the United States and Great Britain" International Studies Quarterly (June 1987).

Anable, David "Media: The Reluctant Participant in Terrorism" in Marie Snyder, ed. Media and Terrorism: The Psychological Impact (North Newton, Kansas: Mennonite Press, 1978), pp. 15-22.

Atwater, Tony "Network Evening News Coverage of the TWA Hostage Crisis" Political Communication and Persuasion (Spring 1987).

Atwater, Tony "Terrorism on the Evening News: An Analysis of Coverage of the TWA Hostage Crisis on 'NBC Nightly News'" (Baton Rouge: Louisiana State University, Manship School of Journalism, Terrorism and the News Media Research Project, 1987).

Ball, George "Jet Planes, Television, and Foreign Policy" 1 SAIS Review (1981), pp. 5-9.
A look at US media handling of the Camp David accords and the Tehran US Embassy takeover.

Bassiouni, M. Cherif "Terrorism, Law Enforcement and the Mass Media: Perspectives, Problems, Proposals" 72, 1 Journal of Criminal Law and Criminology (Spring 1981), pp. 1-52.

Bazalgette, C. and R. Paterson "Real Entertainment: The Iranian Embassy Siege, 1980" 37 Screen Education (1980), pp. 55-67.
How the British Media handled the takeover of the Iranian Embassy in London.

Berger, A. A. Television as an Instrument of Terror: Essays on Media,Popular Culture and Everyday Life (New Brunswick, New Jersey: Transaction Books, 1980), 214 pp.

de Boer, Connie "The Polls: Terrorism and Hijacking" 43, 3 Public Opinion Quarterly (Fall 1979), pp. 410-418.
The author reports the results of polls in the US, UK, West Germany, Spain and the Netherlands on the seriousness of the terrorist problem, how terrorists are perceived, the causes of terrorism, how to prevent terrorism, its effects on civil rights, and the role of the media and sympathizers.

de Borchgrave, Arnaud "Censorship by Omission" in Benjamin Netanyahu, ed. Terrorism: How the West Can Win (New York: Farrar, Straus, Giroux, 1986), pp. 117-119.

Bormann, Ernest G. "A Fantasy Theme Analysis of the Television Coverage of the Hostage Release and the Reagan Inaugural" 68, 2 Quarterly Journal of Speech (1982), pp. 133-145.

Bottom, N. R., Jr. "Anti-Terrorism Film Survey" 2, 1-2 Journal of Security Administration (1979-1980), pp. 50-63.
25 criminal justice students reviewed the films: Postmark: Terror, Surviving Hostage Situations, Kidnapping Executive Style, Bomb Threat: Don't Panic, Public Official Protection, Threat: Car Bomb, Drive For Your Life, and Vehicle Ambush Counter-Attacks.

Clawson, Patrick "Why We Need More But Better Coverage of Terrorism" 30 Orbis (Winter 1987). pp. 701-710.

Clutterbuck, Richard The Media and Political Violence (London: Macmillan, 1981), 191 pp.

Clutterbuck, Richard "Terrorism and Urban Violence" in General Benjamin, ed. The Communications Revolution in Politics (New York: Academy of Political Science, 1982).

Colson, Charles "Terrorism's 'Catch-22'" 30 Christianity Today (January 17, 1986), p. 80.
Moral aspects of media coverage of terrorism.

Consoli, John "Covering Terrorism: Times Mirror's Michael Davies Calls for Conference" 118 Editor and Publisher (November 2, 1985), pp. 11-12.

Crelinsten, Ronald "Power and Meaning: Terrorism as a Struggle Over Access to the Communication Structure" in Paul Wilkinson, ed. Contemporary Research on Terrorism (University of Aberdeen Press, 1987).

Crelinsten, Ronald "Terrorism as Political Communication: The Relationship Between the Controller and the Controlled" in Paul Wilkinson, ed. Contemporary Research on Terrorism (University of Aberdeen Press, 1987).

Cunningham, Ann Marie "The Outer Limits of Fear" 3 Savvy (August 1982), pp. 50-57.

A discussion of the problems female correspondents face in covering terrorism in Latin America.

Diamond, Edwin "The Coverage Itself: Why it Turned into 'Terrorvision'" 33 TV Guide (September 21, 1985), pp. 6-11. A discussion of how television handled the TWA hijacking.

Doyle, Edward John "Propaganda by Deed: The Media's Response to Terrorism" Police Chief (June 1979), pp. 40-41.

Elliott, Deni "Family Ties: A Case Study of Families and Friends During the Hijacking of TWA Flight 847" (Baton Rouge: Louisiana State University, Manship School of Journalism, Terrorism and the News Media Research Project, 1987).

English, Deirdre "The Unprintable Picture" 10 Mother Jones (April 1985), p. 5. A discussion of ethics and editorial decisions in covering terrorism.

"Evolution in Hijack Coverage: NBC's Brokaw Says Reporting on Achille Lauro Incident Shows Networks Learned from Mistakes in TWA Flight 847 Story" 109 Broadcasting (November 11, 1985), pp. 92-93.

Fetscher, Irving Terrorism and the Reaction of the European Publishing Community (Cologne: 1977).

Fields, Howard "New FOIA Bill Would Exempt Terrorism Data" 225 Publishers Weekly (May 4, 1984), p. 16.

Friedlander, Robert A. "Iran: The Hostage Seizure, The Media, and International Law" in Abraham A. Miller, ed. Terrorism, The Media, and the Law (Dobbs Ferry, New York: Transnational Publishers, 1982), pp. 51-66.

Friedlander, Robert A. "Public Information--A Deadly Weapon in Terrorist Hands" 4, 10-12 TVI Journal (Winter 1983), pp. 4-6.

Friedlander, Robert A. Terrorism and the Media: A Contemporary Assessment (Gaithersburg: International Association of Chiefs of Police, 1981), 22 pp.

Gerbner, George Violence and Terror in the Mass Media: A Consolidated Report of Existing Research (New York: UNESCO, 1987).

Gersh, Debra "Media Worldwide Was Cursed by Terrorism in 1985; International Press Institute issues its Annual Report" 119 Editor and Publisher (February 22, 1986), pp. 18-23.

Greer, Herb "Terrorism and the Media: Myths, Illusion, Abstractions" 59 Encounter (August 1982), pp. 67-74.

Grigg, William "Does Publicity in the Media Cause Waves of Food Tampering?" Editor and Publisher (February 21, 1987), pp. 68ff.

Grossman, Lawrence K. "Television and Terrorism: A Common Sense Approach" 6, 4 TVI Report (1986), pp. 1-6.

Harris, Louis "Terrorism" Harris Survey Press Release (December 5, 1977), 3 pp.

Heid, Robin "Should Government Control Media Reporting of Terrorism?" 6, 4 TVI Report (1986), pp. 6-10.

Hertsgaard, Mark "TV, Terrorism, and the White House" 11 American Film (December 1985), pp. 38-39.
A discussion of television broadcasting policy regarding the TWA hijacking incident.

Hester, Al "From La Paz to Beijing--The Many Voices of Shortwave News" 2 Topic (June 1982).
Hester looks at how terrorism and crime are covered in the media.

Hickey, Neil "The Battle for Northern Ireland: How TV Tips the Balance" 29 TV Guide (September 26, 1981), pp. 8-27.

Hill, Frederic B. "Media Diplomacy" Washington Journalism Review (May 1981), pp. 27ff.

Hoeber, Francis P. "Terrorism, Sabotage and Telecommunications" 7 International Security Review (Fall 1982), pp. 289-304.

Hoge, James W. "The Media and Terrorism" in Abraham A. Miller, ed. Terrorism, The Media, and the Law (Dobbs Ferry, New York: Transnational Publishers, 1982).
The author is publisher of the Chicago Sun-Times.

"How Would You Rate Press Coverage of These Events?" Washington Post (September 26, 1986), p. A19.
The Times Mirror network reports the results of their second "People and the Press" poll taken by the Gallup firm on media coverage. Respondents rated good-to-excellent media coverage of the US strikes against Libya, the Achille Lauro hijack, the TWA flight 847 hijack, and the Karachi Pan Am flight 73 takeover.

Jackman, Robert W. and William A. Boyd "Multiple Sources in the Collection of Data on Political Conflict" 23, 2 American Journal of Political Science (May 1979), pp. 434ff.

Jaehnig, Walter "Terrorism in Britain: The Limits of Free Expression" in Terrorism: The Media and the Law (Dobbs Ferry: Transnational Publishers, 1982), pp. 106-122.

Jenkins, Brian Michael "The Psychological Implications of Media-Covered Terrorism" (Santa Monica: The Rand Corporation, P-6627, August 1981), 11 pp.

Jones, Juanita and Abraham Miller "The Media and Terrorist Activity: Resolving the First Amendment Dilemma" 6, 1 Ohio Northern University Law Review (1979), pp. 70-81.
The authors argue that the problem of media intrusion

justifies the most commonly imposed police restrictions during terrorist incidents, and that these restrictions do not interfere with freedom of expression. Supreme Court rulings on press freedom and access are examined.

Jones, Nancy "Constitutionality of Federal Legislation Which Would Restrict Public Access Through the Media to Details About Terrorist Activities While Such Activities Are in Progress" (Washington, D.C.: Library of Congress, CRS, March 25, 1977), 13 pp.

Kelly, Micheal J. and Thomas H. Mitchell "Transnational Terrorism and the Western Elite Press" paper presented to the annual meeting of the Canadian Political Science Association, Saskatoon, Saskatchewan, May 30, 1979, published in 1, 3 Political Communication and Persuasion (1981), pp. 269-296.

Killgore, James "Debate over How the Media Covers Terror; Why Do Some Critics Fault the Electronic and Print Media for the Way They Report Terrorist Incidents?" 118 Scholastic Update (May 16, 1986), p. 12.

Knight, Graham and Tony Dean "Myth and the Structure of the News" 32, 2 Journal of Communication (1982), pp. 144-161. A look at Canadian media coverage of the SAS raid on terrorists who seized the Iranian Embassy in London in 1980.

Kopkind, Andrew "Publish and Perish" 8 More (April 1978), pp. 12-21.
Provides a list of journalists which have been targetted by extra-legal violence since January 1, 1977.

Krauthammer, Charles "Partners in Crime" in Benjamin Netanyahu, ed. Terrorism: How the West Can Win (New York: Farrar, Straus, Giroux, 1986), pp. 111-113.

Latham, Aaron "The Bravest Journalist in the World" 89 Esquire (May 9, 1978), pp. 48-54.
A look at Arrigo Levi, editor of La Stampa.

Livingstone, W. D. "Terrorism and the Media Revolution" in Neil C. Livingstone and Terrell E. Arnold, eds. Fighting Back: Winning the War Against Terrorism (Lexington: Lexington Books, 1986), pp. 213-228.

Lord Chalfont "The Price of Sympathy" in Benjamin Netanyahu, ed. Terrorism: How the West Can Win (New York: Farrar, Straus, Giroux, 1986), pp. 126-130.

Lule, Jack "The Myth of My Widow: A Dramatistic Analysis of News Portrayals of a Terrorist Victim" (Baton Rouge: Louisiana State University, Manship School of Journalism, Terrorism and the News Media Research Project, 1987).

Lumley, Bob and Philip Schlesinger "The Press, the State and its Enemies: The Italian Case" 30, 4 Sociological Review (Great Britain) (1982), pp. 603-626.
Italian press coverage of terrorism in 1978-1982.

Martin, L. John "The Media's Role in International Terrorism" 8, 2 Terrorism (1985), pp. 127-146.

Mazur, Allan "Bomb Threats and the Mass Media: Evidence for a Theory of Suggestion" 47, 3 American Sociological Review (June 1982), pp. 407-410.

"Media Guideline Documents" in Abraham A. Miller, ed. Terrorism, The Media, and the Law (Dobbs Ferry, New York: Transnational Publishers, 1982).

"Media Reporting of Consumer Terrorism" Media Institute Forum (Winter 1986).
This issue of the newsletter is devoted to product tampering.

"Media Reporting of Terrorism Implicated as Accessory to Crimes" 144 Gallup Opinion Index (July 1977), pp. 13-15.

Merari, Ariel and N. Friedland "Public Attitude to Terrorism: A Survey" (Tel Aviv University, Center for Strategic Studies, 1980).

Midgley, Sarah and Virginia Rice, eds. Terrorism and the Media in the 1980's: Proceedings of a Conference held April 14, 1983, Cosponsored by Transnational Communications Center, The Media Institute and the Institute for Studies in International Terrorism, State University of New York (Washington, D.C.: The Institute, TCC, 1984), 67 pp.

Miller, Abraham A. "Terrorism and the Media: Observations from the American and British Experiences" 8, 3 Clandestine Tactics and Technology (Gaithersburg, Maryland: International Association of Chiefs of Police, n.d.), also available in Patrick J. Montana and George S. Roukis, eds. Managing Terrorism: Strategies for the Corporate Executive (Westport, Conn.: Quorum Books, 1983), pp. 91-108.

Miller, Abraham A. "Terrorism, The Media and Law Enforcement" in Abraham A. Miller, ed. Terrorism, The Media, and the Law (Dobbs Ferry, New York: Transnational Publishers, 1982).

Miller, Abraham A., ed. Terrorism, The Media, and the Law (Dobbs Ferry, New York: Transnational Publishers, 1982), 221 pp.

Miller, Abraham A. "Terrorism, The Media, and the Law: A Discussion of the Issues" in Abraham A. Miller, ed. Terrorism, The Media, and the Law (Dobbs Ferry, New York: Transnational Publishers, 1982).

Miro Quesada, Alejandro, Jr., "Covering Terrorism Abroad: Peruvian Journalists Ask 'Foreign Press' to Scale Down Reporting of Terrorist Acts" Editor and Publisher (October 4, 1986), p. 28.

Monday, M. "Insurgent War: A Backgrounder Book for Reporters" (San Diego: TVI mimeo, 1980), 34 pp.

Murphy, Patrick V. "The Police, The News Media, and the Coverage of Terrorism" in Abraham A. Miller, ed. Terrorism, The Media, and the Law (Dobbs Ferry, New York: Transnational Publishers, 1982).

National Advisory Committee on Criminal Justice Standards and Goals "News and Entertainment Media Responsibility for the Prevention of Extraordinary Violence" in Terrorism: The Media and the Law (Dobbs Ferry: Transnational Publishers, 1982).

National News Council "Paper on Terrorism" in Abraham A. Miller, ed. Terrorism, The Media, and the Law (Dobbs Ferry, New York: Transnational Publishers, 1982).

"News Judgement, Professionalism are Guides to Crisis Coverage" 110 Broadcasting (February 17, 1986), pp. 57-58. Lawrence K. Grossman's views on broadcast standards regarding coverage of terrorism.

O'Donnell, Wendy M. "Prime Time Hostages: A Case Study of Coverage of the Hijacking and Hostage-Taking on TWA Flight 847" (Baton Rouge: Louisiana State University, Manship School of Journalism, Terrorism and the News Media Research Project, 1987).

O'Sullivan, John "Deny Them Publicity" in Benjamin Netanyahu, ed. Terrorism: How the West Can Win (New York: Farrar, Straus, Giroux, 1986), pp. 120-125.

Paletz, David L., Peter A. Fozzard, and John Z. Ayanian "The IRA, the Red Brigades, and the FALN in the New York Times" 32, 2 Journal of Communication (1982), pp. 162-171.
A look at how New York Times coverage of these terrorist groups "generally ignores the motivations, objectives, and long-term goals of violent organizations, thereby preventing their causes from gaining legitimacy with the public."

Peterson, Sophia "Foreign News Gatekeepers and Criteria of Newsworthiness" 56 Journalism Quarterly (Spring 1979), pp. 116-125.

Peterson, Sophia "News Selection and Source Validity" in Donald Munton, ed. Measuring International Behavior: Public Sources, Events, and Validity (Halifax, Nova Scotia: Centre for Foreign Policy Studies, Dalhousie University, 1978), pp. 43-66.

Picard, Robert G. "The Conundrum of News Coverage of Terrorism" Toledo Law Review (Spring 1987).

Picard, Robert G. "News Coverage as the Contagion of Terrorism: Dangerous Charges Backed by Dubious Science" 3, 4 Political Communication and Persuasion (1986), pp. 385-400.

Picard, Robert G. "Stages in Coverage of Incidents of Political Violence" (Baton Rouge: Louisiana State University, Manship School of Journalism, Terrorism and the News Media Research Project, 1987).

Picard, Robert G. and Paul D. Adams "Characterization of Acts and Perpetrators of Political Violence Elite US Daily Newspapers" (Baton Rouge: Louisiana State University, Manship School of Journalism, Terrorism and the News Media Research Project, 1987).

Picard, Robert G. and Nicola Page Researchers on Terrorism and Terrorism and Media (Baton Rouge: Louisiana State University, Manship School of Journalism, Terrorism and the News Media Research Project, 1987).
The paper offers names and addresses.

Picard, Robert G. and Rhonda S. Sheets Terrorism and the News Media Research Bibliography (Baton Rouge: Louisiana State University, Manship School of Journalism, Terrorism and the News Media Research Project, 1987).
Offers 450 citations.

Pohlmann, Marcus D. and Thomas P. Foley "Terrorism in the 70s: Media's Connection" 61 National Forum (Summer 1981), pp. 33-35.
A discussion of a preemptive approach to media coverage of terrorism.

"The Police, The News Media, and the Coverage of Terrorism" in Abraham A. Miller, ed. Terrorism: The Media and the Law (Dobbs Ferry: Transnational Publishers, 1982), pp. 76-86.

"Political Violence and the Role of the Media: Some Perspectives" 1, 1 Political Communication and Persuasion (1980), pp. 79-99.
Based on comments at the Jerusalem Conference on International Terrorism held at the Jonathan Institute, July 2-5, 1979.

Pyle, Christopher "Defining Terrorism" Foreign Policy (Fall 1986), pp. 63-78.

Quester, George H. "Cruise-Ship Terrorism and the Media" 3, 4 Political Communication and Persuasion (1986), pp. 355-370.

Rabe, Robert L. "The Journalist and the Hostage: How Their Rights Can be Balanced" in Abraham A. Miller, ed. Terrorism, the Media, and the Law (Dobbs Ferry: Transnational Publishers, 1982), pp. 69-75.

Reimer, Rita "Restricting Right of Newsmen to Negotiate with Those Holding Hostages" (Washington, D.C.: Library of Congress, CRS, March 28, 1977), 4 pp.

Richardson, Lucy E., ed. The Middle East: Press Perspectives and National Policies (Washington, D.C.: Center for Middle East Policy, 1983).

Rickey, Carrie "Terrorist Chic" 6 American Film (September 1981), p. 14.
A discussion of Bernardo Bertolucci and Tragedy of a Ridiculous Man.

Rubin, Jeffrey Z. and Nehemia Friedland "Terrorists and Their Audience: Theater of Terror" Current (July-August 1986), pp. 36-39.

Schlesinger, Philip "Princess Gate 1980: The Media Politics of Siege Management" 37 Screen Education (1980), pp. 29-54.

Schlesinger, Philip "'Terrorism,' The Media, and the Liberal-Democratic States: A Critique of the Orthodoxy" 48, 1 Social Research (Spring 1981), pp. 74-99, reprinted in Yonah Alexander and Alan O'Day, eds. Terrorism in Ulster and Eire.

Schlesinger, Philip, Graham Murdock and Philip Elliott Televising "Terrorism": Political Violence in Popular Culture (London: Comedia Publishing Group, 1983), 181 pp.

Schmid, Alex Peter "Terrorisme en de Jacht op Publiciteit (Terrorism and the Search for Publicity)" 17, 49 Intermediair (December 4, 1981), pp. 1-7, 13.

Schmid, Alex Peter and Janny de Graff Insurgent Terrorism and the Western News Media: An Exploratory Analysis With a Dutch Case Study (Dutch State University, Leiden, Netherlands, Center for the Study of Social Conflicts, November 1980), 477 pp.

Schmid, Alex Peter and Janny de Graff Insurgent Terrorism and the Western Mass Media (Leiden: C.O.M.T., 1980).

Schmid, Alex Peter and Janny de Graff Violence as Communication: Insurgent Terrorism and the Western News Media (Beverly Hills and London: Sage, 1982), 283 pp.

Schorr, Daniel "The Encouragement of Violence" in Benjamin Netanyahu, ed. Terrorism: How the West Can Win (New York: Farrar, Straus, Giroux, 1986), pp. 114-116.

Schroth, Raymond A. "'These People are Fighting for my Mind'-- Reflections on Hijackings and the Press" 154 America (February 1, 1986), pp. 65-67.

Scotti, A. "The Media Doesn't Really Cover Terror-Violence" 4, 10-12 TVI Journal (Winter 1983), p. 2.

Shales, Tom "Terrorvision: The Hostage Speaks: Prime Time in TV-Savvy Tehran" Washington Post (December 11, 1979), pp. C1, C3.
Shales discusses how the Iranian government attempted, with some success, to exploit American news coverage of the siege of the American Embassy.

Sommer, Michael and Heidi Sommer "The Project on Media Coverage of Terrorism: A Summary of National Surveys and Other Investigations, 1977-1979" in Abraham A. Miller, ed. Terrorism, The Media, and the Law (Dobbs Ferry, New York: Transnational Publishers, 1982).

Stein, M. L. "Covering Terrorism" 119 Editor and Publisher (April 26, 1986), pp. 18-19.

Stein, M. L. "Covering Terrorism Abroad; Peruvian Journalist Asks 'Foreign Press' to Scale Down Reporting of Terrorist Acts" 119 Editor and Publisher (October 4, 1986), pp. 28-29.

Stephens, Lowndes F. "Implications of Terrorism for Planning the Public Relations Function" (Baton Rouge: Louisiana State University, Manship School of Journalism, Terrorism and the News Media Research Project, 1987).

Stoil, Michael J. and J. R. Brownell "Research Design for a Study of Threat Communication and Audience Perception of Domestic Terrorism" 1, 2 Political Communication and Persuasion (1981).

"Terrorism and the Media" in Benjamin Netanyahu, ed. Terrorism: How the West Can Win (New York: Farrar, Straus, Giroux, 1986), pp. 229-240.

Terrorism and the Media: An International Seminar Held in Florence, Italy, 1978, Organized by the International Press Institute in Association with Affari Esteri, Rome Italy (Zurich: International Press Institute, 1980), 94 pp.

Terrorism and the Media: Symposium Report (New York: Overseas Press Club, 1986).

"Terrorism Bombs Damage French TV, Radio Headquarters" 320 Variety (October 16, 1985), pp. 3-4.

Terrorism: The Media and the Law (Dobbs Ferry: Transnational Publishers, 1982), 221 pp.

Terry, Herbert A. "Television and Terrorism: Professionalism Not Quite the Answer" 53 Indiana Law Journal (1978), pp. 754ff.

Theberge, Leonard and Yonah Alexander "Terrorism and the Media in the 1980s--Conference Report" 2, 3 Political Communication and Persuasion (1984) pp. 283-332.

Tugwell, Maurice "Terrorism and Propaganda: Problem and Response" 6 Conflict Quarterly (Spring 1986), pp. 5-15.

US Department of State "Guidelines for United States Government Spokespersons During Terrorist Incidents" in Abraham A. Miller, ed. Terrorism, The Media, and the Law (Dobbs Ferry, New York: Transnational Publishers, 1982).

van der Vat, Dan "Terrorism and the Media: Publicity is One of the Aims of Terrorism: Should the Media be Prevented from Providing it?" 11 Index on Censorship (April 1982), pp. 25-27.

Vanocur, Sander "The Role of the Media" in Uri Ra'anan, Robert L. Pfaltzgraff, Jr., Richard H. Shultz, Ernst Halperin, and Igor Lukes Hydra of Carnage: International Linkages of Terrorism: The Witnesses Speak (Lexington, Mass.: Lexington Books, 1986), pp. 259-264.

Vitale, Joseph "TV and Terrorism"6   Channels of Communications (July-August 1986), pp. 12-13.
The article notes that the fear of terrorism limits foreign location filming.

Walzer, Michael "Follow That Network" 194 New Republic (June 2, 1986), p. 8.
A discussion of the ethics of NBC in televising an interview with wanted terrorist Abu Abbas.

Weimann, Gabriel "Media Events: The Case of International Terrorism" 31 Journal of Broadcasting and Electronic Media (Winter 1987), pp. 21-39.

Weimann, Gabriel "The Theater of Terror: Effects of Press Coverage" 33 Journal of Communication (Winter 1983), pp. 38-45.
Exposure to press coverage redefines the image of terrorists.

Weimann, Gabriel "Terrorists or Freedom Fighters? Labeling Terrorism in the Israeli Press" Political Communication and Persuasion (January 1985).

Weisman, John "TV and Terrorism: When Reporting Can Blow up in Your Face (How to Cover Terrorist Activities Without Encouraging Others)" 33 TV Guide (February 23, 1985), pp. 2ff.

Weisman, John "Why American TV is so Vulnerable to Foreign Propaganda" 30 TV Guide (June 12, 1982), pp. 4-6, 10, 12, 14, 16.
Includes a look at network news coverage in late 1981 of the story of a Libyan hit team sent to assassinate US leaders.

Wilkinson, Paul "Relationship Between Freedom of Press and Information and Publicity Given by the Mass Media" paper presented at the Council of Europe Conference on the Defence of Democracy Against Terrorism in Europe, Noember 1980.

Wilkinson, Paul "Terrorism, The Mass Media and Democracy" Contemporary Review (Great Britain) 239 (July 1981), pp. 35-44.

Winter, Bill "Media Taken to Task for Terrorism Coverage" 66 American Bar Association Journal (December 1980), p. 1510.

Wurth-Hough, Sandra "Network News Coverage of Terrorism: The Early Years" 6, 3 Terrorism (1983), pp. 403-421.
A look at how the 3 US television networks covered terrorism in 1968-1971 regarding depiction, frequency, length of coverage, and location.

Psychological
and Medical Approaches

Apter, David "The Legitimation of Violence" paper presented to the second annual meeting of the International Society of Political Psychology, Washington, D.C., May 24-26, 1979.

Baeyer-Katte, Wanda "A Left-Wing Terrorist Indoctrination Group" paper presented to the 1983 annual meeting of the International Society of Political Psychology, Oxford, England, July 1983.

Baeyer-Katte, Wanda, et al. Gruppenprozesse: Analysen zum Terrorismus 3 (Opladen, West Germany: Westdeutscher Verlag, 1982).

Bastiaans, J. "Consequences of Modern Terrorism" in L. Goldberger and S. Breznitz, eds. Handbook of Stress: Theoretical and Clinical Aspects (New York: Free Press, 1982).

Bastiaans, J., D. Mulder, W. K. van Dijk, and H. M. van der Ploeg Mensen bij Gijzelingen: Alphen aan den (Rijn: Sijthoff, 1981), 304 pp.
Four psychiatrists discuss their followup counseling of freed Dutch hostages.

Benedek, E.P. "The Psychiatric Aspects of Terrorism" (Washington, D.C.: American Psychiatric Association, 1979-1980).
The $19,600 contract was designed to develop a conference which would include law enforcement and government officials, consultants to government agencies, and psychiatrists and psychologists in the US and abroad.

Blanchard, William H. Revolutionary Morality: A Psychosexual Analysis of 12 Revolutionaries (Santa Barbara, California: ABC-Clio Information Services, 1984), 281 pp.

Brismar, B. and L. Bergenwald "The Terrorist Bomb Explosion in Bologna, Italy, 1980: An Analysis of the Effects and Injuries Sustained" 22, 3 Journal of Trauma (1982), pp. 216-220.
Cannon, W. B. Bodily Changes in Pain, Hunger, Fear and Rage, second edition (Boston: Charles T. Bradford Company, 1929).

Crenshaw, Martha "The Subjective Reality of the Terrorist: Ideological and Psychological Factors in Terrorism" in Robert O. Slater and Michael Stohl, eds. Current Perspectives on International Terrorism (London: Macmillan, 1987).

Coleman, L. S. "Perspectives on the Medical Study of Violence" 44 American Journal of Orthopsychiatry (1974), pp. 675-687.

Corrado, Raymond R. "A Critique of the Mental Disorder Perspective of Political Terrorism" 4, 3-4 International Journal of Law and Psychiatry (1981), pp. 293-309.

Crelinsten, Ronald C. "The Root Causes of Terrorism" paper presented to the second annual meeting of the International Society of Political Psychology, Washington, D.C., May 24-26, 1979.

Daly, L. N. "Terrorism: What Can the Psychiatrist Do?" paper presented at the 32nd annual meeting of the American Academy of Forensic Sciences, New Orleans, February 22, 1980, published in 26, 1 Journal of Forensic Sciences (January 1981), pp. 116-122.

Davies, J. S. "Biological Perspectives on Human Conflict" in Ted Robert Gurr, ed. Handbook of Political Conflict: Theory and Research (New York: The Free Press, 1980), pp. 19-61.

Davies, James Chowning "Ions of Emotion and Political Behavior" in A. Somit, ed. Biology and Politics (Paris: Mouton, 1976), pp. 97-125.

Denno, Deborah W. and Ruth M. Schwarz, compilers Biological, Psychological, and Environmental Factors in Delinquency and Mental Disorder: An Interdisciplinary Bibliography (Westport, Conn.: Greenwood Press, 1985), 222 pp.
Prepared under the auspices of the Center for Studies in Criminology and Criminal Law, University of Pennsylvania, the bibliography provides material on the role of biological, psychological, and environmental explanations of deviant behavior in the development of crime and violence and in the control, treatment, and rehabilitation of offenders. Its 2200 citations cover child development, brain functions, and crime.

Dreman, S.B. and E. C. Cohen "Children of Victims of Terrorist Activities: A Family Approach to Dealing with Tragedy" 10, 2 American Journal of Family Therapy (1982), pp. 39-47.

Eichelman, Burr, David A. Soskis and William H. Reid, eds. Terrorism: Interdisciplinary Perspectives (Washington, D.C.: American Psychiatric Association, 1982), 186 pp.

Eitinger, Leo "The Effects of Captivity" in Frank M. Ochberg and David A. Soskis, eds. Victims of Terrorism (Boulder: Westview Special Studies in National and International Terrorism, 1982).

Eitinger, Leo "The Stress of Captivity" in R. D. Crelinsten, ed. The Dimensions of Victimization in the Context of Terroristic Acts (Montreal: International Centre for Comparative Criminology, 1977), pp. 69-85.

Fattah, Ezzat A. "Some Reflections on the Victimology of Terrorism" 3, 1-2 Terrorism (1979), pp. 81-108.
Fattah looks at the criteria of selection of victims, arguing that terrorists generally single out targets, rather than launch indiscriminate attacks. He also notes the dynamics of the victim-terrorist relationship, and the victim's reactions to this experience during and after the incident.

Fattah, Ezzat A. "The Use of the Victim as an Agent of Self-Legitimization" 1 Victimology (1976), pp. 29-53.

Ferracuti, Franco "La Prevendibilita del Terrorismo e della Destabilizzaione" paper presented to the 31st Riunione Scientifica della Societa Italiana di Statistica, Torino, April 5-7, 1982, 24 pp.

Ferracuti, Franco "Psychiatric Aspects of Italian Left Wing and Right Wing Terrorism" paper presented to the Seventh World Congress of Psychiatry, Vienna, Austria, July, 1983.
The psychiatric characteristics of left-wing terrorists are far different from typical right-wing terrorists.

Ferracuti, Franco "A Sociopsychiatric Interpretation of Terrorism" paper presented to the 85th annual meeting of the American Academy of Political and Social Science, Philadelphia, April 23-24, 1982, 22 pp., published in 463 Annals of the American Academy of Political and Social Science (September 1982), pp. 129-140.

Ferracuti, Franco and F. Bruno "Psychiatric Aspects of Terrorism in Italy" in I. L. Barak-Glantz and C. R. Huff, eds. The Mad, the Bad and the Different: Essays in Honor of Simon Dinitz (Lexington: Lexington Books, 1981), pp. 199-213.

Fields, Rona M. "Psychological Sequelae of Terrorization" paper presented to the second annual meeting of the International Society of Political Psychology, Washington, D.C., May 24-26, 1979, published in Yonah Alexander and John M. Gleason, eds. Behavioral and Quantitative Perspectives on Terrorism (New York: Pergamon, 1981), p. 51-72.

Fields, Rona M. "Research on the Victims of Terrorism" in Frank M. Ochberg and David A. Soskis, eds. Victims of Terrorism (Boulder: Westview Special Studies in National and International Terrorism, 1982).

Fields, Rona M. "Victims of Terrorism: The Effects of Prolonged Stress" Evaluation and Change (1980), pp. 76-83.
Paper presented at the Second Annual Conference of the International Society for Political Psychology, Washington, D.C., May 24, 1979.

Figley, Ch. R. "Mobilization I: The Iranian Crisis: Final Report of the Task Force on Families of Catastrophe" (West Lafayette: Purdue University, 1980). How the families of hostage victims handled the stress.

Foreman, P. B. "Panic Theory" 37 Sociology and Social Research (1953), pp. 295-304.

Frederick, C. "Effects of Natural vs. Human-Induced Violence Upon Victims" Evaluation and Change (1980).

Freedman, Lawrence Zelic "Terrorism and Change" paper presented to the second annual meeting of the International Society of Political Psychology, Washington, D.C., May 24-26, 1979.

Freedman, Lawrence Zelic "Why Does Terrorism Terrorize?" 6, 3 Terrorism (1983), pp. 389-402.

Fried, Risto "The Psychology of the Terrorist" in Brian Michael Jenkins, conference director Terrorism and Beyond: An International Conference on Terrorism and Low-Level Conflict (Santa Monica: The Rand Corporation, R-2714-DOE/DOJ/DOS/RC, December 1982), pp. 119-124.

Friedlander, Robert A. "The Psychology of Terrorism: Contemporary Views" in Patrick J. Montana and George S. Roukis, eds. Managing Terrorism: Strategies for the Corporate Executive (Westport, Conn.: Quorum Books, 1983), pp. 41-54.

Giegerich, W. "Terrorism as Task and Responsibility: Reflections of a Depth Psychologist" 10, 3 Analytische Psychologie (1979), pp. 190-215.

Goleman, Daniel "The Roots of Terrorism Are Found in Brutality of Shattered Childhood" New York Times (September 2, 1986), pp. C1, C8.

Greaves, Douglas "The Definition and Motivation of Terrorism" 13 Australian Journal of Forensic Science (June 1981), pp. 160-166.

Grings, W. and M. E. Dawson Emotions and Bodily Responses: A Psychophysiological Approach (New York: Academic Press, 1978).

Groebel, Jo "The Social Motivation of Western Terrorists" paper presented to the 7th Biennial Meeting of the International Society for Research on Aggression, Evanston, Illinois, July 1986.

Guttman, D. "Killers and Consumers: The Terrorist and His Audience" 46 Social Research (1979), pp. 517-526.

Hacker, Frederick J. "Contagion and Attraction of Terror and Terrorism" in Yonah Alexander and John M. Gleason, eds. Behavioral and Quantitative Perspectives on Terrorism (New York: Pergamon, 1981), pp. 73-85.

Hacker, Frederick J. "Devils and Poor Devils (Perpetrators, Victims, and Perpetrator Victims Among Terrorists and Cultists)" paper presented to the second annual meeting of the International Society of Political Psychology, Washington, D.C., May 24-26, 1979.

Hacker, Frederick J. "Terror and Terrorism: Modern Growth Industry and Mass Entertainment" 4, 1-4 Terrorism (1980), pp. 143-160.

Hassel, Conrad V. "Interactions of Law Enforcement and Behavioral Science Personnel" in Frank M. Ochberg and David A. Soskis, eds. Victims of Terrorism (Boulder: Westview Special Studies in National and International Terrorism, 1982).

Heskin, Ken Northern Ireland: A Psychological Analysis (New York: Columbia University Press, 1980), 174 pp.

Hillman, R. G. "The Psychopathology of Being Held Hostage" 138 American Journal of Psychiatry (1981), pp. 1193-1197.

Hubbard, David G. "Organic Factors Underlying the Psychology of Terror" in Yonah Alexander and John M. Gleason, eds. Terrorism: Behavioral and Quantitative Perspectives (New York: Pergamon, 1980).

Hubbard, David G. "The Psychodynamics of Terrorism" in Yonah Alexander and T. Adeniran, eds. International Violence (New York: Praeger, 1983), pp. 45-53.

Hulsman, Louk "Terrorism and Criminal Justice Systems" paper presented to the second annual meeting of the International Society of Political Psychology, Washington, D.C., May 24-26, 1979.

Jager, Schmidtchen, and Suellwold, eds. Analysen zum Terrorismus: Volume 2: Lebenslauf-Analysen (Westdeutscher Verlag, 1981).

Jenkins, Brian Michael "The Terrorist Mindset and Terrorist Decisionmaking: Two Areas of Ignorance" (Santa Monica: The Rand Corporation, P-6340, June 1979), 6 pp.

Jessen, F. W. "Communicated Threat Assessment" (Lawrence Livermore Laboratory, California, for the US Nuclear Regulatory Commission, 1981).
The research aims at developing a capability to perform comprehensive technical and psychological assessment of threat messages which communicate the intent to commit criminal acts using nuclear material.

Jones, Peter M. "A Psychiatrist Examines the Terrorist Mind" 118 Scholastic Update (May 16, 1986), p. 6.

Kampf, Herbert A. "On the Appeals of Extremism to the Youth of Affluent, Democratic Societies" 4, 1-4 Terrorism (1980), pp. 161-194.

Kaplan, Abraham "The Psychodynamics of Terrorism" in Yonah Alexander and John M. Gleason, eds. Behavioral and Quantitative Perspectives on Terrorism (New York: Pergamon, 1981), pp. 35-50.

Katwan, Jakov, ed. "The International Scientific Conference on Terrorism, Berlin" 3, 3-4 Terrorism (1980).

Kellen, Konrad "Terrorists--What Are They Like? How Some Terrorists Describe Their World and Actions" (Santa Monica: The Rand Corporation, N-1300-SL, November 1979), reprinted in Brian Michael Jenkins, conference director Terrorism and Beyond: An International Conference on Terrorism and Low-Level Conflict (Santa Monica: The Rand Corporation, R-2714-DOE/DOJ/DOS/RC, December 1982), pp. 125-173.

Knutson, Jeanne N. "Report from Belfast: Agony, Rage and the Process of Denial" paper presented to the International Society of Political Psychology, Mannheim, 1981.

Knutson, Jeanne N. "Social and Psychodynamic Pressures Toward a Negative Identity: The Case of an American Revolutionary Terrorist" paper presented to the second annual meeting of the International Society of Political Psychology, Washington, D.C., May 24-26, 1979, published in G. Calvi, M. Martini and A. Schwanke, eds. Psicologia dell-estermismo Politico (Milan: Franco Angeli Editore, 1981), and in Yonah Alexander and John M. Gleason, eds. Behavioral and Quantitative Perspectives on Terrorism (New York: Pergamon, 1981), pp. 105-150.

Knutson, Jeanne N. "The Terrorists' Dilemmas: Some Implicit Rules of the Game" 4 Terrorism (1980), pp. 195-222.

Krupnick, J. L. and M. J. Horowitz "Victims of Violence: Psychological Responses, Treatment Implications" Evaluation and Change (1980), pp. 42-46.

Kudat, Ayse "Effects of Terrorism on Children" paper presented to the second annual meeting of the International Society of Political Psychology, Washington, D.C., May 24-26, 1979.

Leibstone, Marvin "Terror and Its Survival: Discussions About Manipulable Operational Conditions Which Have Favored the Political Terrorist" 5 Clandestine Tactics and Technology (Gaithersburg, Maryland: International Association of Chiefs of Police, n.d.).

Lichter, S. Robert "A Psychopolitical Study of West German Male Radical Students" 12 Comparative Politics (October 1979), pp. 27-48.

Mann, L. "The Social Psychology of Terrorism" paper presented at the Sixth National Symposium on the Forensic Science, Adelaide, March 1979.

Middendorf, Wolf "Bank Robbers and Their Victims: Historical and Criminological Perspectives" paper presented to the International Seminar on Dimensions of Victimization in the Context of Terrorist Acts, Evian, France, 1977.

Miller, Abraham H. "Psychological Dimensions of Political Terrorism: Some Notes on Victimization" paper presented to the annual convention of the International Studies Association, Los Angeles, March 18-22, 1980.

Milte, Kerry L., Allen A. Bartholomew, Dennis J. O'Hearn, and Andrew Campbell "Terrorism: Political and Psychological Considerations" 9, 2 Australian and New Zealand Journal of Criminology (June 1976), pp. 89-94.

Miron, Murray S. "Psycholinguistic Analysis of the SLA" 1 Assets Protection (1976), pp. 14-19.

Monahan, John Predicting Violent Behavior: An Assessment of Clinical Techniques (Beverly Hills: Sage Library of Social Research, volume 114, 1981), 184 pp.

Montor, Karel and Douglas Afdahl "Brain Wave and Biochemical Research Findings" in Joel J. Kramer, ed. The Role of Behavioral Science in Physical Security: Proceedings of the Third Annual Symposium, May 2-4, 1978 (Washington, D.C.: National Bureau of Standards Special Publication 480-38, 1979), pp. 75-80.

Moreno, Francisco J. "Some Psychodynamics of Terrorists in Spain and El Salvador" paper presented to the second annual meeting of the International Society of Political Psychology, Washington, D.C., May 24-26, 1979.

Moyer, K. E. The Psychobiology of Aggression (New York: Harper and Row, 1976)

Moyer, K. E., ed. Physiology of Aggression and Implications for Control (New York: Raven Press, 1976).

Nadelson, C. C., et al. "A Follow Up Study of Rape Victims" 139 American Journal of Psychiatry (1982), pp. 1266-1270.

Nass, Gustav Medical and Psychological Aspects in the Forensic Assessment of Deviant Behavior, Addicts, Transsexualism and Terrorism; proceedings of the Academy for Fundamental Criminological Research, 4th Installment (Kassel: Society for the Preventive Suppression of Crime Publishers, n.d.), 123 pp, in German.
  Some of the articles focus on the book Anarchoterrorism: A Developmental Psychological Phenomenon: Psychological Analysis of a Specific Category of Behavior.

Niederlander, W. G. "The Survivor Syndrome: Further Observations and Dimensions" 29 Journal of the American Psychoanalytic Association (1981), pp. 413-425.

Ochberg, Frank M. "A Case Study: Gerard Vaders" in Ochberg, Frank M. and David A. Soskis, eds. Victims of Terrorism (Boulder: Westview Special Studies in National and International Terrorism, 1982).

Ochberg, Frank M. "Hostages in Teheran" 10, 5 Psych. Annals (May 1980).

Ochberg, Frank M. "Victims of Terrorism" 41, 3 Journal for Clinical Psychiatry (March 1980).

Ochberg, Frank M. and David A. Soskis "Planning for the Future: Means and Ends" in Frank M. Ochberg and David A. Soskis, eds. Victims of Terrorism (Boulder: Westview Special Studies in National and International Terrorism, 1982).

Ochberg, Frank M. and David A. Soskis, eds. Victims of Terrorism (Boulder: Westview Special Studies in National and International Terrorism, 1982), 201 pp.
The chapters focus on stress, captivity, and coping mechanisms as they relate to terrorist hostage victims. Most of the discussion centers on the victim's psychological and physiological reactions to the experience.

Oots, Kent Layne and Thomas C. Wiegele "Terrorist and Victim: Psychiatric and Physiological Approaches from a Social Science Perspective" 8, 1 Terrorism (1985), p. 1-32.

Ottenberg, Perry "Terrorism: 'No Hostages are Innocent'" 10, 5 Psychiatric Annals (1980), p. 11-22.

Parenti, F. Assieme Per Uccidere: Psicologia della Violenza di Gruppo (Together to Kill: The Psychology of Group Violence) (Rome: Armando, 1978).

Pearce, K. I. "Police Negotiations: A New Role for the Community Psychiatrist" 22, 4 Canadian Psychiatric Association Journal (June 1977), pp. 171-175.
The article notes the type of individual involved in a hostage situation--the mentally ill, the criminal, and the terrorist. Those clinic characteristics important in determining the management of the negotiations are examined and psychiatrists are asked to become involved in an advisory role.

Post, Jerrold M. "Notes on a Psychodynamic Theory of Terrorist Behavior", paper presented to the Seventh World Congress of Psychiatry, Vienna, Austria, July, 1983, 21 pp., published in 7, 3 Terrorism (1984), pp. 241-256.

Post, Jerrold M. "Psychological Insights on Political Terrorism", paper presented to the 24th annual convention of the International Studies Association, Mexico City, April 5-9, 1983.

"The Psychology of Terrorism" 18 Security Digest (Washington, D.C.: The Wilson Center International Security Studies Program, May 1987), 4 pp.
A summary of an international conference held March 16-18, 1987. A shorter version appeared in Wilson Center Reports (June 1987), pp. 5-7.

"The Psychology of the Terrorist" (Final Report from Committee A of the Berlin Conference, November 1978).

Rader, Herschel "The Child as Terrorist: Seven Cases" 84, 1 School Review (November 1975), pp. 5-41.

Raffay, A. V. "Hope, A Principle of Terrorism" 1 _Analytische Psychologie_ (1980), pp. 38-52.

Rasch, Wilfried "Individual Career and Group Formation in the German Terrorist Scene" paper presented to the second annual meeting of the International Society of Political Psychology, Washington, D.C., May 24-26, 1979.

Rasch, Wilfried "Psychological Dimensions of Political Terrorism in the FRG" 2 _International Journal of Law and Psychiatry_ (1979, pp. 79-85.

Rice, Berkeley "Between the Lines of Threatening Messages" 15 _Psychology Today_ (September 1981), pp. 52-59.
A discussion of Murray Miron's research on psycholinguistic aspects of terrorism and anonymous letters.

Rich, R. and S. Stenzel "Mental Health Services for Victims: Policy Paradigms" _Evaluation and Change_ (1980).

Rogers, R. "On Emotional Responses to Nuclear Issues and Terrorism" 5, 3 _Psychiatric Journal of the University of Ottawa_ (1980), pp. 147-152.

Ronfeldt, David and William Sater "The Mindsets of High-Technology Terrorists: Future Implications from an Historical Analog" (Santa Monica: The Rand Corporation, N-1610-SL, 1981), 33 pp., also available in Yonah Alexander and Charles K. Ebinger, eds. _Political Terrorism and Energy: The Threat and Response_ (New York: Praeger, 1982).

Roth, Walton T. "The Meaning of Stress" in Ochberg, Frank M. and David A. Soskis, eds. _Victims of Terrorism_ (Boulder: Westview Special Studies in National and International Terrorism, 1982).

Rovner, Sandy "The Mind of the Terrorist" _Washington Post Health_ (November 11, 1986), p. 16.
An interview with Dr. Jerrold Post and Conrad V. Hassel, who argue that leftist terrorists are children of the upper middle class, while rightwing terrorists are working-class, and that the best way to deal with terrorist groups is to ignore them and offer preferable alternatives for their membership, rather than confront the group head-on.

Rubin, Jeffrey Z. and Nehemia Friedland "Threat of Terror: Political Terrorism is Not Likely to Disappear from the Stage, but Viewing it as Theater May Help Prevent Mindless Tragedies" 20 _Psychology Today_ (March 1986), pp. 18-24.
Includes a related article on the Achille Lauro hijacking.

Rupprecht, Reinhard "Description of a Research Project to Study the Causes of Terrorism" in Brian Michael Jenkins, conference director _Terrorism and Beyond: An International Conference on Terrorism and Low-Level Conflict_ (Santa Monica: The Rand Corporation, R-2714-DOE/DOJ/DOS/RC, December 1982), pp. 115-118.

Salewski, Wolfgang D. "The Latest Theory Recognized by Sociological Science Research in Terrorism and Violence" 3, 3-4 Terrorism (1980), pp. 297-301.

Schneider, Hans Joachim "Opfer des Terrorismus" 63, 6 Mschr Kriminologie und Strafrechtsreform (1980), pp. 407-412.

Silverstein, Martin "Surviving Terrorism" 5 Washington Quarterly (Autumn 1982), pp. 175-180.

Skove, Cynthia "Victims of Terrorism" Georgetown (Winter 1987), pp. 10-13, 39.

Soskis, David A. and Ofra Ayalon "A Six-Year Follow-Up of Hostage Victims" 7, 4 Terrorism (1985), pp. 411-416.

Soskis, David A. and Frank M. Ochberg "Concepts of Terrorist Victimization" in Frank M. Ochberg and David A. Soskis, eds. Victims of Terrorism (Boulder: Westview Press, 1982).

Strentz, Thomas "Proxemics and Interview" 44, 9 Police Chief (1977), pp. 74-76.

Strentz, Thomas "The Stockholm Syndrome: Law Enforcement Policy and Ego Defenses of the Hostage" 347 Annals of the New York Academy of Sciences (June 20, 1980), pp. 137-150.

Strentz, Thomas "The Stockholm Syndrome: Law Enforcement Policy and Hostage Behavior" in Frank M. Ochberg and David A. Soskis, eds. Victims of Terrorism (Boulder: Westview Special Studies in National and International Terrorism, 1982).

Strentz, Thomas "The Terrorist Organizational Profile: A Psychological Evaluation" in Yonah Alexander and John M. Gleason, eds. Behavioral and Quantitative Perspectives on Terrorism (New York: Pergamon, 1981), pp. 86-104.

Symonds, Martin "Acute Responses of Victims to Terror" Evaluation and Change (1980).

Symonds, Martin "Victim Responses to Terror" 347 Annals of the New York Academy of Sciences (June 20, 1980), pp. 129-136.

Symonds, Martin "Victim Responses to Terror: Understanding and Treatment" in Frank M. Ochberg and David A. Soskis, eds. Victims of Terrorism (Boulder: Westview Special Studies in National and International Terrorism, 1982).

Terr, L. C. "Chowchilla Revisited: The Effects of Psychic Trauma Four Years After a School-Bus Kidnapping" 140 American Journal of Psychiatry (1983), pp. 1543-1550.

Tinklenberg, Jared R. "The Effects of Captivity" in Frank M. Ochberg and David A. Soskis, eds. Victims of Terrorism (Boulder: Westview Special Studies in National and International Terrorism, 1982).

Tinklenberg, Jared R., P. Murphy and P. Murphy "Adaptive Behavior of Victims of Terrorism" in R. D. Crelinsten, ed. The Dimensions of Victimization in the Context of Terroristic Acts (Montreal: International Centre for Comparative Criminology, 1977), pp. 92-107.

"Thwarting Terrorists: Can Psychiatry Help?" 117 Science News (May 17, 1980), p. 308.

Turk, Austin T. "Social Dynamics of Terrorism" paper presented at the annual meeting of the American Academy of Political and Social Science, Philadelphia, April 22-24, 1982, 20 pp.

Turner, James "A Systematic Conceptualization Concerning Acts of Terror" paper presented to the second annual meeting of the International Society of Political Psychology, Washington, D.C., May 24-26, 1979.

Turner, James "Uses and Misuses of the Hostage Identification Syndrome" paper presented to the second annual meeting of the International Society of Political Psychology, Washington, D.C., May 24-26, 1979.

Watts, M. W. and D. Sumi "Attitudes and Physiological Response to Audiovisual Display of Aggressive Social Behavior" paper presented to the annual meeting of the Midwest Political Science Association, Chicago, April 29--May 1, 1976.

Wolk, R. L. "Psychoanalytical Conceptualization of Hostage Symptoms and Their Treatment" (Napanoch, New York: Forensic Services, New York Department of Mental Hygiene, Eastern New York Correctional Facility, 1977).

Woods, Colin "Problems of International Terrorism" paper presented at the 43rd plenary Scientific Session of the Australian Academy of Forensic Sciences, Sydney, May 30, 1980, published in O. Schmalzbach, ed. 12, 2-3 Australian Journal of Forensic Sciences (Sydney: Butterworths, 1979/1980), pp. 67-74.

Wykert, John "A Meeting on Terrorism" 14, 8 Psychiatric News (April 20, 1979), pp. 1-13.

Wykert, John "Psychiatry and Terrorism" 14 Psychiatric News (February 2, 1979), pp. 1, 12-14.

Zonis, Marvin "Seminar on the Psychological Roots of Shiite Muslim Terrorism" (unpublished manuscript, March 1, 1984).

Related Studies

Abel, Charles Frederick <u>Punishment as Restitution;</u> <u>Definitions, Justification, and Questions of Equity</u> (University of Maryland, Department of Political Science, Ph.D. dissertation, 1979).

Adeniran, Tunde and Yonah Alexander, eds. <u>International</u> <u>Violence</u> (New York: Praeger, 1982), 265 pp.

Archer, Dane and Rosemary Gartner <u>Violence and Crime in Cross</u> <u>National Perspective</u> (New Haven: Yale University Press, 1984), 352 pp.
  The ad reads "Does the level of domestic violence in a society increase after that nation has participated in a war? Do large cities always have higher homicide rates than smaller cities? The data Archer and Gartner have assembled on rates of major crimes for 110 nations and 44 major international cities make it possible, for the first time, to examine these and other significant issues regarding the patterns and causes of violent crime."

Barnard, Neil "The Role of the Population in a Guerrilla War" 26, 3 <u>Roeping en Riglyne</u> (September 1978), pp. 5-6.
  Barnard soon afterwards became the chief of the South African National Intelligence Service.

Beattie, Robert "ICPSR: Resources for the Study of Conflict Resolution: The Inter-University Consortium for Political and Social Research" 23, 2 <u>Journal of Conflict Resolution</u> (June 1979), pp. 337-345.
  Beattie notes the holdings of data sets which can be used for analyzing conflicts, including events compilations (the ITERATE dataset is the only one mentioned on terrorism), voting records, aggregate data on countries, and polls.

Ben-Rafael, Eliezar and Moshe Lissak <u>Social Aspects of</u> <u>Guerrilla and Anti-Guerrilla Warfare</u> (Jerusalem: The Magnes Press, 1979).

Blumstein, Alfred and Soumyo Moitra "An Analysis of the Time Series of the Imprisonment Rate in the States of the United States: A Further Test of the Stability of Punishment Hypothesis" 70, 3 Journal of Criminal Law and Criminology (Fall 1979), p. 376-390.

Bordenkircher, D. E. "Prisons and the Revolutionary" paper presented to the Annual Congress of Correction, American Correctional Association, Houston, August 18-22, 1974.

Brodsky, Stanley L. and H. O'Neal Smitherman, eds. Handbook of Scales for Research in Crime and Delinquency (New York: Plenum, 1982), 550 pp.
Blurb reads: "Brings together information about 388 scales used for research into crime, law, justice, corrections, and delinquency."

Brown, Geoff Sabotage: A Study of Industrial Conflict (Bristol: Spokesman, 1977).

Carrere, Rene and Pierre Valat-Morio "La Violence Politique Mondiale en 1978-1979-1980: Comparaison avec 1968-1977 (Political Violence in the World in the Years 1978-79-80: A Comparison with the Years 1968-77)" 24 Etudes Polemologiques (1981), pp. 120-166.
Foreign interventions and holy wars are becoming more frequent.

Castro, J. A. M. "Crime Trends and Crime Prevention Strategies in Latin American Countries" 35 International Review of Criminal Policy (1979), pp. 38-43.

Chang, Y-M and I. Ehrlich "Insurance, Protection from Risk and Risk-Bearing" 18 Canadian Journal of Economics (August 1985), pp. 574-586.

Coles, Robert "Jim Jones: The Piper of Doom" 11, 14 Washington Post Book World (April 5, 1981, pp. 1-2.
A review of George Klineman, Sherman Butler and David Conn The Cult That Died: The Tragedy of Jim Jones and the Peoples Temple (New York: Putnam), 372 pp.; James Reston, Jr. Our Father Who Art in Hell (New York: Times Books), 338 pp.; Kenneth Wooden The Children of Jonestown (New York: McGraw-Hill), 238 pp.; Ethan Feinsod Awake in a Nightmare: Jonestown: The Only Eyewitness Account (New York: Norton), 223 pp.; Min S. Yee and Thomas N. Layton In My Father's House: The Story of the Layton Family and the Reverend Jim Jones (New York: Holt, Rinehart and Winston), 361 pp.; and Shiva Naipaul Journey to Nowhere: A New World Tragedy (New York: Simon and Schuster), 320 pp.

Coyle, Dominick J. Minorities in Revolt (Rutherford, New Jersey: Fairleigh Dickinson University Press and London: Associated University Presses, 1983), 253 pp.

Davis, James R. Street Gangs: Youth, Biker, and Prison Groups (Dubuque, Iowa: Kendall/Hunt Publishing Company, 1982), 150 pp.

Day, Alan J., ed. <u>Political Dissent: An International Guide to Dissident, Extra-Parliamentary, Guerrilla and Illegal Political Movement</u> (London: Longman House, 1983).

De Sola, Ralph <u>Crime Dictionary</u> (New York: Facts on File, 1982), 219 pp.

Dugan, Maire A. <u>The Relationships Between Pre-Independence Internal Violence and Nonviolence and Post-Independence Internal Violence, External Belligerency and International Governmental Repressiveness</u> (Syracuse University, Department of Political Science, Ph.D. dissertation, 1979).

Dugan, Maire A. "The Relationships Between Pre-Independence Violence and Nonviolence and Post-Independence Political Repression" paper presented at the 20th annual convention of the International Studies Association, Toronto, March 21-24, 1979, 29 pp.
Dugan uses quantitative methods to test Gandhi's views of the efficacy of nonviolence.

Erlander, Howard S. "Estrangement, Machismo and Gang Violence" 60, 2 <u>Social Science Quarterly</u> (September 1979), pp. 235-248.

Friedlander, Robert A. "United States Policy Towards Armed Rebellion" <u>Yearbook of World Affairs 1983</u> (London: London Institute of World Affairs, 1983), pp. 39-62.

Frye, Charles A., ed. <u>Values in Conflict: Blacks and the American Ambivalence Toward Violence</u> (Washington, D.C.: University Press of America, 1980), 169 pp.

Gaylin, Willard, Ruth Macklin, and Tabitha M. Powledge, eds. <u>Violence and the Politics of Research</u> (New York: Plenum, 1981), 272 pp.
The blurb reads: "This book tells the story of three major research programs organized to study violence and aggressive behavior, programs that were aborted because they were politically and socially controversial."

Gibbs, Jack P. "Assessing the Deterrence Doctrine: A Challenge for the Social and Behavioral Sciences" 22, 6 <u>American Behavioral Scientist</u> (July-August, 1979), pp. 653-677.

Gurr, Ted Robert, ed. <u>Handbook of Political Conflict: Theory and Research</u> (New York: Free Press, 1980), 566 pp.

Halachmi, Arie "Community Disaster: Implications for Management" 12, 4 <u>Midwest Review of Public Administration</u> (December 1978), pp. 271-279.

Hall, John R. "Apocalypse at Jonestown" 16, 6 <u>Society</u> (September-October, 1979), pp. 52-61.

Hoggart, Richard "1968-1978: The Student Movement and its Effects in the Universities" 50, 2 <u>Political Quarterly</u> (April-June 1979), pp. 172-181.

Hough, M., ed. Revolutionary Warfare and Counter-Insurgency (Pretoria, South Africa: Institute for Strategic Studies, University of Pretoria, 1984), 47 pp.

Jones, R. V. "Nonmilitary Conflict" 9, 88 Washington Papers (1981), pp. 33-40.

Kampf, Herbert A. "On the Appeals of Extremism to the Youth of Affluent, Democratic Societies" 4 Terrorism (1980), pp. 161-194.

Kasturi, D. G. Typological Analysis of Collective Political Violence (Louisiana State University, Ph.D. dissertation, 1979), 285 pp.

Kegley, Charles W., Jr., and Richard A. Skinner "The Case-for-Analysis Problem" in James N. Rosenau, ed. In Search of Global Patterns (New York: Free Press, 1976), pp. 303-317.
The authors note that whatever one's level-of-analysis, one may look solely at the behavior of a single actor, or the dyadic relationships between actors. It is their belief that the most promising area lies in looking at the directed dyad, i.e., behavior directed from A to B.

Kegley, Charles W., Jr. and Eugene Wittkopf Transformation of World Politics (New York: St. Martins, 1981).

Knorr, Steven J. "Deterrence and the Death Penalty: A Temporal Cross-Sectional Approach" 70, 2 Journal of Criminal Law and Criminology (Summer 1979), pp. 235-254.

Krippendorff, Ekkehart "Minorities, Violence, and Peace Research" 16, 1 Journal of Peace Research (1979), pp. 27-40.

LeJeune, R. and N. Alex "On Being Mugged: The Event and Its Aftermath" 2 Urban Life and Culture (October 1973), pp. 259-287.

Lewis-Beck, Michael S. "Some Economic Effects of Revolution: Models, Measurement, and the Cuban Evidence" 84, 5 American Journal of Sociology (1984), pp. 1127-1149.

Li, Richard P. "Political Risk Assessment: Framework, Methods and Strategies", paper presented to the annual convention of the International Studies Association, Atlanta, March 27-31, 1984.

Margarita, Mona "Killing the Police: Myths and Motives" 452 Annals of the American Academy of Political and Social Science (November 1980), pp. 63-71.

Mason, Thomas David The Causes of Urban Racial Violence: An Empirical Examination (University of Chicago, Department of Political Science, Ph.D. dissertation).

Meurer, Emil M., Jr. "Violent Crime Losses: Their Impact on the Victim and Society" 443 Annals of the American Academy of Political and Social Science (May 1979), pp. 54-62.

Midlarsky, Manus I. "Boundary Permeability as a Condition of Political Violence" 1 Jerusalem Journal of International Relations (Winter 1975), pp. 53-70.

Moczarski, Kazimierz "Document: Poland: Confessions of an SS General: The Destruction of the Warsaw Ghetto" 23, 4 Survey (Autumn, 1977-78), pp. 163-180.

Nagin, Daniel "General Deterrence: A Review of the Empirical Evidence" in Alfred Blumstein, Jacqueline Cohen and Daniel Nagin, eds. Deterrence and Incapacitation: Estimating the Effects of Criminal Sanctions on Crime Rates (Washington: National Academy of Sciences, 1978).

O'Brien, John T. and Marvin Marcus, eds. Crime and Justice in America: Critical Issues for the Future (Elmsford, New York: Pergamon, 1979), 381 pp.

Pitcher, Brian L., and Robert L. Hamblin "Collective Learning in Ongoing Political Conflicts" 3, 1 International Political Science Review (1982), pp. 71-90.

Purchell, Hugh Revolutionary War: Guerrilla Warfare and Terrorism in our Time (London: H. Hamilton, 1980), 96 pp.

Raab, Earl "Anti-Semitism in the 1980's" 29, 2 Midstream (1983), pp. 11-18.
A look at the increase in terrorist attacks against Jews worldwide.

Rankin, Joseph H. "Changing Attitudes Toward Capital Punishment" 58, 1 Social Forces (September 1979), pp. 194-211.

Rofe, Yacov and Isaac Lewin "Attitudes Toward an Enemy and Personality in a War Environment" 4, 1 International Journal of Intercultural Relations (1980), pp. 97-105.
A study of Israeli high school students living in towns which have been differentially affected by terrorist attacks.

Rothman, David J. "Doing Time: Days, Months and Years in the Criminal Justice System" 19, 1-2 International Journal of Comparative Sociology (March-June 1978), pp. 130-138.

Sarkesian, Sam C. "The Open Society: Defensive Measures" paper prepared for the Conference on Terrorism and Other "Low Intensity" operations: International Linkages, Fletcher School of Law and Diplomacy, Tufts University, Medford, Massachusetts, April 1985.

Schneider, H. J. "Crime and Criminal Policy in Some Western European and North American Countries" 35 International Review of Criminal Policy (1979), pp. 55-65.

Shultz, Richard "Low Intensity Conflict" in Stuart M. Butler, Michael Sanera, and W. Bruce Weinrod, eds. Mandate for Leadership II (Washington, D.C.: Heritage Foundation, 1984).

Smith, Michael D. "Precipitants of Crowd Violence" 48, 2 Sociological Inquiry (1978), pp. 121-132.

Strinkowski, Nicholas "The Organizational Behavior of Revolutionary Groups" (Evanston, Illinois, Department of Political Science, Northwestern University, Ph.D. dissertation, 1985).

Susini, J. "Crime Trends and Crime Prevention Strategies in Western Europe" 35 International Review of Criminal Policy (19790), ppl. 67-70.

Suhrke, Astri, Lela Garner Noble and Robert L. Beckman "Ethnic Conflict and International Relations" 9, 4 Plural Societies (Winter 1978), pp. 3-22.

Takahasi, Sadahiko and Carl B. Becker "Organized Crime in Japan" paper presented at the annual meeting of the Academy of Criminal Justice Sciences, 1985.

Tarr, David "The Strategic Environment: US National Security and the Nature of Low Intensity Conflict" paper delivered at the annual meeting of the Midwest Political Science Association, Chicago, April 19-21, 1979.

Taylor, William J., Jr., and Steven A. Maaranen, eds. The Future of Conflict in the 1980s (Lexington, Mass.: Lexington Books, 1983).

Tedeschi, James T. and Thomas V. Bonoma "Measures of Last Resort: Coercion and Aggression in Bargaining" in Daniel Druckman, ed. Negotiations: Social-Psychological Perspectives (Beverly Hills: Sage, 1978), pp. 213-241.

Tiffany, Willard T. and James M. Ketchel "Psychological Deterrence in Robberies of Banks and Its Application to Other Institutions" in Joel J. Kramer, ed. The Role of Behavioral Science in Physical Security: Proceedings of the Third Annual Symposium, May 2-4, 1978 (Washington, D.C.: National Bureau of Standards Special Publication 480-38, 1979), pp. 81-88.

Tovar, Hugh "Low-Intensity Conflict: Active Responses in an Open Society" paper prepared for the Conference on Terrorism and Other "Low Intensity" Operations: International Linkages, Fletcher School of Law and Diplomacy, Tufts University, Medford, Massachusetts, April 1985.

Turk, A. T. Political Criminality: The Defiance and Defense of Authority (London: Sage, 1982), 232 pp.

Wheatcroft, Andrew The World Atlas of Revolution (New York: Simon and Schuster, 1983), 208 pp.

Wilber, Charles D., ed. Contemporary Violence: A Multi-Disciplinary Examination (Springfield: Thomas, 1975).

Williams, Colin H., ed. National Separatism (Cardiff: University of Wales, 1982), 317 pp.

Wilson, Colin and Donald Seaman Encyclopedia of Modern Murder, 1962-82 (New York: Putman, 1985).

Wolfgang, Marvin E. and Neil Alan Weiner, eds. <u>Criminal Violence</u> (Beverly Hills: Sage, 1982).

Yough, Syng Nam <u>A Cross-National Analysis of Political Violence: A Model Specification and Its Empirical Test</u> (Texas Tech University, Political Science Department, Ph.D. dissertation, 1979).

Zawodny, J.K. "How to Capture a City by Insurgency and How to Combat Insurgents Fighting for Such a City: Two Combat Reports from World War II" 3, 1-2 <u>Terrorism</u> (1979), pp. 147-155.
  Zawodny translated documents by a German and a Polish commander involved in fighting during the Warsaw Uprising of 1940.

Zimmermann, Ekkart <u>Political Violence, Crises and Revolution: Theories and Research</u> (Cambridge, Mass.: Schenkman, 1983).

Fiction

Aaron, David <u>State Scarlet</u> (New York: Putnam, 1987), 351 pp. Reviewed by Rory Quirk "One of Our Bombs is Missing!" <u>Washington Post Book World</u> (May 10, 1987), p. 7. The KGB and CIA team up to find an individual who stole a US nuclear weapon and threatens to destroy a West European city if all US nuclear weapons are not removed from Europe.

Ambler, Eric <u>The Levanter</u> (New York: Atheneum, 1972). Palestinians plan terrorist attacks in Tel Aviv.

Ardies, Tom <u>Kosygin is Coming</u> (Garden City: Doubleday, 1974).

Ardies, Tom <u>This Suitcase is Going to Explode</u> (Garden City: Doubleday, 1973).
A group plants several suitcases hiding nuclear bombs in US cities.

Aricha, Amos <u>Hour of the Clown</u> (New York: Signet, 1981).
The KGB tasks an agent to lead international terrorists who are to assassinate 15 leading pro-Israeli figures, including Henry Kissinger and Senator Scoop Jackson.

Arrighi, Mel <u>Navona 1000</u> (Indianapolis: Bobbs-Merrill, 1976).

Arvay, Harry <u>Operation Kuwait</u> (New York: Bantam, 1975).
Israelis attempt to halt hijackers via preemptive attacks.

Arvay, Harry <u>The Piraeus Plot</u> (New York: Bantam, 1975).
Israel aids Arafat against his radical foes.

Atles, Philip <u>The Underground Cities Contract</u> (New York: Pinnacle, 1974).
A fictional account of Turkish terrorists.

Awin, Margery <u>Silence Over Sinai</u> (New York: Pyramid, 1976).
Arab terrorists hope to take hostage members of an Egyptian-Israeli negotiating meeting.

Ballard, J. G. <u>High Rise</u> (New York: Holt, 1977).

Bell, Madison Smartt Waiting for the End of the World (New York: Ticknor and Fields, 1985), 322 pp.
Reviewed by David Remnick "The Bomb Beneath Times Square" Washington Post Book World (September 1, 1985), pp. 3-4.

Bickham, Jack M. The Regensburg Legacy (New York: Doubleday, 1980), 287 pp.
An intact Nazi CBW laboratory is discovered beneath a former Wehrmacht base in West Germany.

Black, Lionel Arafat is Next (New York: Stein and Day, 1975).
Private individuals attempt to assassinate Arafat.

Block, Thomas H. Forced Landing (New York: Coward McCann, 1983), 303 pp.
Reviewed by Douglas B. Feaver "Scare in the Air: Predictable Fun" Washington Post (August 27, 1983), p. C6. A novel of a $20 million hijacking of a DC9 which lands on an aircraft carrier.

Burmesiter, Jon Running Scared (New York: St. Martins, 1973).

Caidin, Martin Almost Midnight (New York: Morrow, 1971).
Terrorists steal nuclear weapons.

Caidin, Martin Operation Nuke (New York: McKay, 1973).

Caillou, Alan Death Charges (New York: Pinnacle, 1973).

Callison, Brian A Plague of Sailors (New York: Putnam, 1971).

Calmer, Ned The Peking Dimension (Garden City: Doubleday, 1976).
The daughter of a US and a Chinese diplomat is kidnapped.

Cartwright, Justin The Horse of Darius (New York: Macmillan, 1980).
An assassin plots to kill Shah Reza Pahlavi.

Chandler, David T. The Capablanca Opening (New York: St. Martins, 1977).
A novel of Tupamaro kidnappers.

Charles, Robert Flight of the Raven (New York: Pinnacle, 1975).

Chesterton, G.K. The Man Who Was Thursday (1908).

Clancy, Ambrose Blind Pilot (New York: Morrow, 1980), 384 pp.
Reviewed by Douglas Bauer "Visions of the Irish War" Washington Post (October 24, 1980), p. B7.

Cohen, William S. and Gary Hart The Double Man (New York: Morrow, 1985), 348 pp.
Reviewed by Jack Beatty in Washington Post Book World (April 7, 1985, pp. 1, 6. Written by two US Senators.

Collins, L. and D. LaPierre The Fifth Horseman (New York: Simon and Schuster, 1981), 478 pp.

A novel about Libyan-supported nuclear terrorism, reviewed by Richard Helms "Specter of Nuclear Blackmail" 10, 32 Washington Post Book World (August 10, 1980), pp. 1-2.

Condon, Richard Whisper of the Axe (New York: Dial, 1976). Black revolutionaries fund their operations via the Haitian drug trade.

Cooper, H. H. A. "Fiction May Become Fact" 4, 1-3 TVI Journal (1982), pp. 10-13.
A review of dozens of terrorism novels.

Cox, Richard Sam Seven (New York: Reader's Digest, 1977). Terrorists destroy an airliner with a heat-seeking missile.

Dan, Uri and Peter Mann Ultimatum: Pu 94 (New York: Leisure, 1977).
Terrorists attempt to make a nuclear weapon based upon publicly available literature.

de Mille, Nelson Cathedral (New York: Delacorte/Bernard Geis, 1981), 483 pp.
Reviewed by Terence Winch "A Fantastic Tale of Feisty Fenians" Washington Post (June 23, 1981), p. C6.

DiMona, Joe To The Eagle's Nest (New York: William Morrow, 1980), 311 pp.
Leftwing terrorists kidnap a American movie crew working on a film about Hitler in Berchtesgaden.

Driscoll, Peter In Connection with Kilshaw (Philadelphia: Lippincott, 1974).

Duncan, Robert L. Fire Storm (New York: William Morrow, 1978). US oil executives hire Japanese terrorists to kill a Senator.

Eachus, Irv Raid on the Bremerton (New York: Viking, 1980), 244 pp.
Reviewed by Nancy and Allan Ryan Washington Post Book World (October 5, 1980), p. 11. Terrorists take over a US nuclear submarine.

Fairbairn, Douglas Street 8 (New York: Delacorte, 1977). A novel of anti-Castro terrorists.

Faust, Ron The Long Count (New York: Fawcett, 1979), 223 pp. Reviewed by L. J. Davis Washington Post Book World (January 6, 1980), p. 6. A boxer stranded in a South American country is kidnapped with the US Ambassador and a pretty girl by leftist guerrillas.

Fleming, H. K. The Day They Kidnapped Queen Victoria (New York: St. Martin's, 1978).
Irish terrorists kidnap the Queen.

Flynn, J.M. Warlock (New York: Pocket, 1976).

Foster, Tony Zigzag to Armageddon
Another novel about nuclear terrorism.

Fuentes, Carlos The Hydra Head, translated by Margaret Sayers Penden (New York: Farrar, Straus and Giroux, 1978).

Gibian, George "Terror in Russian Culture and Literary Imagination" 5, 2 Human Rights Quarterly (May 1983), pp. 191-198.
With "Comments" by Norman Naimark, pp. 199-202.

Gill, Bartholomew McGarr and the Politician's Wife (New York: Scribners, 1977).
A novel about Irish terrorism.

Gilman, Dorothy Mrs. Pollifax on Safari (Garden City: Doubleday, 1977).
A novel of terrorism in Zambia.

Godey, John The Talisman (New York: Putnam, 1976).
Vietnam vets threaten to destroy the Unknown Soldier if an anti-war activist is not pardoned by the President.

Gosling, Paula The Zero Trap (New York: Coward, McCann and Geoghegan, 1980).

Graves, Richard L. Cobalt 60 (New York: Stein and Day, 1975).

Graves, Richard L. C.L.A.W. (New York: Stein and Day, 1976).
US-trained Vietnamese attack US Presidential candidates.

Haddad, C. A. Bloody September (New York: Harper and Row, 1976).

Haldeman, Joe "To Howard Hughes: A Modest Proposal" in Joe Haldeman, ed. Study War No More (New York: Avon, 1977), pp. 305-323.
A short story of how a billionaire could co-opt scientists into creating nuclear weapons and blackmail governments into disarming.

Hall, Adam The Kobra Manifesto (Garden City: Doubleday, 1976).
The daughter of the US Secretary of Defense is kidnapped.

Hamilton, Donald The Vanishers (New York: Fawcett/Gold Medal, 1986), 295 pp.
Reviewed by Michael Dirda "Matt Helm, Vanishing Breed" Washington Post (August 16, 1986), p. D3.

Harper, David Hijacked (New York: Dodd, Mead, and Company, 1970).

Harrison, Harry Queen Victoria's Revenge (Garden City: Doubleday, 1975).

Hebden, Mark March of Violence (New York: Harcourt, 1970).

Henissart, Paul Margin of Error (New York: Simon and Schuster, 1980), 334 pp.
An East German terrorist plans to assassinate a world leader at a Swiss hospital.

Henissart, Paul <u>Narrow Exit</u> (New York: Simon and Schuster, 1974).

Herbert, Frank <u>The White Plague</u> (New York: Putnam's, 1982). Reviewed by Craig Shaw Gardner <u>Washington Post Book World</u> (August 29, 1982), p. 7. A man who has seen his wife and children killed by an IRA bomb plants an extremely contagious disease--which is fatal to women--in countries which he believes help the IRA.

Herbert, Frank and Charles Pfahl "The White Plague, Part 2 of 2" 4 <u>Omni</u> (August 1982), pp. 50-60. Biological warfare by the Irish Republican Army.

Herrick, William <u>Love and Terror</u> (New York: New Directions, 1981), 250 pp. Reviewed by Michael Bishop "A Terrorist Romance, Cool, Raw and Heartily Real" <u>Washington Post</u> (July 23, 1981), p. C6.

Herron, Shaun <u>Through the Dark and Hairy Wood</u> (New York: Random House, 1972).

Hesky, Olga <u>A Different Night</u> (New York: Random House, 1971).

Higgins, George V. <u>The Patriot Game</u> (New York: Knopf, 1982), 237 pp. Reviewed by Jonathan Yardley "Macho and Murder in the IRA's World: George Higgins' Novel of Crime and Corruption" <u>Washington Post</u> (April 14, 1982), pp. B1, B9.

Higgins, Jack <u>The Savage Day</u> (New York: Holt, 1972). A novel of IRA arms smuggling.

Higgins, Jack <u>Solo</u> (New York: Stein and Day, 1980).

Higgins, Jack <u>Wrath of the Lion</u> (Greenwich: Fawcett, 1977). Terrorism by the French rightwing.

Himmel, Richard <u>The Twenty-Third Web</u> (New York: Random House, 1977). Terrorists in the US attempt to thwart support of Israel.

Hoffenberg, Jack <u>17 Ben Gurion</u> (New York: Putnam, 1977). A novel of terrorism in the Middle East.

Holder, Dennis "When Terrorists Attack America" 34 <u>TV Guide</u> (February 8, 1986), pp. 42-46. A discussion of Hal Holbrook's "Under Siege" television drama.

Household, Geoffrey <u>High Place</u> (Boston: Little Brown, 1955).

Household, Geoffrey <u>Hostage: London</u> (1977). A novel of nuclear terrorism.

Hoyle, F., and G. Hoyle <u>The Westminster Disaster</u> (1977). A novel of nuclear terrorism.

Hunt, E. Howard The Gaza Intercept (New York: Stein and Day, 1981), 302 pp.
A PLO splinter group plans to explode an atomic device over Tel Aviv at the height of the national birthday celebration.

Hyde, Christopher Maxwell's Train (Villard, 1985), 273 pp.
Reviewed by Martin Morse Wooster Washington Post (March 11, 1985), p. B4. Members of the Japanese Red Army, Sandinistas, Baader-Meinhof Group, Red Brigades, and Libyans united as the World People's Army to steal $35 million from the Amtrak Night Owl.

Ing, Dean "Very Proper Charlies" in Isaac Asimov, Charles G. Waugh, and Martin Harry Greenberg, eds. TV: 2000 (New York: Fawcett, 1982), pp. 282-335.
American television networks cooperate in fighting terrorism by portraying their deeds satirically, refusing to broadcast their motives.

Jepson, Selwyn A Noise in the Night (Philadelphia: Lippincott, 1957).

Kane, Henry The Tripoli Documents (New York: Simon and Schuster, 1976).
Robert Kennedy's Palestinian assassin targets the US Secretary of State.

Kartun, Deker Beaver to Fox (New York: St. Martin's, 1986), 256 pp.
Reviewed by Charles Willeford "Taking on the Terrorists" Washington Post (September 12, 1986), p. F10. Rightwing terrorists in France attempt to destabilize the government and bring back WWII fascism.

Katz, Robert Ziggurat (Boston: Houghton Mifflin, 1977).
A novel of nuclear terrorism.

Kosinski, Jerzy Cockpit (Boston: Houghton Mifflin, 1975), pp. 95-96.
An episode includes an individual who taints consumer products.

Lambert, Derek The Yermakov Transfer (New York: Saturday Review, 1974).
Jewish terrorists plan to kidnap the Soviet Premier.

Lathan, Emma Going For the Gold (New York: Simon and Schuster, 1981).

Leather, Edwin The Mozart Score (New York: Doubleday, 1979).

Lessing, Doris The Good Terrorist (New York: Knopf, 1985), 375 pp.
Reviewed by Marilynne Robinson "Doris Lessing's Gentrified Revolutionaries" Washington Post Book World (September 22, 1985), p. 4.

Lindstrom, Bob "White-Collar Terrorism" 5 <u>A+</u> (July 1987), pp. 97-98.
A review of a microcomputer game which involves interaction fiction by Douglas Adams entitled "Bureaucracy".

Lippincott, David <u>The Voice of Armageddon</u> (New York: Putnam, 1974).

Littell, Robert <u>The Amateur</u> (New York: Simon and Schuster, 1981), 252 pp.
A CIA cryptologist seeks to avenge the terrorist murder of his fiancee.

Ludlum, Robert <u>The Bourne Identity</u> (New York: Richard Marak, 1980).
A novel of a Carlos-like figure and the mechanics of plotting international assassinations.

Lyall, Gavin <u>Judas Country</u> (New York: Viking, 1975).

MacDonald, John D. <u>The Green Ripper</u> (Philadelphia: Lippincott, 1979).
Travis McGee uncovers a terrorist gang masquerading as a religious cult in Florida.

MacInnis, Helen <u>Cloak of Darkness</u> (New York: Harcourt, Brace and Jovanovich, 1982).

MacLaverty, Bernard <u>Cal</u> (New York: George Braziller, 1983), 170 pp.
Reviewed by Anatole Broyard "Domesticated Violence" <u>New York Times</u> (August 20, 1983). A look at the war between the Catholics and the Protestants in Ulster.

MacLean, Alistair <u>Floodgate</u> (New York: Doubleday, 1984).
Another novel of "the ultimate terrorist act."

MacLean, Alistair <u>Athabasca</u> (New York: Doubleday, 1980).
A terrorist attack on the oil industry.

MacLean, Alistair <u>Goodbye California</u> (New York: Doubleday, 1978).
Terrorists take over a nuclear power plant, hoping to cause an earthquake which will destroy California.

Markov, Georgi <u>The Assassins</u> (1969).
A drama of a plot to kill a general in a police state, written by a Bulgarian author who was murdered by a man who stabbed him with a poisoned umbrella tip.

Marshall, William <u>Gelignite</u> (New York: Holt, 1977).
Terrorists threaten to destroy the Chinese cemetery in Hong Kong.

Mason, Colin <u>Hostage</u> (New York: Walker, 1973).
Israelis destroy Cairo with stolen US nuclear weapons. The Soviets respond with a counter-city strategy.

McAlister, Ian Strike Force 7 (Greenwich: Fawcett, 1974).
Mercenaries vs. terrorists.

McClure, James Rogue Eagle (New York: Harper and Row, 1976).
A novel of terrorism by South African whites.

McDonald, Hugh C. Five Signs from Ruby (New York: Pyramid, 1976).
The PLO funds the building of five nuclear weapons, which are used to blackmail Israel.

Melman, Bili "The Terrorist in Fiction" 15, 3 Journal of Contemporary History (July 1980), pp. 559-576.

Mewshaw, Michael Year of the Gun (New York: Atheneum, 1984), 273 pp.
Reviewed by Oliver Banks "Terrorism of Words" Washington Post (June 1, 1984), p. B4.
A novel of Italian Red Brigades terrorism set in 1977.

Nelson, Walter The Siege of Buckingham Palace (Boston: Little, Brown, 1980), 239 pp.
Reviewed in Washington Post Book World (April 6, 1980), p. 10.

Nessen, Ron The First Lady (Chicago: Playboy, 1979), 328 pp.
Reviewed by L.J. Davis "Tales for Twelfth Night" Washington Post Book World (January 6, 1980), p. 6. The President's wife is kidnapped by a crazed Puerto Rican, a psychotic black, a girl and a Japanese.

Orde, Lewis and Bill Michaels The Night They Stole Manhattan (New York: G.P. Putnam's Sons, 1980).

O'Neill, Edward A. The Rotterdam Delivery (New York: Coward, 1975).
Terrorists hijack an oil tanker.

Pace, Eric Any War Will Do (New York: Random House, 1972).

Parker, Robert B. The Judas Goat (Boston: Houghton Mifflin, 1978).
Rightwing Americans strike at the 1976 Olympic Games.

Patterson, James Black Market (New York: Simon and Schuster, 1986).
The Green Band bombs 14 buildings on Wall Street.

Patterson, Richard North Private Screening (New York: Villard, 1985), 322 pp.
Reviewed by Dennis Drabelle "On the Trail of a Terrorist" Washington Post Book World (November 17, 1985), p. 9.

Peters, Stephen The Park is Mine (New York: Doubleday, 1981).
A deranged Vietnam vet takes over Central park. The book shows weaknesses in society's defenses and response mechanisms.

Pieczenik, Steve <u>Terror Counter Terror</u> (1981).
Pieczenik, a psychiatrist, resigned as a Deputy Assistant
Secretary of State in November 1979 over the handling of the
Iranian hostage crisis.

Pitts, Denis <u>This City is Ours</u> (New York: Mason Charter,
1975).
Terrorists threaten to destroy New York City with a hijacked
oil tanker.

Power, M. S. <u>The Killing of Yesterday's Children</u> (New York:
Viking, 1986), 264 pp.
Reviewed by Dennis Drabelle in <u>Washington Post Book World</u>
(April 11, 1986), p. C2.

Prager, Emily "Traveler's Update" 17 <u>Penthouse</u> (November
1985), p. 35.
A satire on how travellers should prepare for a terrorist
attack.

Price, Anthony <u>The Alamut Bomb</u> (Garden City: Doubleday, 1972).

Rance, Joseph and Arei Kato <u>Bulletin Train</u> (New York: William
Morrow, 1980), 248 pp.
Reviewed by Nancy and Allan Ryan <u>Washington Post Book World</u>
(October 5, 1980), p. 11. Terrorists hide a bomb aboard the
supertrain Hikari 109 between Tokyo to Hakata; if a $5 million
payment isn't made, the bomb will go off when the train slows
to 50 mph.

Rayner, William <u>Day of Chaminuka</u> (New York: Atheneum, 1977).

Reed, J. D. <u>Free Fall</u> (New York: Delacorte, 1980).
A novel of the D.B. Cooper legend--a skyjacker who parachutes
with his loot.

Reiss, Bob <u>Divine Assassin</u> (Boston: Little, Brown, 1985), 297
pp.
Reviewed by Martin Morse Wooster "Capital Thriller"
<u>Washington Post</u> (June 8, 1985), p. G-8. An American military
officer seeks vengeance for the murder by a Libyan hit team of
his fiancee.

Ritner, Peter <u>The Passion of Richard Thynne</u> (New York: William
Morrow, 1976).
American Indians attack the Widener Library.

Ross, Frank <u>Dead Runner</u> (New York: Atheneum, 1977).
Arab terrorists threaten to explode a nuclear device if the
British do not release a colleague.

Royce, Kenneth <u>The Third Arm</u> (New York: McGraw-Hill, 1980),
205 pp.
A group of international terrorists plan to blow up the
Concorde carrying Margaret Thatcher and Helmut Schmidt.

Sapir, Richard and Warren Murphy <u>The Terror Squad</u> (New York:
Pinnacle, 1973).
A fictional account of an international terrorist network.

Seaman, Donald <u>The Terror Syndicate</u> (New York: Coward, McCann, 1976).

Sela, Owen <u>An Exchange of Eagles</u> (New York: Pantheon, 1977). An attempt to prevent World War II via assassination.

Seymour, Gerald <u>The Harrison Affair</u> (New York: Summit, 1980), 352 pp.
Reviewed by Stanley Ellin "In the Grip of Terror" <u>Washington Post Book World</u> (February 17, 1980), p. 12.

Shaara, Michael <u>The Herald</u> (New York: McGraw-Hill, 1981), 229 pp.
A novel of genetic weaponry aimed at defective genes.

Shabtai, Sabi H. <u>5 Minutes to Midnight</u> (New York: Delacorte, 1980), 377 pp.
Terrorists attempt to seize a US nuclear facility.

Sharp, Marilyn <u>False-Face</u> (New York: St. Martin's/Marek, 1984).
Reviewed by Frances A. Koestler "Of Spies and Hostages" <u>Washington Post</u> (October 6, 1984), p. B5.
The advertising blurb reads: "CIA agent Richard Owen (Sunflower) is back--and does he have his hands full:
--He and a group of US Congressmen are being held hostage by terrorists in Mexico
--His arch rival (and master assassin) is one step ahead of him", etc.

Sharpe, Tom <u>The Wilt Alternative</u> (New York: St. Martin's, 1979), 212 pp.
A humorous novel about how an English professor manages to save his family from terrorists holding them hostage in his home.

Smith, Wilbur <u>The Delta Decision</u> (New York: Doubleday, 1980).

Stevenson, William <u>Booby Trap</u> (New York: Doubleday, 1987).
Blurb in <u>Washington Post Book World</u> (April 12, 1987), p. 13 reads: "The Windfall Islands, lazing in the brilliant tropical sun of the Caribbean, seem like an unlikely target for the world's premier terrorist. But then, Zia Gabbiya has been dangerously unpredictable from the moment he began his murderous rise to power in the oil-rich desert of North Africa. So when he arrives in the balmy, sedate island paradise in America's backyard, the CIA suspects it's no vacation. And when operative Pete Casey uncovers the first clues to Gabbiya's astonishing plan, it's up to an ill-equipped team of civilians armed only with their wits and a battered old WWII biplane to thwart a daring and ingenious plot to destroy the security of the Western World."

Szulkin, Robert "The Terror of Transformation in Varlam Shalamov's Stories" 5, 2 <u>Human Rights Quarterly</u> (May 1983), pp. 207ff.

Thomas, Gordon and Max Morgan-Witts <u>Pontiff</u> (New York: Doubleday, 1983), 461 pp.
Reviewed by Joseph McLellan "Plot Against the Pope" <u>Washington Post</u> (June 21, 1983), p. B-2.

Thomas, Michael <u>Green Monday</u> (New York: Wyndham Books, 1980).
A terrorist vignette is included.

Thomas, Michael <u>Someone Else's Money</u> (New York: Simon and Schuster, 1982).
One episode includes a terrorist attack.

Tiger, Virginia "Alice and Charlie and Vida and Sophy: A Terrorist's Work is Never Done" 90 <u>New York Times Book Review</u> (November 10, 1985), p. 11.

Tippin, G. Lee <u>The Arab</u> (Canton, Ohio: Daring Books, 1985), 210 pp.
A man whose pregnant wife is murdered by terrorists is sent to avenge the murder of the US Marines in Beirut.

Titley, Alan "Rough Rug-Headed Kerns: The Irish Gunman in the Popular Novel" 15, 4 <u>Eire-Ireland</u> (1980), pp. 15-38.
A look at anti-Irish and anti-IRA stereotypes in Irish and British literature in the 1970s.

Wallace, Irving <u>The Almighty</u> (New York: Doubleday, 1982).
Reviewed by Jonathan Yardley "Ah, 'The Almighty' Malaprop: Irving Wallace's New Embarrassment" <u>Washington Post</u> (November 17, 1982), pp. B1, B4. A novel which includes a mad kamikaze pilot targetting Air Force One.

Washburn, Mark <u>The Armageddon Game</u> (New York: Putnam, 1977).

Watkins, Leslie <u>The Killing of Idi Amin</u> (New York: Avon, 1977).
A novel of an attempt by Sanity International to kill the Ugandan dictator.

Way, Peter <u>Belshazzar's Feast</u> (New York: Atheneum, 1982), 320 pp.
Reviewed by Carolyn Banks <u>Washington Post Book World</u> (April 4, 1982), p. 8. A novel of terrorist use of botulism in London.

West, Morris <u>The Clowns of God</u> (New York: William Morrow, 1981).

West, Morris <u>Harlequin</u> (Markham, Ontario: Pocket Books, 1975).

Wickbom, Kaj "Diskussion om Nazismen och Dagens Terrorism i Tyska Forbundsrepubliken. Aktuella Speloch Dokumentarfilmer (Discussion of Nazism and Contemporary Terrorism in West Germany: Current Fictional and Documentary Films" 84, 2 <u>Statsvetenskaplig Tidskrift (Sweden)</u> (1981), pp. 101-103.
A review of the debate about three current films.

Williams, Alan <u>Shah-Mak</u> (New York: Coward, McCann, 1976).
A novel of a faked assassination which becomes real.

Williams, John Click Song (Boston: Houghton Mifflin, 1982).

Williamson, Tony The Doomsday Contract (New York: Simon and Schuster, 1978).
A novel involving thefts of plutonium and nuclear bombs and the kidnapping of nuclear scientists.

Wingate, John Avalanche (New York: St. Martin's, 1977).

Wolfe, Michael The Panama Paradox (New York: Harper and Row, 1977).
Panamanian terrorists conduct attacks on the Panama Canal.

Wylie, Philip The Smuggled Atom Bomb (Garden City: Doubleday, 1965).
A novel of nuclear blackmail.

Wyllie, John Death is a Drum...Beating Forever (Garden City: Doubleday, 1977).

Yates, Brock Dead in the Water (New York: Farrar, 1975).
A novel about an attempt to kidnap the Canadian Prime Minister.

Yerby, Frank A Rose for Ana Maria (New York: Dial, 1976).

Bibliographies

Atiyeh, George N. The Contemporary Middle East 1948-1973: A Selective and Annotated Bibliography (Boston: G.K. Hall, 1975), 664 pp.

Blackey, Robert Revolutions and Revolutionarists: A Comprehensive Guide to the Literature (Santa Barbara: ABC-CLIO, 1982), 488 pp.

Bonanate, Luigi, ed. La Violenza Politica nel Mondo Contemporaneo: Bibliografia Internationale sul Terrorismo, i Movimenti di Ribellione, la Guerriglia Urbana, le Guerre di Liberazione, le Lotte Antiimperialistiche; La Mappa del Terrorismo nel Mondo Contemporaneo (University of Turin, Italy, Institute di Scienze Polit., 1979), 253 pp. The text in English and Italian covers 1954-1977.

Friedlander, Robert A. "Terrorism in the 70s -- A Selective Bibliography" 11, 6 TVI: Terrorism Violence Insurgency Journal (July 1981), pp. 2-9.

Janke, Peter with Richard Sim Guerrilla and Terrorist Organisations: A World Directory and Bibliography (Brighton: The Harvester Press, and New York: Macmillan, 1983), 531 pp. The bibliographic work appears as a literature review at the beginning of each regional section.

Khalidi, Walid and Jill Khadduri Palestine and the Arab-Israeli Conflict (Beirut: Institute for Palestine Studies and Kuwait: University of Kuwait, 1974). A bibliography containing 4500 entries.

Lakos, Amos Terrorism, 1970-1978, A Bibliography (Waterloo, Ontario: University of Waterloo Library, 1979), 73 pp.

Lakos, Amos International Terrorism: A Bibliography (Boulder, Colorado: Westview Press, 1986).

Lutz, Robert E., Susan L. Streiker, and Debra S. Johnson-Champ "International Terrorism: A Legal Bibliography of Selected Issues and Sources" 20 International Lawyer (Summer 1986).

Manheim, J. B. and M. Wallace <u>Political Violence in the US,</u> <u>1875-1974: A Bibliography</u> (New York: Garland, 1975).

Mickolus, Edward F. <u>The Literature of Terrorism: A</u> <u>Selectively Annotated Bibliography</u> (Westport: Greenwood, 1980), 553 pp.
The present volume updates this listing, which has 3890 entries, cross-indexed by author and title, with numerous annotations.

Moreland, Richard L. and Michael L. Berbaum "Bibliography" in Abraham A. Miller, ed. <u>Terrorism, The Media, and the Law</u> (Dobbs Ferry, New York: Transnational Publishers, 1982).

Norton, Augustus R. "Terror-Violence: A Critical Commentary and Selected Annotated Bibliography" <u>Clandestine Tactics and</u> <u>Technology</u> (Gaithersburg, Maryland: International Association of Chiefs of Police, 1980), 16 pp.

Ontiveros, Suzanne Robitaille <u>Global Terrorism: A Historical</u> <u>Bibliography</u> (New York: ABC CLIO, 1986), 168 pp.
The bibliography includes abstracts of 598 items which appeared in scholarly journals published between 1970 and 1984. Citations are organized by region. A short chronology of the decade is included.

Reid, Edna Ferguson <u>An Analysis of Terrorism Literature: A</u> <u>Bibliometric and Content Analysis Study</u> (University of Southern California: Doctor of Library Administration Dissertation Presented to the Faculty of the School of Library and Information Management, May 1983), 357 pp.
A study of "invisible colleges": which authors influence other authors?

Silverburg, Sanford R. "The Arab-Israeli Conflict: A Legal Bibliography" <u>Law Library Journal</u> (February 1979), pp. 12-20.

Silverburg, Sanford R. "An International Legal Bibliography on the Palestinian-Israeli Conflict" 10, 2 <u>Denver Journal of</u> <u>International Law and Policy</u> (Winter 1981), pp. 263-278.

Silverburg, Sanford R. "A Selected International Law Bibliography on the Arab-Israeli Conflict" 4 <u>Suffolk</u> <u>Transnational Law Journal</u> (1980), pp. 47-88.

<u>Terrorism</u> (Quantico, Virginia: FBI Academy Library, June 1980, mimeo), 12 pp.

Watson, Francis M., Sr. "The Textbooks of Political Violence: A Selected Bibliography" 3 <u>Clandestine Tactics and Technology</u> (Gaithersburg, Maryland: International Association of Chiefs of Police, 1976), 20 pp.

Wilcox, Laird M. <u>Bibliography on Terrorism and Assassination</u> (Kansas City: Editorial Research Service, 1980), 24 pp.

Author Index

Wilson, A.   131
Wilson, Clifton E.   185
Wilson, Colin   216
Wilson, James Q.   28
Wilson, R. D.   124
Wingate, John   230
Winkler, H. B.   163
Winn, Gregory F. T.   112
Winter, Bill   197
Wise, Charles Dean   124
Wohl, James P.   141
Wolf, John B.   28, 29, 47,
   81, 112, 124, 141, 153,
   154, 167
Wolfe, Michael   230
Wolffers, Arthur   63
Wolfgang, Marvin E.   29, 217
Wolk, R. L.   209
Wolman, B. B.   63
Woods, B. F.   29
Woods, Colin   209
Woods, Randall B.   141
Woolf, S. J.   63, 112
Wooton, Barbara   29
Wright, C.D.   29
Wright, Claudia   186
Wright, Jeffrey W.   167
Wright, Robin B.   124
Wright, Steve   112, 164
Wurth, Don E.   141
Wurth-Hough, Sandra   197
Wykert, John   209
Wylie, Philip   230
Wyllie, John   230
Yallop, J.H.   164
Yaniv, Avner   124
Yates, Brock   230
Yerbury, J. C.   113
Yerby, Frank   230
Yermakov, N.   113
Yoder, Amos   186
Yodfat, Aryeh Y.   113, 124
Yonay, Ehud   124
Yough, Syng Nam   217
Young, P. Lewis   131
Young, Robert   63
Zabih, Sepehr   124
Zafren, Daniel   168
Zamir, Meir   124
Zamoyskiy, Lelliy Petrovich
   29
Zasulic, Vera   63
Zawodny, J. K.   29, 67, 217
Zerb, Milton R.   154
Zimmermann, Ekkart   29, 113,
   217
Zofka, Z.   55
Zonis, Marvin   209
Zoppo, Ciro E.   64, 113

Title Index

About the Compilers

EDWARD F. MICKOLUS is President of Vinyard Software, Inc. In addition to *Literature of Terrorism: A Selectively Annotated Bibliography* (Greenwood Press, 1980), his previous works include *Transnational Terrorism: A Chronology of Events, 1968-1979*, also published by Greenwood Press.

PETER A. FLEMMING is a doctoral candidate in Political Science at Purdue University, Indiana, and holds his Masters Degree from the University of Windsor. His research interests are in political violence and the quantitative analysis of international terrorism.